# STUDY GUIDE

Prepared by

Teresa Merrells
*Mount Royal University*

Anna L. Moro
*McMaster University*

# CONTEMPORARY LINGUISTIC ANALYSIS
## An Introduction

### Seventh Edition

Edited by
William O'Grady
*University of Hawaii*

John Archibald
*University of Victoria*

**Pearson Canada**
Toronto

*For Chris and his girls, especially J., M., and D.*

*T.M.*

*I gratefully acknowledge the assistance of Stephanie Kelly, and the invaluable suggestions of Catherine Anderson, John Connolly, Ivona Kučerová, Melanie Pothier, and Elisabet Service. I would also like to thank Tae-Jin Yoon for many helpful comments on hangul, and David Kanatawakhon for his assistance with Mohawk.*

*A.L.M.*

ISBN 978-0-321-62426-0

Senior Acquisitions Editor: Lisa Rahn

Sponsoring Editor: Carolin Sweig

Senior Developmental Editor: Darryl Kamo

Lead Project Manager: Söğüt Y. Güleç

Production Editor: Avivah Wargon

Copy Editor: Joyce Hildebrand

Proofreader: Jennifer Abel

Composition: MPS Limited, a Macmillan Company

Data sets for Russian (p. 48), Tojolabal and Sindhi (p. 50), Turkish (p. 93), Bontoc and Michoacan Aztec (p. 94), Isleta (p. 95), Isthmus Zapoteco (p. 96), and Luiseño (p. 98) are reprinted by permission from *Language Files: Materials for an Introduction to Language and Linguistics*, 9th Edition by The Ohio State University Department of Linguistics (Ohio State University Press, 2007). Used with permission from Ohio State University Press.

Data sets for Ganda (p. 91) and Kanuri (p. 92) are reprinted by permission from *The Study of Langua* 3rd Edition, by George Yule. Copyright © 2006 George Yule. Reprinted with the permission of Cambridge University Press.

6   15 14

Printed and bound in Canada.

# CONTENTS

# PREFACE

This study guide is intended to accompany the seventh edition of *Contemporary Linguistic Analysis: An Introduction*. It began as a series of worksheets distributed to students in class and gradually expanded to include brief explanations of course content and additional practice exercises. This material was eventually linked together with reminders and review sheets. As the study guide evolved, it became more generic and all-encompassing. As a result, the study guide is of potential use to any instructor of introductory linguistics using *Contemporary Linguistic Analysis: An Introduction*.

The study guide originally contained a preview of major concepts followed by chapters on the core components of theoretical linguistics: phonetics, phonology, morphology, syntax, and semantics, as well as historical linguistics. For the seventh edition of *Contemporary Linguistic Analysis: An Introduction*, the study guide has been expanded to include Chapters 8 to 15 of the text. The study guide continues to focus on the core aspects of theoretical linguistics, since these are areas of introductory linguistics in which students typically require a great deal of practice in order to better understand the methods of analysis used within each of these branches of linguistics. Incorporating the remaining text chapters into the study guide will allow students to practice applying these methods of analysis in other branches of linguistics (e.g., language classification, language acquisition, sociolinguistics, psycholinguistics, etc.). The study guide also continues to be closely linked to the text through references to tables, figures, examples, and diagrams of syllable structure, word trees, and syntactic structure.

Each chapter in the study guide begins with a list of the main topics found in that chapter. The sections in each chapter correspond to this list. Each section contains brief explanations of important concepts and questions for students about these concepts, along with numerous exercises. Each chapter also includes general questions aimed at getting students to actively think about the concepts presented in the text. This feature is designed to complement the text's ability to engage students with the material. All chapters include reminders of important concepts and conclude with a review checklist that students can use to prepare for exams. Students who wish to work and study independently will find an Answer Key to this study guide on the Companion Website at **www.pearsoncanada.ca/ogrady** (access code protected).

I gratefully acknowledge Anna Moro's contribution to the study guide in the form of Chapters 9 (Aboriginal Languages of Canada), 12 (Psycholinguistics: The Study of Language Processing), 14 (Language in Social Contexts), and 15 (Writing and Language). Without her, the study guide could not have been expanded.

I also acknowledge contributions made by Carrie Dyck, Elaine Sorensen, Leone Sveinson, Joyce Hildebrand, and Lorna Rowsell to Chapters 1 through 7. I would like to thank all the reviewers for their comments, especially Carrie Dyck and William O'Grady, whose invaluable suggestions and advice have improved the overall quality of the study guide. Thanks also go to Elizabeth Ritter for using an early version of the study guide with her students and providing valuable feedback. Finally, I extend my sincere thanks and gratitude to Michael Dobrovolsky and John Archibald for their continued support.

Teresa Merrells

# CHAPTER 1. LANGUAGE: A PREVIEW

The following are some of the important concepts found in this chapter. Make sure you are familiar with them.

1. Specialization
2. Creativity
3. Linguistic Competence
4. Grammar

## SPECIALIZATION

Humans are specialized for language. The characteristics below illustrate some of the aspects of our special capacity for language.

### 1. Speech Organs

> Our lungs, vocal cords, tongue, teeth, lips, and nasal passages are used both for survival (e.g., breathing and eating) and for producing the sounds of our language.

### 2. Speech Perception

> We are also equipped for speech perception, and we have this ability at birth. Studies have shown that newborns are able to perceive subtle differences between sounds, even sounds they have never heard before.

### 3. The Human Mind

> Our minds form words, build sentences, and interpret meanings in ways not found in other species.

This specialization for language sets us apart from all other creatures!

# CREATIVITY

Human language is creative. That is, language does not provide us with a set of pre-packaged messages. Rather, it allows us to produce and understand new words and sentences whenever needed. However, there are limitations on both the form and interpretation of new words and sentences. Linguists attempt to identify, understand, and explain these limitations.

**Exercise!**  Think about the limitations on the creativity of language while answering the following questions.

1. Put a checkmark beside those words that are possible English words.

   a. tlim _____   e. plog _____ ✓ _____

   b. stuken ____ ✓ _____   f. skpit _____

   c. tseg _____   g. ngan _____

   d. fomp ____ ✓ _____   h. breb _____

   *Phonology*

   Think about why some of the above are not possible English words. (HINT: Look at the combination of sounds found at the beginning of the words.)

2. Put a checkmark beside those words that are possible English words.

   a. speakless _____   d. reglorify _____ ✓ _____

   b. beautifulness ____ ✓ _____   e. horseable _____

   c. unrug _____   f. weedic _____ ✓ _____

   *morphology*

   Think about why some of the above are not possible English words. (HINT: Think about the prefix or suffix and its contribution to the meaning of the word.)

3. Put a checkmark beside those sentences that are possible English sentences.  *syntax*

   a. The building was tossed yesterday away. _____

   b. The building is swept every morning. _____ ✓ _____

   c. Every child should obey parents his. _____

   d. Somebody left their gloves in the theatre. _____ ✓ _____

   e. George surprised Mary with a party. _____ ✓ _____

   f. Joe surprised the stone. _____

For those that are not possible English sentences, try to explain why.

4. Now try this!

   a. Arrange the words "bird", "worm", "catches", "early", "every", and "a" into an English sentence.

*A worm catches every early bird.*

   b. Think of other arrangements of the same words that result in different sentences from the one you just put together.

*Every early bird catches a worm.*

   c. How could you arrange the words so that the sentence you create is not an acceptable English sentence?

*A bird every early worm catches.*

## LINGUISTIC COMPETENCE

*Linguistic competence* can be defined as subconscious knowledge that enables the native speakers of a language to produce and understand an unlimited number of both familiar and novel utterances. The native speakers of a language are those who acquired it as children in a home rather than in a classroom.

Linguists divide the subconscious knowledge that the native speakers of a language share into the following fields of study:

1.  Phonetics:    the study of the articulation and perception of speech sounds

2.  Phonology:   the study of how speech sounds pattern in language

3.  Morphology: the study of word structure and word formation

4.  Syntax:      the study of sentence structure

5.  Semantics:    the study of the meaning of words and sentences

This subconscious knowledge allows the speakers of a language to produce an infinite number of sentences, many of which they have never uttered or heard before. We don't memorize language: we create it.

Go back to the exercise on creativity. For each data set, determine which aspect of your linguistic competence allows you to decide which are possible English words and sentences.

## GRAMMAR

Grammar, to a linguist, refers to all the elements of our linguistic competence: phonetics, phonology, morphology, syntax, and semantics. In very general terms, grammar can be defined as the mental system of knowledge needed to form and interpret the sounds, words, and sentences of our language. The study of grammar is central to understanding language and to what it means to know a language. This is because all languages have sounds, words and sentences, all grammars allow for the expression of any thought, all grammars share common principles and tendencies called universals, all grammars are equal, and all grammars change over time. However, our grammatical knowledge is subconscious: we can decide what sounds right and what does not, even though we may not be sure why this is so.

There are two perspectives on grammar: prescriptive and descriptive. A prescriptive grammar gives the socially accepted rules for language use, while a descriptive grammar is an objective description of the knowledge that native speakers share. Examine the table below and see if you can tell which type of grammar is being exemplified.

| | |
|---|---|
| "Between you and I …" is **WRONG.** | My friend Malvolio says, "Many believe that there's an enormous rivalry between Orsino and I." That may sound correct, but the pronoun *I* is wrong here. |
| "Between you and me …" is **RIGHT.** | *Between* is a preposition, and prepositions are followed by objects. *I* is a subject or nominative pronoun. Objective pronouns which follow a preposition are *me, you, him, her, us,* and *them.* |

| | |
|---|---|
| "She is older than me" is **WRONG.** | The word *than* is a conjunction. It joins two sentences, words, or phrases. There are two sentences here: (1) "She is older" and (2) "I am." |
| "She is older than I" is **RIGHT.** | In a comparison joined by *than* or *as*, complete the sentence with *am* as in sentence two, above. You wouldn't say "She is smarter than me am," so it must be "She is smarter than I." |

| | |
|---|---|
| "Who do I ask?" is **WRONG.** | *Who* and *whom* will never cause you trouble if you remember that *who* is generally appropriate whenever you use *he, she,* or *they,* and *whom* acts as a substitute for *him, her,* or *them.* |
| "Whom do I ask?" is **RIGHT.** | It helps to recast a question into a statement. In this example, you would not say "I ask he," so the correct wording is "Whom do I ask?" (Yes, that sounds stuffy—which is why the incorrect "Who do I ask?" is sometimes used in informal speech.) |

| | |
|---|---|
| "The list of home upgrades such as cabinets and appliances were unchanged from the previous list" is **WRONG.** | Matching a plural verb with a singular subject is a mistake. The subject of the sentence, *list*, is singular, but it is separated from the verb by the plural phrase *such as cabinets and appliances.* |
| "The list of home upgrades such as cabinets and appliances was unchanged from the previous list" is **RIGHT.** | Distraction by particulars may cause you to forget that you were speaking in the singular and lead you to use a plural verb. Keep your mind on what you're talking about (the subject). |

The preceding are all examples of a prescriptivist view of language. While a prescriptivist grammar is useful in helping people learn a foreign language, in that it contains the socially accepted rules for language use, linguists are more interested in descriptive grammar.

**Spot the Difference!**  Each of the following aspects of linguistic competence contains two statements. See if you can identify which statement is prescriptivist and which is descriptivist. Do this by writing either D.G. (Descriptive Grammar) or P.G. (Prescriptive Grammar) beside each statement.

①  Sounds

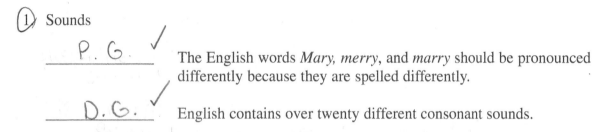

_____P. G.____ ✓  The English words *Mary, merry*, and *marry* should be pronounced differently because they are spelled differently.

_____D. G.____ ✓  English contains over twenty different consonant sounds.

Think about how many different vowel sounds are found in English.

Do all languages have the same consonant and/or vowel sounds? Think of a language that has different vowel or consonant sounds from English.

②  Words

_____P. G____  The use of *thunk* and not *thought* as the past tense of the verb *think* is an example of how change is causing the English language to deteriorate.

_____D. G____ ✓  Many nouns in English are formed by adding the suffix *-ment* to words (e.g., achievement, government, judgment).

Think about why no English speaker would construct the word *chairment*.

3./ Sentences

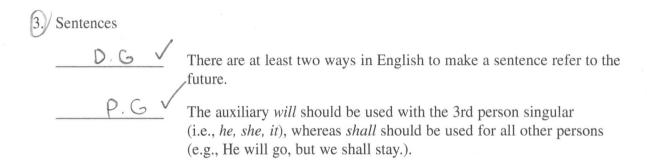

___D.G ✓___   There are at least two ways in English to make a sentence refer to the future.

___P.G ✓___   The auxiliary *will* should be used with the 3rd person singular (i.e., *he, she, it*), whereas *shall* should be used for all other persons (e.g., He will go, but we shall stay.).

Think of how to change the sentence *The horses eat hay* to refer to the future.

Think about how other languages make statements refer to future time.

4.) Meaning

___P.G. ✓___   The word *cool* should only be used to refer to temperature.

___D.G ✓___   Many words in a language often have opposite meanings (e.g., hot/cold, light/dark).

Think about how the meaning of a sentence is different from the meaning of the words that it is composed of.

---

**QUICK REMINDER!**

Linguistics is the study of the structure of human language, and linguists attempt to describe and explain, in an objective and non-judgmental fashion, the internalized and unconscious knowledge that the native speakers of a language share and that allows them to both speak and understand their language. While the primary focus of this guide is on Canadian English, many of the principles and theories discussed apply to all other languages as well.

# REVIEW EXERCISE

Each of the statements below illustrates a concept found in Chapter 1. For each statement, determine which concept is being illustrated. Write the number of the concept beside the appropriate statement. The first is done for you.

Concepts:

1. Linguistic competence
2. Prescriptive grammar
3. Descriptive grammar
4. Universal (i.e., something common to all languages)

Statements:

a.   4          All languages have a way of making negatives.

b.   2  x 1     Speakers of Canadian English know that one way to make questions is to move an auxiliary verb to the position before the subject noun phrase.

c.   3  ✓       Many nouns in English are formed by adding -ness to an adjective: for example, sadness, silliness, and happiness.

d.   2  ✓       'Brung' should never be used as the past tense of 'bring'.

e.   4, ✓       Every language has a set of vowels and consonants.

f.   4  x 1     Speakers of any language are capable of producing an unlimited number of novel sentences.

g.   1  x 3     In English, there is theoretically no limit on the number of adjectives that can occur before a noun.

h.   1  x 2     In the sentence "My friend is smarter than me", 'me' is incorrect because it is an object pronoun and this comparative construction requires the subject pronoun 'I'.

I.   3  ✓       In English, the plural is formed by adding either [-s], [-z] or [-əz] to the end of nouns.

J.   4  ✓       Every language has a way of forming questions.

K.   2  x 1     Speakers of Canadian English know that the different vowel sounds in the words bat, bet, but, and bit are crucial to their meanings.

**REVIEW! REVIEW!** Make sure you understand the terms listed below.

- creativity
- descriptive grammar
- generality
- grammar
- the human mind
- inaccessibility
- linguistic competence
- mutability
- native speaker
- parity

- prescriptive grammar
- speech organs
- speech perception
- universality

## QUESTIONS? PROBLEMS? DIFFICULTIES?

_____

_____

_____

_____

_____

_____

_____

# CHAPTER 2. PHONETICS:
# THE SOUNDS OF LANGUAGE

Phonetics is the study of the articulation and perception of speech sounds. Important topics and concepts found in this section include the following:

1. International Phonetic Alphabet
2. Segments
3. Sound producing system
4. Consonant articulation
5. Vowel articulation
6. Phonetic transcription
7. Suprasegmentals
8. Processes

## PHONETIC TRANSCRIPTION

The speech sounds of language are transcribed using the symbols found in the International Phonetic Alphabet (IPA). Here are some things to keep in mind when using the IPA:

- Each IPA symbol represents one and only one speech sound.
- Each speech sound found in language corresponds to one and only one IPA symbol.
- Since symbols represent sounds, the same symbols can be used in whatever language that sound occurs. See table 2.1 on p. 15 of the text for some examples of how the symbol [ð] can be used in different languages.

⇒ The focus in this chapter is on learning the sounds of English and their corresponding IPA symbols. For examples of some sounds not found in English and their IPA symbols, see tables 2.28 and 2.29 on p. 51.

⇒ It is important to remember that IPA symbols represent sounds and not how that sound is spelled in a particular language. To indicate this difference, symbols are enclosed in [ ] brackets. Don't forget to use them!

## SEGMENTS

Words typically consist of a number of segments (individual speech sounds). Doing phonetic transcription involves determining what these segments are, along with their corresponding phonetic symbols. In doing transcription, it can be useful, as a starting point, to determine the number of segments in a word. But don't be fooled by spelling! Each of the following boxes illustrates a reason why we can't rely on spelling to determine the number of speech sounds in an English word.

9

Some letters or combinations of letters have more than one speech sound associated with them. In each of the example sets below, determine if the underlined letter (or letters) is pronounced the same way for all the words presented.

⇒      'o'         as in        h<u>o</u>t          ech<u>o</u>          w<u>o</u>man

⇒      'c'         as in        <u>c</u>areful          <u>c</u>entury

⇒      'ou'       as in        sh<u>ou</u>ld          t<u>ou</u>gh          s<u>ou</u>nd

Sometimes one speech sound can be represented using different letters or combinations of letters. In each of the example sets below, determine if the underlined letters have the same or different speech sounds.

⇒      thr<u>ough</u>      cl<u>ue</u>      sh<u>oe</u>      t<u>oo</u>

⇒      r<u>ea</u>l          s<u>ee</u>          sorr<u>y</u>          Sh<u>ei</u>la

⇒      str<u>aw</u>      t<u>a</u>lk      f<u>ough</u>t      l<u>o</u>st

Many words in English contain double letters. Double letters do not necessarily mean that there are two speech sounds. Say each of the words below and determine if you pronounce the double letter twice.

            str<u>ee</u>t          b<u>oo</u>k          mi<u>tt</u>en          ki<u>ll</u>er

Finally, many words in English contain silent letters. These are letters that we do not pronounce and that therefore do not correspond to a speech sound. Say each of the words below and determine if you pronounce all of the letters.

            knife          leave          pneumonia          thumb

The above points also illustrate some of the reasons for using IPA rather than conventional spelling for doing phonetic transcription. In IPA, unlike in spelling, each symbol corresponds to only one sound and always the same sound. The lesson is . . . when you are doing phonetic transcription, you need to forget about spelling!

**Practice! Practice!**  To get ready for transcription, try the following exercises.

1. Determine the number of speech sounds in each of the following words.

   a.  thing ___3___           d.  phosphate ___6___

   b.  comb ___3___            e.  scene ___3___

   c.  psychic ___5___         f.  fright ___4___

2. Say each of the following words. Which letter(s) correspond to the first sound in each word?

   a.  Thomas ___th___         d.  knee ___n___

   b.  unemployed ___u___      e.  choice ___ch___

   c.  committee ___c___       f.  ease ___ea___

3. Say each of the following words. Which letter(s) correspond to the last sound in each word?

   a.  laugh ___gh___          d.  lamb ___m___

   b.  sang ___ng___           e.  use ___s___

   c.  bow ___ow___            f.  choice ___c___

## SOUND-PRODUCING SYSTEM

Human language contains a finite number of speech sounds, or phones. The system that produces these sounds includes the following.

⇒ **Lungs.**  The lungs provide the moving air necessary for speech.

⇒ **Larynx.**  The larynx contains the vocal folds (or cords) that provide the source of the sound. See figure 2.2 on p. 18 of the text for a representation of the larynx. The vocal folds can be positioned in different ways. The space between the vocal folds is called the glottis. The different positions of the vocal folds are called glottal states. There are four glottal states that you should be familiar with; see figure 2.3 on p. 19 for a representation of each of these states.

- Voiced
- Voiceless
- Whisper
- Murmur

⇒ **Pharynx.**  This is the tube of the throat between the larynx and the oral cavity.

⇒ **Oral cavity.**  This is the mouth.

⇒ **Nasal cavity.**  This is also known as the nasal passages. The velum controls airflow through the nasal passages. Raising the velum cuts off airflow through the nasal passages. Lowering the velum allows air to flow through the nasal passages.

The pharynx, oral cavity, and nasal cavity act as filters that modify the sound in various ways. Together they constitute the vocal tract.

**Try This!**  Label the different elements of the sound-producing system on the diagram on the opposite page. You can also label the trachea (windpipe) and the velum. If you're having difficulty, refer to figure 2.1 on p. 17 of the text.

## SOUND CLASSES

Sounds can be divided into three major classes: consonants, vowels, and glides. Each class of sounds shares some phonetic properties. The defining characteristics of each class are given below.

⇒  **Consonants.**  Consonants are sounds that can be either voiced or voiceless and that are made with a narrow or complete obstruction in the vocal tract. This is an articulatory characteristic of consonant sounds.

⇒  **Vowels.**  Vowels are sounds that are typically voiced and that are made with little obstruction in the vocal tract. Vowels tend to be more sonorous than consonants. As a result, we perceive vowels as louder and longer lasting. This is an acoustic characteristic of vowels. Vowels are also classified as syllabic sounds, meaning that they can form the nucleus of a syllable.

⇒  **Glides.**  Glides are sounds that have characteristics of both consonants and vowels. They are sometimes called semivowels or semiconsonants. Glides are like vowels in their articulation, but they are like consonants in that they never form the nucleus of a syllable.

**Exercise!**  Each of the following words has one or more letters underlined. The underlined letters correspond to one sound. Identify this sound as a consonant, vowel, or glide. The first is done for you.

1.  rottweiler _____consonant_____          5.  myth ___consonant___

2.  through _____          6.  whistle ___glide___

3.  lovely _____          7.  suffer ___vowel___

4.  year ___glide___          8.  judge ___glide___

---

### REMINDER!

Some types of consonants can also be syllabic (i.e., function as the nucleus of a syllable). For this reason, you should think of sounds not just as being consonants, vowels, or glides, but as being syllabic or non-syllabic elements. This will be useful in doing phonetic transcription and also when doing phonology (Chapter 3).

# CONSONANT ARTICULATION

Consonants are sounds that are made with obstruction in the vocal tract. Consonants do not normally form the nucleus of a syllable and can be voiced or voiceless. The following pages contain information about consonants that you should become very familiar with.

## Articulatory Description

All sounds, regardless of whether they are consonants, vowels, or glides, are described in terms of how they are articulated. This information is contained in the sound's articulatory description. Consonants and vowels are described differently. There are three parameters necessary to describe consonant (and glide) articulations.

1. Glottal state
2. Place of articulation
3. Manner of articulation

⇒ Glottal state refers to whether a sound is voiced or voiceless.

⇒ Place of articulation refers to where in the vocal tract an obstruction occurs. Places of articulation are found

- at the lips (labial)
- within the oral cavity (dental, alveolar, alveopalatal, palatal, velar, uvular)
- in the pharynx (pharyngeal)
- at the glottis (glottal)

See figure 2.5 on p. 23 of the text for diagrams of places of articulation at the lips (labial) and at some points within the oral cavity (alveolar, interdental, palatal, and velar).

**Try This!** Each place of articulation has an articulatory term used to describe sounds made at that particular spot in the vocal tract. For example, sounds made with the lips are called labial sounds. Give the articulatory term describing sounds made at each of the following places of articulation.

    a.  lips and teeth   _labiodental_

    b.  hard palate   _palatal_

    c.  uvula   _uvular_

    d.  alveolar ridge   _alveolar_

**Now ...** Label all places of articulation on the diagram on the following page. For each place of articulation, give the corresponding articulatory term. You can also label the different parts of the tongue (tip, blade, body, back, and root). If you are having difficulty, refer to figure 2.4 on p. 22 of the text.

⇒ Manner of articulation refers to the different types of sounds resulting from different positions of the lips, tongue, velum, and glottis. Manners of articulation include

- Stops (see tables 2.3 and 2.4 on p. 26)
- Fricatives (see tables 2.5 and 2.6 on pp. 27 and 28)
- Affricates (see table 2.7 on p. 28)
- Nasals (see tables 2.3 and 2.4 on p. 26)
- Liquids (see table 2.10 on p. 31)
- Glides

**Now ...** Fill in the chart on the following page with the consonant and glide sounds of Canadian English. If you are having difficulty, refer to table 2.12 on p. 33.

## Now Try This!

1. Give the phonetic symbol for the first consonant in each of the following words.

   a. through   [θ]          d. whistle   [w]

   b. shave     [ʃ]          e. phone     [f]

   c. knee      [n]          f. queen     [k]

2. Give the phonetic symbol for the last consonant in each of the following words.

   a. laugh     [f]          d. myth      [θ]

   b. sang      [ŋ]          e. lamb      [m]

   c. choice    [s]          f. box       [s]

---

### QUICK REMINDER!

Every sound has one and only one articulatory description. And every articulatory description corresponds to one and only one symbol in the International Phonetic Alphabet (IPA).

---

# CANADIAN ENGLISH CONSONANT CHART

| | | PLACE OF ARTICULATION | | | | | | | |
|---|---|---|---|---|---|---|---|---|---|
| | GLOTTAL STATE | Bilabial | Labiodental | Interdental | Alveolar | Alveopalatal/Palatal | Velar | Glottal |
| Stop | voiceless | | | | | | | |
| | voiced | | | | | | | |
| Fricative | voiceless | | | | | | | |
| | voiced | | | | | | | |
| Affricate | voiceless | | | | | | | |
| | voiced | | | | | | | |
| Nasal | voiced | | | | | | | |
| Liquid a. lateral | voiced | | | | | | | |
| b. retroflex | voiced | | | | | | | |
| Glide | voiced | | | | | | | |

MANNER OF ARTICULATION

Some more about …

**Voiceless Stop Articulations**

⇒ **Aspiration.** Sometimes when the voiceless stops [p, t, k] are pronounced, they are produced with a small puff of air. This puff of air is called aspiration and is represented as [ʰ]. Aspiration is caused by a delay in voicing. See figures 2.6, 2.7, and 2.8 on pp. 29 and 30 for some diagrams outlining when and why aspiration does and does not occur in English.

**Try This!** Say the words in the boxes below. Pay close attention to the first sound, and see if you can feel when aspiration does and does not occur. You can feel this extra release of air by putting your hand close to your mouth as you produce the words.

| Voiceless Aspirated Stops | | Voiceless Unaspirated Stops | |
|---|---|---|---|
| [pʰ] | pit<br>punk | [p] | spit<br>spunk |
| [tʰ] | take<br>tab | [t] | stake<br>stab |
| [kʰ] | kill<br>car | [k] | skill<br>scar |

⇒ **Unreleased Stops.** Sometimes when the voiceless stops [p, t, k] are pronounced, they are not released. That is, the articulation ends with either the lips closed or the tongue on the place of articulation. The symbol for this articulation is a raised [ ˥ ].

**Try This!** Say the words in the boxes below. For the words in the first column, pay close attention to the first sound, and see if you can feel your lips opening or your tongue moving away from the place of articulation. For the words in the second column, pay close attention to the final sound and see if your lips remain closed or if your tongue remains at the place of articulation.

| Voiceless Aspirated Stops | | Voiceless Unreleased Stops | |
|---|---|---|---|
| [pʰ] | pit<br>punk | [p˥] | cap<br>leap |
| [tʰ] | take<br>tab | [t˥] | pot<br>most |
| [kʰ] | kill<br>car | [k˥] | back<br>sack |

### Fricative and Affricate Articulations

⇒ **Strident/Sibilant.** Some fricatives and affricates are noisier than others. Say the words in the box below. See if you can hear which fricatives and affricates are noisier. The noisier fricatives and affricates are considered to be strident (sibilant). The quieter fricatives and affricates are considered non-strident. This is an acoustic criterion used in describing fricatives and affricates.

| Non Strident Fricatives | | Strident Fricatives & Affricates | |
|---|---|---|---|
| [f] and [v] | fit<br>vat | [s] and [z] | sip<br>zen |
| [θ] and [ð] | thick<br>though | [ʃ] and [ʒ] | ship<br>pleasure |
| | | [tʃ] and [dʒ] | cherub<br>gem |

**Now ...** Go back to the Canadian English consonant chart on p. 17 and put a box around the group of fricatives and affricates considered to be strident. If you are having difficulty, see table 2.8 on p. 28.

### Liquid and Nasal Articulations

### *l* and *r* Articulations

⇒      *l*. Since [l] is normally voiced, *lateral* usually means voiced lateral. However, [l] can also be voiceless, in which case it is represented as [l̥]. Say the words in the table below and see if you can hear the difference between the voiced and voiceless laterals.

| Voiced Lateral | | Voiceless Lateral | |
|---|---|---|---|
| [l] | lip<br>love<br>lullaby<br>lamp | [l̥] | please<br>play<br>clean<br>clever |

⇒      *r*. Like [l], [r] (or less commonly, [ɹ]) is normally voiced. *Retroflex* therefore usually means voiced retroflex. Like [r], it can also be voiceless, in which case it is represented as [r̥]. English also has a flap sound, which is another type of sound commonly identified with *r*. A flap is made when the tip of the tongue strikes the alveolar ridge as it passes by. [ɾ] represents a flap. Say the words in the following table and see if you can hear the difference between the voiced and voiceless [r], and the flap.

| Voiced Retroflex | | Voiceless Retroflex | | Flap | |
|---|---|---|---|---|---|
| [ɹ] | ride<br>right<br>car | [ɹ̥] | pray<br>train<br>crayon | [ɾ] | bitter<br>butter |

⇒    **Alveolar and Velarized *l*.**  Not every lateral [l] is pronounced in the same way. Say the words in the table below. Pay close attention to where your tongue is when you articulate the [l] sound. See if you can feel if your tongue is more towards the front or back of your mouth. The [l] in the first group is considered to have an alveolar articulation, while the [l] in the second group is considered to be velarized. The alveolar [l] is often called "clear l" and the velarized [l] "dark l".

| Alveolar *l*  (clear) | | Velarized *l*  (dark) | |
|---|---|---|---|
| [l] | lip<br>love<br>lullaby | [ɫ] | swallow<br>guilt<br>silk |

⇒  **Syllabic and Non-syllabic.**  Liquid and nasal articulations can be either syllabic or non-syllabic. Remember that a syllabic sound (e.g., a vowel) forms the nucleus of a syllable. It is only when a liquid or nasal forms the nucleus of a syllable that it is considered to be syllabic. If the liquid or nasal does not form the nucleus of a syllable, it is considered to be non-syllabic. Say the words in the table below and see if you can hear when the liquid or nasal is syllabic and when it is non-syllabic. See table 2.11 on p. 32 for some more examples of English syllabic and non-syllabic liquids and nasals.

| | Some syllabic sounds | Some non-syllabic sounds |
|---|---|---|
| **Liquids** | twinkle<br>father | lawn<br>rain |
| **Nasals** | glutton<br>winsome | hamburger<br>master |

## Exercise!

1. Say the following words. Put a checkmark beside those words containing aspirated voiceless stops.

   1. scratch _____   4. pending _____✓_____

   2. talk _____✓_____   5. stripe _____

   3. segments _____   6. careful _____✓_____

2. Say the following words. Put a checkmark beside those words containing a syllabic liquid or nasal.

   a. laugh _____   e. kitten __✓_____
   f- fricative          ✓                    nasal

   b. bottom ____✓_____   f. bushel ___✓_____
        nasal                              liquid

   c. mad _____   g. rugby _____
        stop

   d. suffer ____✓_____   h. note _____
        liquid                             t - stop

3. Say the following words. Put a checkmark beside those words containing a velarized (dark) [l].

   a. malign _____   d. pull ____✓_____

   b. silly ____✓_____   e. lamb _____

   c. allow _____   f. meal ____✓_____

# VOWEL ARTICULATION

Vowels are sounds that are sonorant, are articulated with little obstruction in the vocal tract, and are syllabic (can form the nucleus of a syllable). Vowels are also usually voiced.

## Articulatory Description

Four parameters are necessary to describe vowel articulations.

1.  Height
2.  Backness
3.  Tenseness
4.  Roundness

⇒  Different vowel sounds are made by varying the position of the body of the tongue. High, mid, and low (height), and front and back (backness) are used to describe tongue placement.

⇒  Tenseness refers to the amount of constriction in the vocal tract muscles when the sound is articulated. Vowels made with greater constriction are described as tense. Vowels made with less constriction are described as lax. Tense vowels tend to be longer than lax vowels.

⇒  Roundness refers to whether the lips are rounded. Vowels with the lips rounded are described as rounded; vowels without lip rounding are described as unrounded.

## Simple Vowels and Diphthongs

⇒  Simple vowels are vowels whose quality does not change during their articulation, while diphthongs are vowels that exhibit a change in quality within a single syllable. This change in quality is the result of the tongue moving away from a vowel articulation to a glide articulation. Say the words in the table below and see if you can hear the change in quality during a diphthong articulation.

| Some simple vowels | Some diphthongs |
| --- | --- |
| sit | boy |
| lost | now |
| cup | cry |
| met | pray |
| bat | sew |

⇒  Diphthongs can be classified as either major or minor. The major diphthongs are those whose quality change is easy to hear. The quality change in the minor diphthongs is harder to hear. Say the words containing diphthongs in the above table again, and see if you can tell which are the major diphthongs and which the minor diphthongs.

See table 2.13 on p. 35 of the text for some examples of simple vowels, and major and minor diphthongs in Canadian English.

**Some other vowels ...**

⇒  [a] is found in Canadian English as a single vowel only before [r] in words such as *car*.

⇒  [ɔ] is found in Canadian English only before [r] in words such as *more*.

**Now ...** Fill in the chart on the following page with the phonetic symbols corresponding to both the simple vowels and diphthongs found in Canadian English. Circle all tense vowels. See figure 2.11 on p. 37 if you are having difficulty.

 **Practice!**  Give the phonetic symbol for the vowel sound in each of the following English words.

a.  stool _____ [u] _____          d.  pot _____ [a] _____

b.  sight _____ [aj] _____          e.  sit _____ [ɪ] _____

c.  meet _____ [i] _____          f.  put _____ [ʊ] _____

---

## QUICK REMINDER

For every articulatory description, you need to be able to provide the corresponding phonetic symbol:

e.g.,  voiceless bilabial stop      →      [p]

For every phonetic symbol, you need to be able to provide the corresponding articulatory description:

e.g.,  [p]      →      voiceless bilabial stop

You need to be able to do this for both consonants and vowels!

# CANADIAN ENGLISH VOWEL CHART

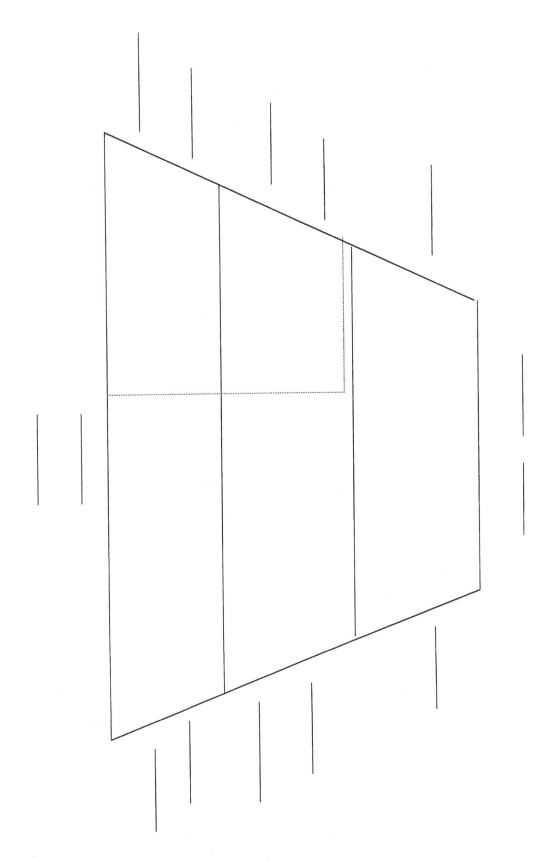

# FACIAL DIAGRAMS FOR CONSONANTS

There are four important parts to either completing or deciphering facial diagrams for consonants.

**Glottal State.** Voiced sounds are shown by two wavy lines where the larynx would be. Voiceless sounds are represented by two lines shaped like an ellipse.

Voiced                                                                 Voiceless

**Place of Articulation.** The narrowest point in the airstream passage is the place of articulation.

**Manner of Articulation.** If no air escapes past a given articulator (i.e., in a stop), then the articulator must touch the place of articulation. If the air does escape (i.e., in a fricative), then there is a space between the articulator and the place of articulation. If the sound is an affricate, then the diagram is shown with the articulator touching the place of articulation and an arrow indicating the direction in which the articulator moves.

Stop                              Fricative                              Affricate

**Nasal Passage.** For oral sounds, the nasal passage is closed, while for nasal sounds the nasal passage is open.

✳ Complete the following diagrams so that each of the sounds listed below is depicted.

1. [s]        3. [ʧ]        5. [g]
2. [p]        4. [n]        6. [ð]

To complete the diagrams, you must do the following:

- Draw in the glottal state: either voiced or voiceless.
- Draw in the lips: either closed or open.
- Draw the tongue to indicate the place of articulation (see figure 2.5 on p. 23 for some examples) and the manner of articulation.
- Draw in the velum: either raised or lowered.

The first sound has been done for you.

[ s ]          [ ʧ ]          [ g ]

[ p ]          [ n ]          [ ð ]
                              as in though

For each drawing presented below, there is only one sound that could be produced by the vocal tract position. You are to figure out which consonant sound is represented and write the phonetic symbol for that sound between square brackets below the drawing.

Make sure that you pay attention to voicing, place and manner of articulation, and the position of the velum.

The first drawing has been labelled for you.

# FACIAL DIAGRAMS FOR VOWELS

There are four important parts to either completing or deciphering facial diagrams for vowels.

**Glottal State.**  Vowels are always voiced. As on facial diagrams for consonants, voicing is shown by two wavy lines where the larynx would be.

**Nasal Passage.**  For oral vowels, the nasal passage is closed, while for nasal vowels, the nasal passage is open.

**Lip Position.**  Vowels are either rounded or unrounded. For rounded vowels, the lips are closer together, while for unrounded vowels, the lips are more spread apart.

Unrounded:

Rounded:

**Tongue Placement.**  The height and position of the tongue determine the particular vowel articulation being depicted. For example, if the front of the tongue is high in the mouth, then a high front vowel results. If the main body of the tongue is neither high nor low, then a mid central vowel results. If the back of the tongue is low, then a low back vowel results.

Complete the following diagrams so that each of the sounds listed below are depicted.

1. [æ]                    2. [ʌ]                    3. [ĩ]

To complete the diagrams, you must do the following:

- Draw in the glottal state.
- Draw in the velum: either raised or lowered.
- Draw in the lips: either rounded or unrounded.
- Draw the appropriate portion of the tongue to the appropriate height.

low front

[ æ ]

central mid

[ ʌ ]

high front

[ ĩ ]

For each drawing presented below, determine which vowel sound is represented and write the phonetic symbol for that sound between the brackets below the drawing.

mid back

[ o ] or [ow]

low back

[ ã ]

mid front

[ ej ]

# PRACTICE WITH SOUNDS

1. Give the phonetic symbol for each of the following articulatory descriptions.

   a. [ ʔ ]   voiceless glottal stop

   b. [ i ]   high front unrounded tense vowel

   c. [m ]   voiced bilabial nasal
              *lips*

   d. [ θ ]   voiceless interdental fricative
              *teeth   more airflow!*

2. Give the articulatory description that corresponds to each of the following phonetic symbols.

   a. [æ]   *low front unrounded lax*

   b. [f]   *voiced labiodental fricative.*

   c. [j]   *voiced palatal glide.*
            *back ridge*

   d. [ʌ]   *mid central unrounded lax*

3. Each of the following groups of sounds contains at least one shared phonetic property (e.g., glottal state, place of articulation, manner of articulation, tongue height, lip position, etc.). For each group of sounds, give some phonetic properties that the sounds have in common. Include as many as possible.

   a. [b, d, g]   *voiced oral stops*

   b. [ʃ, ʧ, ʒ]   *strident alveopalatal*
                  *back ride.*

   c. [j, r, n]   *voiced sonorants.*

   d. [ɑ, o, ʊ]   *back vowels.*

   e. [æ, ɪ, ɛ]   *front lax unrounded vowels.*

4. For each of the following groups of sounds, circle the sound that does not belong and state a phonetic property that the remaining sounds share. There may be more than one possible answer!

   a. [f ð v (z)]   *non-strident fricatives*

   b. [d t (ŋ) g]   *oral stops.*

   c. [ɑ o (ɪ) u]   *back tense vowels.*

# TRANSCRIPTION HINTS

Each of the boxes below contains some examples of sounds that often cause difficulty when students are beginning to do transcription. For more examples of transcribed words containing Canadian English vowel and consonant symbols, see tables 2.16 and 2.17 on pp. 39 and 40.

## SYLLABIC CONSONANTS

| | |
|---|---|
| r | [r] for the 'r' sound in 'real', 'right', etc. <br> [ər], [r̩], or [ɚ] for the syllabic 'r' sound in 'butt**er**', 'b**ir**d', 'p**urr**', etc. <br> [ ɾ ] for the 't' sound in words like 'bu**tt**er', 'wri**t**er', 'pu**tt**er', 'po**tt**er', etc. |
| l | [l] for the 'l' sound in 'light', 'pill', 'please', etc. <br> [əl] or [l̩] for the syllabic 'l' in 'bott**le**', 'pudd**le**', 'pood**le**', etc. |
| m | [m̩] for the syllabic 'm' in 'bott**om**', 'wins**ome**', etc. <br> [m] for any other 'm' sound |
| n | [n̩] for the syllabic 'n' in 'butt**on**', 'hidd**en**', etc. <br> [n] for any other 'n' sound |

## DIPHTHONGS

Diphthongs are transcribed as vowel-glide sequences. Remember that diphthongs are a single speech sound. Remember as well that diphthongs are described in terms of the vowel, not the glide.

- Use [a], not [ɑ], for the major diphthongs (i.e., [aj], [aw], not [ɑj], [ɑw]). The symbols [a] and [ɑ] <u>do not</u> represent the same vowel sound.
- The mid tense vowels [e] and [o] are considered to be minor diphthongs and are transcribed as [ej] and [ow].
- The high tense vowels [i] and [u] are sometimes also considered to be minor diphthongs. You may be required to transcribe these as [ij] and [uw].

## VOWELS BEFORE [r]

[r] is a very powerful sound, making it difficult to hear the preceding vowel sound. The following examples may help.

| | | | | | |
|---|---|---|---|---|---|
| [bir] | beer | [bɔr] | boar | [bejr] | bear |
| [bar] | bar | [bur] | boor | [bər], [br̩], or [bɚ] | burr |

## SCHWA AND WEDGE

<table>
<tr><td>

Schwa [ə]

– used for unstressed vowels
    e.g., [əbawt] 'about'
– found before [r]
    e.g., [bərd] 'bird'
– used in the words 'the' and 'a'

</td><td>

Wedge [ʌ]

– used when there is some degree of
  stress on the vowel
    e.g., [sʌpər] 'supper'
– not found before [r]

</td></tr>
</table>

## ASPIRATION

| p, t, k | use [pʰ, tʰ, kʰ] for any 'p', 't', 'k' sound that occurs at the beginning of a syllable followed by a vowel that receives some degree of stress.<br>e.g., [pʰæt] 'pat', [tʰɑt] 'taught', [kʰejk] 'cake'<br>[əpʰír] 'appear', [ətʰǽk] 'attack' |
|---|---|
| | use [p, t, k] for any other 'p', 't', 'k' sound.<br>e.g., [splæt] 'splat', [stown] 'stone', [skejt] 'skate' |

You may also be required to transcribe the following:

⇒ Unreleased voiceless stops. Use the symbol [ ̚ ].

⇒ Velarized *l*. Use the symbol [ɫ].

## TRANSCRIPTION EXERCISES

**A Start!** Transcribe the following words as you would say them in normal everyday speech. Remember to include brackets and remember to forget spelling. Watch out for syllabic consonants!

1. craft  kræft
2. rich  rɪtʃ
3. thought  θɑt
4. sigh  saj
5. tape  tʰejp
6. had  hæd
7. health  hɛlθ
8. vague  vejg
9. exit  ɛgzɪt
10. luge  luʒ
11. rooster  rustr̩
12. sugar  ʃʊgr̩
13. frog  frag
14. instead  ɪnstɛd
15. unit  junɪt
16. paddle  pæɾl̩
17. bottom  baɾm̩
18. question  kwɛstʃn̩
19. angel  endʒl̩
20. church  tʃr̩tʃ

## ✳ Vowel Practice!

1. key  kʰi
2. cheese  tʃiz
3. bone  bown
4. due  du
5. ate  ejt
6. east  ist
7. loaf  lowf
8. wheeze  wiz
9. mainsheet  mejnʃit
10. made  mejd
11. through  θru
12. throw  θrow

## ✳ More Vowels! This time watch out for vowels before *r* sounds.

1. cheer  tʃir
2. there  θejr
3. chair  tʃejr
4. car  kʰar
5. star  star
6. score  skɔr
7. sir  sr̩
8. her  hr̩
9. floor  flɔr
10. oar  ɔr
11. horse  hɔrs
12. course  kʰɔrs
13. heart  hart
14. hard  hard
15. harm  harm
16. sharp  ʃarp
17. shirt  ʃr̩t
18. thwart  θwɔrt

## ✳ Practice with Diphthongs. Transcribe the following words as you would say them in normal everyday speech. Watch out for those diphthongs!

1. voice  vojs
2. trial  trajl̩
3. bicycle  bajsɪkl̩
4. hour  awr̩
5. oily  ojli
6. goat  gowt
7. eyes  ajz
8. prize  prajz
9. embroider  ɪmbrojdr̩
10. sailing  sejlɪŋ
11. crow  krow
12. cried  krajd
13. prowl  prawl̩
14. counter  kʰawntr̩
15. lazy  lejzi
16. knifed  najft
17. down  dawn
18. daze  dejz

**Remember … transcription takes a lot of practice!**

**Practice with Schwa and Wedge.** In this one, pay close attention to the schwa and wedge sounds. You might want to determine which vowel gets primary stress to help you out.

|  |  |  |
|---|---|---|
| 1.  sludge | 2.  thunder | 3.  hung |
| 4.  quality | 5.  behave | 6.  oven |
| 7.  luck | 8.  separate | 9.  stuff |
| 10.  nation | 11.  announce | 12.  understand |

**One More Try!** This one has everything in it. Again, transcribe as you would say the word in normal everyday speech. Watch out . . . they get harder!

|  |  |  |
|---|---|---|
| 1.  days | 2.  agitate | 3.  gnome |
| 4.  Xerox | 5.  roast | 6.  pinstripe |
| 7.  guess | 8.  theatrical | 9.  masculine |
| 10.  yellow | 11.  bargain | 12.  precious |
| 13.  science | 14.  machine | 15.  formula |
| 16.  motorcycle | 17.  surrounded | 18.  comedy |
| 19.  extinguish | 20.  costume | 21.  graduate |
| 22.  implement | 23.  ponder | 24.  irrigate |
| 25.  isolate | 26.  timetable | 27.  unforgivable |
| 28.  frighten | 29.  lemonade | 30.  called |

**Reverse Transcription.** Give the correctly spelled English word for each of the following transcriptions.

|  |  |  |
|---|---|---|
| 1.  [liʒər] | 2.  [ʃaj] | 3.  [pʰajp] |
| 4.  [æks] | 5.  [swit] | 6.  [sɑfənd] |
| 7.  [wərði] | 8.  [tʰub] | 9.  [fowni] |
| 10.  [wʌns] | 11.  [ʧojs] | 12.  [stæʧuw] |
| 13.  [ʃejd] | 14.  [mɛnʃən] | 15.  [skwɛr] |

# SUPRASEGMENTALS

Suprasegmentals refer to inherent properties that are part of all sounds regardless of their place or manner of articulation. The three main suprasegmentals are pitch, length, and stress. Pitch is further divided into tone and intonation.

## Pitch

⇒ Tone languages are languages in which pitch movement is used to signal differences in meaning. Mandarin Chinese is a good example. Tone languages may use register and/or contour tones. A register tone is a level pitch, while a contour tone is a moving pitch. See figure 2.14 on p. 42 for some examples of register and contour tones in Mandarin. Figures 2.12 and 2.15 on pp. 41 and 42 give some examples from other tone languages.

⇒ Intonation is pitch movement that is not related to differences in word meaning. For example, rising pitch is often used to signal a question (an incomplete utterance), and falling intonation a statement (a complete utterance). See figures 2.16 to 2.19 on p. 43 of the text for some examples of different intonations and their representation.

## Length

⇒ Long vowels and consonants are sounds whose articulation simply takes longer relative to other vowels and consonants. Length is indicated with [ː]. See table 2.19 on p. 44 for some examples of short and long vowels in Yapese and table 2.20 on p. 45 for some examples of short and long consonants in Italian.

## Stress

⇒ Stress is associated with vowels. Stressed vowels are perceived as more prominent than other vowels. The most prominent vowel receives primary stress. Primary stress is usually indicated with [ ´ ]. In English, stressed vowels tend to be higher in pitch, louder, and longer than unstressed vowels. See table 2.21 on p. 45 for some examples of differing stress placement in English.

**Exercise!** Mark primary stress on each of the following words.

1. scórnẹd
2. discóvery
3. explósion
4. génius
5. macaróni

6. dúplicate
7. díctate
8. óccupied
9. infórmative
10. ídolize

**Now ...** Go back and transcribe each word.

36    Chapter Two

# PROCESSES

Processes describe articulatory adjustments that occur during speech. Processes typically function to make words easier to articulate. Processes also occur to make speech easier to perceive. The boxes below define and illustrate the different articulatory processes found in language.

---

ASSIMILATION

Assimilation involves sounds changing to become more like nearby sounds. While there are many different kinds of assimilation, in general, assimilation can be divided into three main types:

1. Voicing Assimilation:
   - A sound takes on the same voice as a nearby sound
   - Includes      voicing
                    devoicing

2. Assimilation for Place of Articulation:
   - A sound takes on the same place of articulation as a nearby sound.
   - Includes      palatalization
                   homorganic nasal assimilation . . . and more!

3. Assimilation for Manner of Articulation:
   - A sound takes on the same manner of articulation as a nearby sound
   - Includes      nasalization
                   flapping . . . and more!

**In addition ...** some types of assimilation, such as nasalization, can be either regressive or progressive. In regressive assimilation, a segment takes on some characteristic of the following segment. That is, a sound is influenced by what comes after it. In progressive assimilation, a segment takes on some characteristic of the preceding segment. That is, a sound is influenced by what comes before it. See tables 2.22 and 2.24 on pp. 47 and 48 of the text for examples of progressive assimilation, and table 2.23 on p. 48 for examples of regressive assimilation.

---

DISSIMILATION

A sound changes to become less like a nearby sound so that the resulting sequence of sounds is easier to pronounce: e.g., fifths: [fɪfθs] → [fɪfts].

---

DELETION

The process of deletion simply removes a sound from a phonetic context. Deletion frequently occurs in rapid speech: e.g., fifths: [fɪfθs] → [fɪfs]. See table 2.25 on p. 49 for some examples of schwa deletion in English.

---

EPENTHESIS

The process of epenthesis adds a segment to a phonetic context. Epenthesis is common in casual speech: e.g., warmth: [warmθ] → [warmpθ]. See tables 2.26 and 2.27 on p. 50 for more examples of this process.

---

METATHESIS

Metathesis is a process that changes the order of segments: e.g., prescribe → perscribe. Metathesis is common in the speech of young children: e.g., animal → aminal.

---

VOWEL REDUCTION

In vowel reduction, vowels move to a more central position when they are in unstressed syllables. That is, a vowel is pronounced as a full vowel when in a stressed syllable, and as a schwa when in an unstressed syllable.

---

**Identifying Processes ...** To identify processes, you need to look for differences between the starting and ending pronunciations.

⇒ If a sound is missing, **deletion** has occurred.
⇒ If a sound has been added, **epenthesis** has occurred.
⇒ If the order of sounds has changed, **metathesis** has occurred.
⇒ If a sound has changed, you need to determine if either **assimilation** or **dissimilation** has occurred. To do this, take the following steps:
  • Determine the phonetic property that has changed (voice, place, or manner of articulation).
  • Compare this phonetic property with the phonetic properties of the nearby sounds.
  • If the changed phonetic property matches a phonetic property of a nearby sound, then **assimilation** has occurred. The phonetic property that matches will tell you the specific type of assimilation that has occurred.
  • If the phonetic properties do not match, then **dissimilation** has occurred.

**Remember ...** For assimilation, you also need to be able to identify when processes such as nasalization or place of articulation assimilation are regressive and when they are progressive. To determine this, you need to look at whether the influencing sound comes before (progressive) or after (regressive) the sound that is undergoing the change.

**An example ...**

prince:      [prɪns]      →      [prĩnts]

⇒ [t] occurs in the final pronunciation but not the starting; therefore, epenthesis has occurred.

⇒ [ɪ] has changed to [ĩ]. Remember that [˜] indicates a nasalized sound. The vowel, therefore, has changed from an oral to a nasal sound, and since the following sound is a nasal, assimilation–in particular nasalization–has occurred. The influencing sound is the following nasal, meaning that the nasalization is regressive.

The change in the pronunciation of the word 'prince' from [prɪns] to [prĩnts] involves two processes: epenthesis and regressive nasalization.

**Try These!** Identify the process(es) at work in each of the following:

1. ask:        [æsk]         →      [æks]        *metathesis*

2. winter:     [wɪntər]      →      [wĩnər]      *epenthesis / nasalization (regressive)*

3. clear:      [kl̥ir]         →      [kəlir]       *epenthesis  voice assimilation*

4. puddle:     [pʰʌdəl]      →      [pʰʌɾəl]     *flapping*

5. sixths:     [sɪksθs]      →      [sɪksts]     *dissimulation*

6. wash:       [wɑʃ]         →      [wɑrʃ]       *deletion nasal (regressive)*

7. sandwich:   [sændwɪʧ]     →      [sæmwɪʧ]     *place assimulation*

**REVIEW! REVIEW!**  Make sure you know the following:

- the different parts of the sound-producing system, including the vocal tract
- the difference between voiced and voiceless sounds
- the difference between nasal and oral sounds
- the characteristics of consonants, glides, and vowels
- the places and manners of articulation for consonant sounds
- the different tongue placements required to describe vowels
- the difference between tense and lax, and rounded and unrounded vowels
- the symbols and articulatory descriptions for English consonants
- the strident fricatives and affricates
- the symbols and articulatory descriptions for English vowels
- when and why aspiration occurs
- how to complete and decipher facial diagrams
- how to identify processes
- the suprasegmentals of tone, intonation, length, and stress
- transcription, transcription, transcription!

# QUESTIONS?  PROBLEMS?  DIFFICULTIES?

_____

_____

_____

_____

_____

_____

_____

_____

_____

_____

# CHAPTER 3. PHONOLOGY:
# CONTRASTS AND PATTERNS

Phonology is the study of how languages organize speech sounds into a system of contrasts and patterns. Important terms, concepts, and topics of discussion within this chapter include the following:

1. Contrast
2. Minimal pairs and near minimal pairs
3. Complementary distribution
4. Phonemes and allophones
5. Phonology problems
6. Rules and generalizations
7. Phonetic and phonemic representations
8. Syllables
9. Features
10. Derivations and rule ordering

Since we will be dealing with many languages besides English, you will come across some phonetic symbols that have not been discussed. Articulatory descriptions will be provided for these unfamiliar sounds.


## PHONOLOGICAL STRUCTURE

Three types of structure are relevant to phonological analysis.

**Segments:**    As discussed in Chapter 2, a segment is an individual speech sound. Each IPA symbol represents a segment.

**Syllables:**    Segments can be grouped together to form a syllable. A syllable consists of a syllabic element (e.g., a vowel) plus any preceding or following segments.

**Features:**    Segments are made up of features. A feature is a unit that corresponds to a single piece of either articulatory or acoustic information. Features are the smallest type of phonological structure.

These three units of phonological structure work together to produce the sound patterns of a language. See figure 3.1 on p. 56 for a representation of the hierarchical relationship between the different units of phonological structure.

# CONTRAST

Sounds (or segments) are said to contrast when their presence alone is responsible for forms having different meanings. Both consonant and vowel sounds may contrast with each other. Determining which sounds contrast is a first step in phonological analysis.

⇒ **Minimal Pairs.** A minimal pair is defined as two phonetic forms that have different meanings and that differ by one sound that is in the same environment in both forms. *Environment* refers to the phonetic context in which the sound is found. A minimal pair means that sounds contrast.

   e.g., English [pæt] 'pat' and [bæt] 'bat'

⇒ **Near Minimal Pairs.** A near minimal pair is defined as two phonetic forms that contain differences other than the one involving the key contrast; the extra differences must not involve sounds right next to the contrasting sounds. Like a minimal pair, these forms have different meanings, and like a minimal pair, a near minimal pair means that sounds contrast.

   e.g., Hindi [bara] 'large' and [b̤ari] 'heavy'

⇒ **Phonemes.** Sounds that contrast are said to belong to separate phonemes. Native speakers' phonological knowledge includes knowledge of which sounds are contrastive (distinctive) in their language. Phonemes are used to capture this knowledge. Sounds belonging to separate phonemes can be represented as follows.

/ /                    / /    ⟵_____ knowledge stored in the mind

[ ]                    [ ]    ⟵_____ sounds that the vocal tract produces

**Think ...** Which sounds contrast in the English and Hindi examples above? Put together a phonemic representation of the contrastive sounds in each example.

**Try This ...** Can the sounds [m] and [n] both occur in each of the following environments? What English words result from using [m] and [n] in the same environment? Are these words minimal pairs? If so, what does this tell us about how [m] and [n] pattern in English?

   [____ ajt]    [____ it]    [pʰæ ____]

See table 3.2 on p. 58 for some consonantal contrasts in English, and table 3.3 on p. 58 for examples of vowel contrasts in English. See table 3.5 on p. 60 for some examples of vowel contrasts in Japanese.

**Exercise!** State whether each of the following pairs of words on the next page is a minimal pair, a near minimal pair, or neither. Make sure you pay attention to the meanings provided.

1. [ʧogʊr] 'necklace'  and  [ʧogʊl] 'bracelet'  *minimal pair*

2. [pækt] 'towel'  and  [sægt] 'roof'  *near minimal pair*

3. [telʌm] 'book'  and  [tɛlʌm] 'book'  *minimal pair*

4. [kətɑge] 'letter'  and  [kətage] 'fork'  *Not*

5. [supt] 'bulb'  and  [depts] 'sugar'  *NOt*

6. [nozər] 'frog'  and  [hoʒəlʊp] 'valley'  *near*

7. [fɪθæk] 'rain'  and  [fɪðæk] 'window'  *minimal pair*

# COMPLEMENTARY DISTRIBUTION

Not all sounds found in a language contrast with each other. Some sounds are in complementary distribution. Two phonetically similar sounds are in complementary distribution when they never occur in the same phonetic environment. Remember, the term *environment* refers to the phonetic context in which the sounds occur.

⇒ **Distribution.** Sounds that are in complementary distribution are found in predictable environments. The distribution is simply a statement of the environments in which the sounds are found. In English, for example, oral and nasal vowels are in complementary distribution.

    i.e.,   Nasal vowels occur before nasal consonants.
            Oral vowels occur before oral consonants, after nasal consonants, and in several other types of environments.

⇒ **Allophones.** Sounds that are in complementary distribution are allophones belonging to the same phoneme. Allophones are phonetic variants of a sound. Part of native speaker knowledge is knowledge of which allophones belong to the same phoneme. Remember that phonemes represent native speaker knowledge. Allophones belonging to the same phoneme can be represented as follows.

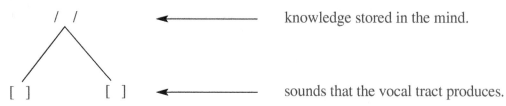

    / /    ⟵    knowledge stored in the mind.

    [ ]    [ ]    ⟵    sounds that the vocal tract produces.

⇒ **Elsewhere.** One allophone is used to represent the phoneme. This is typically the allophone that occurs in the greatest number of phonetic environments and is referred to as "elsewhere". So the distribution of English nasal and oral vowels becomes the following:

        Nasal vowels occur before nasal consonants.
        Oral vowels occur elsewhere.

⇒ **Now ...** Using the above information, put together a representation for English [i] and [ĩ].

**Exercise!** The following exercises are designed to help you understand the predictable nature of complementary distribution.

1.  In English, [p] has (at least) three allophones:

    [p]     – unaspirated
    [pʰ]    – aspirated
    [p˺]    – unreleased

    The following list of words gives examples of each allophone.

    | [p] | [pʰ] | [p˺] |
    |---|---|---|
    | spook | pig | collapse |
    | spirit | police | apt |
    | operate | appear | flipped |
    | happening | repair | ape |
    | | | cop |
    | | | clap |

    Using the data in the above chart, determine which allophone occurs in each of the following environments:

    at the beginning of a word (word initially)

    before a stressed vowel

    before a consonant

    at the end of a word (word finally)w

    after [s]

    after a stressed vowel

    *[p] occurs after s and after a stressed vowel*
    *[pʰ] beginning of a word before a stressed vowel*
    *[p˺] end of a word before a consonant*

**Now ...** Can [p], [pʰ], and [p˺] all occur in each of the following environments? Think about whether the words that result from using each of these sounds in the same environment have different meanings. Then, determine which sound can occur in each of the following environments. Make sure you pay attention to which vowel is stressed.

$$[hɪ \text{\_\_\_\_} i]  [\text{\_\_\_\_} ɑt]  [kɛ \text{\_\_\_\_} t]$$

2.  English [ l ] has (at least) three allophones:

    [l]     – alveolar (clear) l
    [ɫ]     – velarized (dark) l
    [l̩]    – syllabic l

    The following list of words gives examples of each allophone.

    | [l] | [ɫ] | [l̩] |
    |---|---|---|
    | lip | swallow | paddle |
    | love | silly | obstacle |
    | allow | salt | twinkle |
    | malign | ilk | bushel |
    | slip | pull | hurdle |

Using the data in the above chart, determine which allophone occurs in each of the following environments:

at the end of a word after a consonant |

at the end of a word after a vowel +

after a stressed vowel +

before a stressed vowel 1

after [s] 1

at the beginning of a word (word initially) 1

**Now ...** Can [l], [ɫ], and [l̩] all occur in each of the following environments? Think about whether the words that result from using each of these sounds in the same environment have different meanings. Then, determine which sound can occur in each of the following environments. Again, be sure and pay attention to which vowel is stressed.

[s_____ ajd]   [mi ____]   [hæs ____]

**Reminder ...** The environments in the above exercises are not to be taken as a complete list of environments to look for when doing phonological analysis. They are only examples of some possible environments, many of which pertain only to these exercises.

## DETERMINING COMPLEMENTARY DISTRIBUTION

For each data set below, find the complementary distribution and put together a representation of the distribution. Remember: the allophone that occurs in the greater number of environments is chosen as elsewhere and is used to represent the phoneme. All data is given in phonetic transcription.

1.  The following data is from Oneida. Examine the sounds [s] and [z].

[s] *elsewhere*                                    [z] *between vowels*

| [lashet] | 'let him count' | [kawenezuzeʔ] | 'long words' |
| [laʔsluni] | 'white men' | [khaiize] | 'I'm taking it along' |
| [loteswatu] | 'he's been playing' | [lazel] | 'let him drag it' |
| [skahnehtat] | 'one pine tree' | [tahazehteʔ] | 'he dropped it' |
| [thiskate] | 'a different one' | [tuzahatiteni] | 'they changed it' |
| [sninuhe] | 'you buy' | [wezake] | 'she saw you' |
| [wahsnestakeʔ] | 'you ate corn' | | |

2. The following data is also from Oneida. Examine the sounds [s] and [ʃ].

[s] *elsewhere*                                      [ʃ] *before [j]*

| [lashet] | 'let him count' | [ʃjatuhe?] | 'you write' |
|---|---|---|---|
| [la?sluni] | 'white men' | [tehʃja?k] | 'let you break' |
| [loteswatu] | 'he's been playing' | [ja?teʃjatekhahʃjahte?] | 'they would suddenly' |
| [skahnehtat] | 'one pine tree' | | 'separate again' |
| [thiskate] | 'a different one' | | |
| [sninuhe] | 'you buy' | | |
| [wahsnestake?] | 'you ate corn' | | |

3. The following data is from Japanese. Examine the sounds [t], [ʧ] and [ts].

   Note: The symbol [ts] is a single segment representing a voiceless alveolar affricate.

*←before a high front tense vowel*
*elsewhere    before a high tense back vowel*

| [tatami] | 'mat' | [tsukue] | 'desk' |
|---|---|---|---|
| [tegami] | 'letter' | [ato] | 'later' |
| [ʧitʃi] | 'father' | [deguʃi] | 'exit' |
| [ʃita] | 'under' | [tsutsumu] | 'to wrap' |
| [matsu] | 'to wait' | [kata] | 'person' |
| [natsu] | 'summer' | [tatemono] | 'building' |
| [ʧizu] | 'map' | [te] | 'hand' |
| [koto] | 'fact' | [utʃi] | 'house' |
| [tomodatʃi] | 'friend' | [otoko] | 'male' |
| [totemo] | 'very' | [tetsudau] | 'to help' |

## PHONEMES AND ALLOPHONES

Phonemes and allophones are two units of representation used in phonology. These are used to capture native speakers' knowledge about how sounds pattern in their language.

**PHONEME** means ...    1. The way in which sounds are stored in the mind.
2. The contrastive phonological units of a language.
3. The underlying representation.

**ALLOPHONE** means ...    1. The way in which sounds are pronounced.
2. The predictable variants of the language's phonological units.
3. The surface representation.

⇒ **Phonemes.** Phonemes represent the contrastive sounds of a language. Contrastive sounds belong to separate phonemes and are represented on two levels:

| **Phonemic:** | / / | / / |
|---|---|---|
| **Phonetic:** | [ ] | [ ] |

- Contrastive sounds are phonetically different sounds (i.e., they have different articulations) *and* phonologically different sounds (i.e., they are found in the same environment and make meaning differences).

⇒ **Allophones.** Allophones belong to the same phoneme, are in complementary distribution, and are also represented on two levels:

**Phonemic:**        / /

**Phonetic:**      [ ]        [ ]

- Sounds in complementary distribution are phonetically different sounds (i.e., they have different articulations), *but* they are phonologically the same sound (i.e., they do not contrast and are never found in the same environment).

⇒ **Differences in phonemes across languages.** Whether segments contrast or not is determined on a language-by-language basis. Sounds that are contrastive in one language may not be contrastive in another. Consider the following examples.

| Language | Segments | Phonetic Forms |
|----------|----------|----------------|
| Khmer | [kʰ] [k] | [kʰat] 'to polish' and [kat] 'to cut' |
| Turkish | [ɛ] [æ] | [bɛn] 'I' and [bæn] 'I' |
| Japanese | [i] [iː] | [tori] 'bird' and [toriː] 'shrine gate' |

**Think …** Do the sounds [kʰ] and [k] contrast in Khmer? What about in English? Do the sounds [ɛ] and [æ] contrast in Turkish? Think of an English minimal pair containing [ɛ] and [æ]. Do the sounds [i] and [iː] contrast in Japanese? Do they contrast in English? Remember that [ː] indicates a long sound.

⇒ **Differences in allophones across languages.** The patterning of allophones can also vary from language to language. For example, both English and Scots Gaelic have nasal vowels; however, the distribution is different in the two languages. In English, nasal vowels only occur before nasal consonants, while in Scots Gaelic, nasal vowels occur on both sides of a nasal consonant. In both languages, oral vowels occur elsewhere. See tables 3.11 and 3.12 on p. 65 of the text for some examples of nasal vowels in English and Scots Gaelic. See table 3.13 on p. 66 for an example of a different pattern of nasalization.

**Think …** How would the representation of nasal vowels be different for Scots Gaelic than for English? Think of a language in which nasal and oral vowels are separate phonemes (i.e., they are not in complementary, but contrastive distribution).

## SOLVING PHONOLOGY PROBLEMS

The basic goal in solving a phonology problem is to determine if the sounds being examined are separate phonemes or if they are allophones of the same phoneme.

## WHEN SOUNDS ARE SEPARATE PHONEMES, THEY ARE

1. contrastive/distinctive
2. in unpredictable distribution
3. easily perceived as different
4. not necessarily phonetically similar

## WHEN SOUNDS ARE ALLOPHONES OF THE SAME PHONEME, THEY ARE

1. non-contrastive/rule-governed
2. in predictable distribution
3. not easily perceived as different
4. always phonetically similar

## PROBLEM SOLVING FLOWCHART

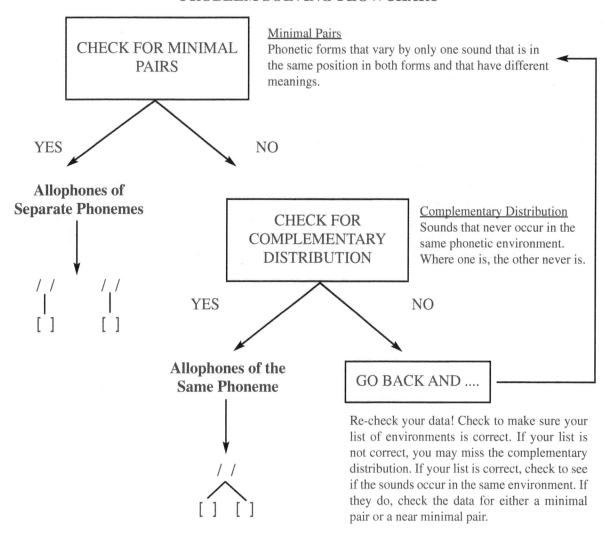

Repeat the above for each pair of sounds you are investigating!

1. Arabic: [h] and [ʔ] *[handwritten: [h] and [ʔ] are allophones of seperate phonemes. They are in contrastive distribution: (a) and (e) is a minimal pair, as is (b) and (f), (c)(g), (d)(h)]*

|     |          |              |     |          |            |
|-----|----------|--------------|-----|----------|------------|
| a.  | [ʔuru:b] | wars         | e.  | [huru:b] | flight     |
| b.  | [fahm]   | understanding| f.  | [faʔm]   | coal       |
| c.  | [habba]  | gust, squall | g.  | [ʔabba]  | grain, seed|
| d.  | [ha:l]   | cardamom     | h.  | [ʔa:l]   | condition  |

*[handwritten annotation at top:]* [θ] and [t] are allophones of the same phoneme. [θ] between vowels [t] Elsewhere.

2.  Hebrew: [θ] and [t]    ([x] represents a voiceless velar fricative)

|   |   |   |   |   |   |
|---|---|---|---|---|---|
| a. | [tafar] | saw | e. | [tannur] | stove |
| b. | [ʃtaim] | two | f. | [oθax] | you |
| c. | [iθi] | with me | g. | [teʃaʔ] | nine |
| d. | [raiθa] | you saw | h. | [tamid] | always |

3.  Slovak: [f] and [v]  *[handwritten:]* allophones of separate phonemes. (a),(b) (e),(f)

|   |   |   |   |   |   |
|---|---|---|---|---|---|
| a. | [vatra] | campfire | d. | [vɔlk] | wolf |
| b. | [farba] | paint | e. | [feltʃar] | paint |
| c. | [faːdni] | monotonous | f. | [vedro] | bucket |

**Think …**   Different languages may contain the same sounds, but these sounds may not pattern in the same way. Think about [t] and [θ] in English. Are these sounds in complementary distribution, or can they be found in a minimal pair? Put together a representation of how these sounds pattern in English. How is the English pattern different from how these sounds pattern in Hebrew?

> Sounds can also be in **free variation**. This refers to sounds that occur in the same phonetic environment but do not create words having different meanings. Say the final *p* in the word *stop* in the following ways: (1) with the lips closed for a moment before releasing them ([stɑp˺]), (2) with a glottal closure ([stɑpʔ]), and (3) forcefully ([stɑp!]). Does the meaning of the word change with the different articulations?

## SOME PHONOLOGY PROBLEMS!

The following pages contain data sets from a number of different languages. Some of the data may have been regularized. Each data set contains sufficient data to make valid conclusions about the sounds under consideration. For each data set, do the following:

- State your conclusion (i.e., separate phonemes or allophones of the same phoneme).
- Provide evidence to support your conclusion.
- Provide a representation of the phoneme(s).

**1. Russian:**   [a] and [ɑ]

[a]    This symbol represents a low central lax unrounded vowel.

Remember, you want to look for minimal pairs involving the sounds that you have been asked to investigate. There may be other minimal pairs in the data, but you only want those that contain the sounds you are asked to examine.

|   |   |   |   |   |   |
|---|---|---|---|---|---|
| 1. | [atəm] | 'atom' | 6. | [pɑɬ] | 'he fell' |
| 2. | [dva] | 'two' | 7. | [dɑɬ] | 'he gave' |
| 3. | [pɑɬkə] | 'stick' | 8. | [dar] | 'gift' |
| 4. | [mas] | 'ointment' | 9. | [matə] | 'mint' |
| 5. | [ukrɑtə] | 'she stole' | 10. | [brɑɬ] | 'he took' |

**2. Inuktitut:** [u] and [a]

> [q]   This symbol represents a voiceless uvular stop.

| | | | | | |
|---|---|---|---|---|---|
| 1. | [iglumut] | 'to a house' | 6. | [aniguvit] | 'if you leave' |
| 2. | [ukiaq] | 'late fall' | 7. | [ini] | 'place, spot' |
| 3. | [iglu] | '(snow)house' | 8. | [ukiuq] | 'winter' |
| 4. | [aiviq] | 'walrus' | 9. | [ani] | 'female's brother' |
| 5. | [pinna] | 'that one up there' | 10. | [anigavit] | 'because you leave' |

**3. English:** [g], [gʲ] and [gʷ]

> [gʲ]   This symbol represents a 'fronted [g]' made with the back of the tongue at or near the hard palate.
>
> [gʷ]   This symbol represents a 'rounded [g]' made with simultaneous lip rounding.

| | | | | | |
|---|---|---|---|---|---|
| 1. | [gɑn] | 'gone' | 7. | [gʲik] | 'geek' |
| 2. | [gʷufi] | 'goofy' | 8. | [igər] | 'eager' |
| 3. | [gli] | 'glee' | 9. | [gejm] | 'game' |
| 4. | [slʌg] | 'slug' | 10. | [gowfər] | 'gopher' |
| 5. | [grin] | 'green' | 11. | [gædʒət] | 'gadget' |
| 6. | [rægʷu] | 'ragout' | 12. | [gʲis] | 'geese' |

**4. Korean:** [l] and [ř]

> [ř]   This symbol represents a flapped [r].
>
> [ʉ]   This symbol represents a high central rounded vowel.

| | | | | | |
|---|---|---|---|---|---|
| 1. | [kal] | 'dog' | 10. | [onelppam] | 'tonight' |
| 2. | [kenel] | 'shade' | 11. | [silkwa] | 'fruit' |
| 3. | [iřumi] | 'name' | 12. | [mul] | 'water' |
| 4. | [kiři] | 'road' | 13. | [seul] | 'Seoul' |
| 5. | [juŋutʃʉm] | 'receipt' | 14. | [kəřiřo] | 'to the street' |
| 6. | [pal] | 'leg' | 15. | [sařam] | 'person' |
| 7. | [ilkop] | 'seven' | 16. | [tatʉl] | 'all of them' |
| 8. | [ipalsa] | 'barber' | 17. | [vəřʉm] | 'summer' |
| 9. | [uři] | 'we' | | | |

**5. Tojolabal** (spoken in Mexico):   [k] and [kʼ]

   [ ʼ ]   This diacritic means the sound has been glottalized.

| | | | | | |
|---|---|---|---|---|---|
| 1. | [kisim] | 'my beard' | 7. | [sak] | 'white' |
| 2. | [tʃakʼa] | 'chop it down' | 8. | [kʼisin] | 'warm' |
| 3. | [koktit] | 'our feet' | 9. | [skutʃu] | 'he is carrying it' |
| 4. | [kʼak] | 'flea' | 10. | [kʼuutes] | 'to dress' |
| 5. | [pʼakan] | 'hanging' | 11. | [snika] | 'he stirred it' |
| 6. | [kʼaʔem] | 'sugar cane' | 12. | [ʔakʼ] | 'read' |

**6. English:**   [l] and [ɫ]

   **Note:**   The English data presented below has been simplified somewhat. For a more challenging (and more accurate) analysis of English [l] and [ɫ], try problem 10 on page 99 of the text!

| | | | | | |
|---|---|---|---|---|---|
| 1. | [lɪp] | 'lip' | 7. | [fɪlθ] | 'filth' |
| 2. | [lʌvli] | 'lovely' | 8. | [wɑɫgrinz] | 'Wallgreens' |
| 3. | [sɪɫk] | 'silk' | 9. | [gɪlt] | 'guilt' |
| 4. | [slajm] | 'slime' | 10. | [tæɫk] | 'talc' |
| 5. | [mɪɫk] | 'milk' | 11. | [hiəl] | 'heal' |
| 6. | [kæɫgri] | 'Calgary' | | | |

**7. Sindhi:**   [p], [b], and [pʰ]

   For these three sounds to be allophones of separate phonemes, you must find a minimal pair for each of the following:

   • [p] and [b]
   • [p] and [pʰ]
   • [b] and [pʰ]

   You may use the same data item in more than one minimal pair.

| | | | | | |
|---|---|---|---|---|---|
| 1. | [pʌnu] | 'leaf' | 7. | [tʌru] | 'bottom' |
| 2. | [vʌdʒu] | 'opportunity' | 8. | [kʰʌto] | 'sour' |
| 3. | [ʃʌki] | 'suspicious' | 9. | [bʌdʒu] | 'run' |
| 4. | [gʌdo] | 'dull' | 10. | [bʌnu] | 'forest' |
| 5. | [dʌru] | 'door' | 11. | [bʌtʃu] | 'be safe' |
| 6. | [pʰʌnu] | 'snakehood' | 12. | [dʒʌdʒu] | 'judge' |

**8.** __Kenyang__ (spoken in Cameroon): [k] and [q]   Then: [b] and [β].

[q]     This symbol represents a voiceless uvular stop.
[β]     This symbol represents a voiced bilabial fricative.

| | | | | | | |
|---|---|---|---|---|---|---|
| 1. | [enoq] | 'tree' | | 7. | [uβit] | 'person's name' |
| 2. | [eβet] | 'house' | | 8. | [nʧiβu] | 'I am buying' |
| 3. | [bag] | 'rope' | | 9. | [etaq] | 'town' |
| 4. | [enok] | 'tree' | | 10. | [nab] | 'brother-in-law' |
| 5. | [nbat] | 'knife' | | 11. | [pobrin] | 'work project' |
| 6. | [etak] | 'town' | | 12. | [ndeβi] | 'European' |

---

## QUICK REMINDER!!

Don't forget to use / / brackets to indicate phonemes and to use [ ] brackets to indicate allophones.

---

## RULES AND GENERALIZATIONS

When a phonological analysis uncovers allophones belonging to the same phoneme, a rule can be put together to capture the distribution.

**Some things to remember ...**

⇒ Allophones belonging to the same phoneme represent a predictable sound change. Such sound changes occur because segments are often affected by the phonetic characteristics of neighbouring sounds. These changes are described using processes such as assimilation. Rules, therefore, are descriptions of articulatory processes.

⇒ The sound changes represented in allophonic distributions usually affect not individual sounds, but groups of sounds that share a common phonetic property – that is, a class of sounds. For this reason, rules are formulated as generally as possible.

**The format and function of rules ...**

⇒ Rules are given in phonological notation.

$$\text{e.g.,} \quad /l/ \rightarrow [\mathring{l}] \; / \left\{ \begin{array}{c} p \\ t \\ k \end{array} \right\} \underline{\quad\quad}$$

⇒ Rules link the phonemic and phonetic levels together and consist of the following three parts:

1. the phoneme (e.g., /l/)
2. the change that takes place as captured by the non-elsewhere allophone (e.g., [l̥])
3. the environment in which the change from the phoneme to the non-elsewhere allophone takes place (e.g., $\begin{Bmatrix} p \\ t \\ k \end{Bmatrix}$ _____ )

- The rule is read as the statement "A voiced lateral liquid becomes voiceless after voiceless stops."

**Now ...** In English, the voiced retroflex liquid also becomes voiceless after voiceless stops, just like the lateral liquid. Write a rule to capture this distribution. Then, combine your rule with the above rule for lateral liquids. Convert your combined rule into one very general statement.

**Think ...** What type of assimilation does your combined rule describe? Think about the phonetic property of the phoneme that changed to arrive at the non-elsewhere allophone.

See figures (22) and (23) on p. 92 for examples of rules involving deletion and epenthesis.

**Exercise!**   Convert these statements into rules. Watch out for classes of sounds!

1. Voiceless stops become voiced at the beginning of words.

2. Alveopalatal affricates become fricatives between vowels.

3. Vowels become nasalized before nasals.

4. Schwa is deleted word finally.

5. A schwa is inserted between a voiceless bilabial stop and a voiced lateral liquid.

**Exercise!**   Convert the following rules into statements. Make your statements as general as possible.

1.        t  ⟶  tˀ   /   ʔ____

___

2.   $\left\{\begin{array}{c} f \\ s \\ \theta \\ \int \end{array}\right\} \longrightarrow \left\{\begin{array}{c} v \\ z \\ ð \\ ʒ \end{array}\right\}$  /   V____V

___

3.   $\left\{\begin{array}{c} i \\ e \end{array}\right\} \longrightarrow \left\{\begin{array}{c} ɪ \\ ɛ \end{array}\right\}$  /   ____#

___

4.   $\left\{\begin{array}{c} t \\ d \end{array}\right\} \longrightarrow$  ɾ   /   V____V

___

## PHONETIC AND PHONEMIC REPRESENTATIONS

There are two types of representation: phonetic and phonemic.

⇒ **Phonetic Representation.**   The phonetic representation is a representation of normal every-day speech. That is, it is a representation of pronunciation. It includes all phonetic information, including that which is predictable. Phonetic representations are always given in [ ] brackets.

⇒ **Phonemic Representation.**   The phonemic representation is a representation that contains only the phonemes of the language. All predictable information is excluded. Phonemic representations are always indicated with / / brackets.

⇒ **Understanding the Difference.**   To help you understand the difference between phonetic and phonemic representations, go back to the Russian problem on p. 48 of this study guide. Remember that in Russian [a] and [ɑ] are allophones of the same phoneme, with [ɑ] occurring before [ɫ], a velarized lateral liquid, and [a] elsewhere. Given this information, we can convert some of the Russian phonetic forms into Russian phonemic representations.

|  | Phonetic |  |  | Phonemic |  |
|---|---|---|---|---|---|
| [mas] | 'ointment' | | /mas/ | 'ointment' | |
| [ukrɑtə] | 'she stole' | | /ukratə/ | 'she stole' | |
| [brɑɫ] | 'he took' | | /braɫ/ | 'he took' | |

• **Think ...**   Does the phonemic representation of Russian use the phoneme or the allophones? What about the phonetic representation? Where is [ɑ] used in the phonetic representation?

See table 3.14 on p. 66 for some examples of phonetic and phonemic representations of English.

**Think ...**   There are two levels of representation: phonetic and phonemic. What links phonetic and phonemic information together? Think about how you go from the phonemic level (knowledge) to the phonetic level (speech).

## MORE PHONOLOGY PROBLEMS!

For each of the following data sets, do the following:

• Determine whether the sounds under consideration are allophones of the same phoneme or whether they are separate phonemes. Provide evidence to support your conclusion, along with a representation of the phoneme.

• If the sounds are allophones of the same phoneme, then provide a phonological rule.

While the data are from hypothetical languages, they exemplify phenomena found in real languages.

1. Storish:          [ʃ] and [ʒ]

| 1. [gasaʃ] | 'mistake' | 5. [trutuʃ] | 'dive' |
|---|---|---|---|
| 2. [ʒipaʃ] | 'head' | 6. [tolʒog] | 'crash' |
| 3. [seʒor] | 'board' | 7. [naʒut] | 'hospital' |
| 4. [tʌʒəkəʃ] | 'ambulance' | 8. [ʧisoʃ] | 'operation' |

2. Nonamb:          [i] and [ĩ]

| 1. [θikig] | 'weasel' | 5. [apĩŋk] | 'fox' |
|---|---|---|---|
| 2. [gorĩm] | 'parrot' | 6. [nuret] | 'knife' |
| 3. [seyit] | 'arrow' | 7. [ʌlĩnd] | 'ferret' |
| 4. [kĩŋglɔn] | 'cave' | 8. [kuʧis] | 'deer' |

3.  Skatik:          [p] and [f]

1.  [pʊnt]       'scale'        5.  [lɔnik]     'scone'
2.  [akog]       'scatter'      6.  [jɪptu]     'scold'
3.  [zifug]      'skelter'      7.  [fʊnt]      'skate'
4.  [jɪftu]      'scare'        8.  [sipək]     'skin'


4.  Severenese:      [i] and [u]

1.  [ubren]      'table'        5.  [ublet]     'never'
2.  [lezun]      'clock'        6.  [seti]      'blue'
3.  [gunob]      'arm'          7.  [iplet]     'stop'
4.  [setu]       'moss'         8.  [ibren]     'snow'


5.  Luru:           [u] and [ʊ],   [m] and [n]

1.  [luska]      'stone'        8.  [sunbu]     'melon'
2.  [holu]       'fly'          9.  [umʊlo]     'they have'
3.  [sʊrak]      'left'        10.  [rukoru]    'singing'
4.  [ketʊl]      'arm'         11.  [uzmaluk]   'road'
5.  [sumbu]      'melon'       12.  [ketuʃ]     'summer'
6.  [ambʊl]      'yellow'      13.  [ʊrkʊl]     'spark'
7.  [mastuf]     'puppy'       14.  [mustʊr]    'wine'

6.  Silliese:        [t] and [d]

1.  [matan]      'joke'         5.  [dar]       'chip'
2.  [dortalu]    'club'         6.  [bontel]    'laugh'
3.  [antar]      'sneeze'       7.  [gotu]      'funny'
4.  [dili]       'drink'        8.  [doko]      'light'


7.  Breakie:         [p] and [b]

1.  [tiktæpe]    'juice'        5.  [lobop]     'milk'
2.  [dob]        'sugar'        6.  [θupaz]     'egg'
3.  [fæbe]       'table'        7.  [bagur]     'bread'
4.  [sepita]     'food'         8.  [gitip]     'salt'


**Now Try This!**   Go back over the above problems and wherever allophones of the same phoneme were found, convert the first few words in the data set from their phonetic to their phonemic representation. See if you can identify the predictable phonetic property that is missing from the phonemic representation.

---

### REMINDER!  REMINDER!

When you find allophones of the same phoneme, there is a quick way to determine if your solution is in all likelihood correct. If your rule and statement describe an articulatory process such as assimilation, which is the result of neighbouring sounds interacting with each other, then your solution is probably correct. If your rule and statement do not describe such a process, then you might want to rethink your analysis!

---

## SYLLABLES

A syllable is another phonological unit of representation. Sounds can be grouped together to form a syllable, which consists of a syllabic element (usually a vowel) plus any preceding or following sounds.

To understand how syllables work, you need to understand the basics of syllable structure (both core and non-core syllables), how to represent syllables, differences in syllable structure across languages, and the role of syllables in phonology.

### Syllable Structure

Syllables have internal structure, which is represented above the individual sounds making up the syllable. A syllable ($\sigma$) consists of an onset (O) and a rhyme (R). The rhyme consists of a nucleus (N) and a coda (C). Here are some things to keep in mind with respect to syllable structure:

⇒ The **nucleus** of a syllable contains a vowel (including diphthongs) or a syllabic conso-nant (either a syllabic liquid or a syllabic nasal; see Chapter 3, p. 69).

⇒ The **onset** contains consonants occurring before the nucleus.

⇒ The **coda** contains consonants occurring after the nucleus.

In any syllable, the nucleus – and therefore, the rhyme – must be included. This is true for all languages. Onsets and codas may not be present in every syllable, although this may also depend on individual languages.

⇒ **Core Syllables.**  Core syllables contain the structure outlined above. In addition, there are two restrictions on the structure of core syllables in languages that allow multiple consonants in either the onset or the coda.

• **Sonority Requirement.**  Not all sounds have the same degree of sonority. Vowels are the most sonorant, while obstruents (stops, fricatives, and affricates) are the least sonorant. Of the sonorant consonants, glides are the most sonorant, followed by liquids, and finally nasals. This can be diagrammed as follows:

increasing sonority

| 0 | 1 | 2 | 3 | 4 |
|---|---|---|---|---|
| Obstruents | Nasals | Liquids | Glides | Vowels |

Consonants must rise in sonority before the nucleus and fall in sonority after the nucleus. This means that sonority must rise and not fall in the onset, and it must fall rather than rise in the coda. For example, *gr* in the word *green* is a permissible onset, since it rises in sonority from 0 to 2. Similarly, *nt* in the word *tent* is a permissible coda, since it falls in sonority from 1 to 0.

See figure 3.11 on p. 70 for an example of a syllable in English that meets this requirement. See table 3.19 on p. 71 for examples of some English onsets that meet the Sonority Requirement.

- **Binarity Requirement.** Each constituent can, at the most, be binary (branching). This means that an onset can have a *maximum* of two consonants. That is, an onset can consist of zero, one, or two consonants. The same is true for codas.

⇒ **Non-Core Syllables.** These are syllables that fail to meet either the Sonority Requirement or the Binarity Requirement. For example, in the word *stop*, the onset *st* does not rise in sonority, since both consonants are obstruents. In *scratch*, the onset *(scr)* contains three sounds, not two. Similarly, in *kept*, the coda does not fall in sonority (again, both consonants are obstruents), while in *tanks*, the coda *(nks)* contains three sounds.

- Sounds that do not meet either the Sonority Requirement or Binarity Requirement are not part of either the onset or the coda. Rather, they are **appendices**.

**Try This!**   Examine the words below. For each word, determine how many syllables are in the word. For each syllable in the word, determine whether it is a core or non-core syllable. Remember to put the words into their phonemic representation first!

| | | | |
|---|---|---|---|
| 1.  garden | 4.  beauty | 7.  understands | 10.  scraps |
| 2.  parks | 5.  twinkle | 8.  triangle | 11.  cleanser |
| 3.  strained | 6.  lovely | 9.  snowfall | 12.  splashdown |

**Think ...**   Compare the onset in *snow* from *snowfall* to the onset in *stands* from *understands*. Which requirement seems to be more important, the Sonority Requirement or the Binarity Requirement?

## Syllable Representations

There are three, sometimes four, steps to putting together a representation of a syllable. These are illustrated for the word *skateboard* /sketbord/.

First:   Assign the nucleus, the rhyme, and the syllable node. Vowels (including diphthongs) and syllabic consonants may occupy the nucleus position.

Second:   Assign the onset. These are sounds to the left of the nucleus. First assign the sound immediately to the left of the nucleus. Assign a second sound to the onset, but only if that sound is less sonorant than the first sound assigned to the onset. Do not assign a third sound to the onset!

Third:   Assign the coda. These are sounds to the right of the nucleus. First assign the sound immediately to the right of the nucleus. Assign a second sound to the coda, but only if that sound is more sonorant than the first sound assigned to the coda. Do not assign a third sound to the coda!

Fourth:   Assign any leftover sounds to the syllable node. These are appendices that are not part of either the onset or coda.

This step is only needed if there are sounds that have not been assigned to either an onset or a coda.

**Some Definitions ...** An open syllable is a syllable that does not include a coda – that is, the rhyme only consists of the nucleus. A closed syllable is a syllable that includes a coda – the rhyme consists of the nucleus plus the coda.

See figures 3.17 to 3.20 on pp. 74 and 75 for an example of the procedure for setting up syllables. See figures 3.21 and 3.22 on p. 75 for an example of the representation of a non-core syllable.

**Now ...** Go back and construct a syllable representation for each of the twelve words above. Remember to always assign onsets before codas. This reflects a universal preference for onsets over codas. Remember that a syllable does not have to have either an onset or a coda, but it must have a nucleus and a rhyme.

**Think ...** Is /s/ always an appendix? When /s/ is an appendix at the end of the syllable, what meaning(s) can often be assigned to it? Are these meanings part of the word's core meaning?

## Differences in Syllable Structure across Languages

All languages have syllables, but not all languages have the same syllable structure. All languages allow onsets, but not all languages allow codas (e.g., Hawaiian). Some languages allow only a single sound to occupy the onset position (e.g., Korean), some allow two sounds (e.g., French), and some three (e.g., English). There are also languages that require every syllable to have an onset! But no language requires that every syllable have a coda. Finally, onsets usually allow a greater range and type of consonants than do codas.

While syllable structure can vary from language to language, the process for building syllable representations, as outlined above, can still be used.

**Exercise!**   In the hypothetical language data below, all syllables have the structure CV(C). This means that all syllables begin with an onset, but do not have to have a coda. That is, codas are optional. Construct syllable representations for the following words. The data has already been transcribed for you.

1. /z ɪ ʧ n o/     'chair'         3. /s e d n a k u/    'sofa'
2. /t a k u g/     'shell'

## Syllable-Based Phonology

Syllables are often relevant to stating generalizations about the distribution of allophones. For example, in English,

- Voiceless aspirated stops are found at the beginning of a syllable that is word initial or stressed and unaspirated stops are found elsewhere.  See tables 3.20 and 3.21 on p. 76 of the text for some examples of English aspiration, as well as the distribution of aspirated stops in English.

- Vowels are long when followed by a voiced obstruent in the coda position of the same syllable.  See tables 3.22 and 3.23 on p. 77 for some examples of long and short vowels in English, including their distribution.

**Exercise! Exercise!**   The data below is from the same hypothetical language as above. In this hypothetical language, stress is predictable and is marked by a [ ´ ] over a vowel. Determine (making reference to syllable structure) where stress occurs.

> Hint:   You might want to first syllabify some of the words using the syllable structure constraints described above.

1. [fémba]         'foot'              8. [póbzuʤi]       'lizard'
2. [hagút]         'month'             9. [gaʧótfobi]     'knee'
3. [fezók]         'music'            10. [talagubiták]   'cowboy'
4. [waláp]         'mole'             11. [páfzuliha]     'thin'
5. [supóspa]       'gravy'            12. [kéllaboga]     'arm'
6. [tugábʧo]       'stone'
7. [jumanumáp]     'armadillo'

> ## MORE ON SYLLABLES
>
> For a more advanced syllable representation, see figures 3.14, 3.15, and 3.16 on pp. 72 and 73 of the text. These figures include a timing tier, which can be also be used to make phonological generalizations.

# FEATURES

Features represent individual aspects of speech production. Features are usually divided into four categories, as shown below.

| Major Class Features | Manner Features |
|---|---|
| ⇒ [+/-consonantal]<br>⇒ [+/-syllabic]<br>⇒ [+/-sonorant] | ⇒ [+/-continuant]<br>⇒ [+/-nasal]<br>⇒ [+/-lateral]<br>⇒ [+/-delayed release] |
| **Laryngeal Features** | **Place Features** |
| ⇒ [+/-voice]<br>⇒ [+/-spread glottis (SG)]<br>⇒ [+/-constricted glottis (CG)] | ⇒ [LABIAL]<br>   [+/-round]<br>⇒ [CORONAL]<br>   [+/-anterior], [+/-strident]<br>⇒ [DORSAL]<br>   [+/-high], [+/-low], [+/-back],<br>   [+/-tense], [+/-reduced] |

**Some important information ...**

⇒ Since features represent articulation, they are always enclosed in phonetic (i.e., [ ]) brackets.

⇒ Features are binary and are specified either as plus (+) or minus (-).

⇒ [LABIAL], [CORONAL], and [DORSAL] are not specified as either plus or minus, but rather are used to represent the articulator that is active in executing the articulation.

- [LABIAL] for the lips
- [CORONAL] for the tongue tip or blade
- [DORSAL] for the body of the tongue

⇒ Place features are used to represent place of articulation features specific to the active articulator. That is, [LABIAL] sounds are [+/-round]; [CORONAL] sounds are [+/-anterior] and [+/-strident]; and [DORSAL] sounds are [+/-high], [+/-low], [+/-back], [+/-tense] and [+/-reduced]. See table 3.28 on p. 86 for the representation of place of articulation features in some English consonants, and table 3.29 on p. 87 for the representation of place of articulation in some English vowels.

**Features are used ...**

⇒ **To represent segments.** Each segment consists of a number of features, each of which represents either some articulatory or some acoustic information about articulation. See figure 3.23 on p. 79 for an example of how features represent segments. See tables 3.30 and 3.31 on pp. 88 and 89 for the feature matrices of English consonants and vowels.

⇒ **To capture natural classes.** Natural classes are classes of sounds that share a feature or features and that pattern together in sound systems. For example, voiceless stops can be considered a natural class, as can rounded vowels. See table 3.24 and 3.25 on p. 80 for examples of how features capture different natural classes.

⇒ **To understand the nature of allophonic variation.** Allophonic variation is not the substitution of one allophone for another, but a change in the specification of a feature of the allophone. For example, voiceless sounds often change and become voiced when near other voiced sounds. This can be captured with the single feature [voice].

**Determining feature representations ...**

⇒ **For segments.** Think about the articulatory description for that sound. Begin with the major class features and include in the matrix the appropriate value for each feature, so that when the features are taken together, they define whether the segment is a consonant (obstruent or sonorant), a glide, or a vowel. Do the same for the manner, laryngeal, and place features. Remember that for the place features, you need to first determine the active articulator and then the features corresponding to the exact position of that articulator.

[p] is a voiceless bilabial unaspirated stop

$$
\begin{bmatrix}
+ \text{ consonantal} \\
- \text{ syllabic} \\
- \text{ sonorant} \\
- \text{ continuant} \\
- \text{ delayed release} \\
- \text{ voice} \\
- \text{ SG} \\
\\
\text{o LABIAL} \\
- \text{ round}
\end{bmatrix}
$$

these features define [p] as an obstruent

these features define [p] as a stop

these features define [p] as voiceless and unaspirated

these features specify LABIAL as the active articulator for [p] and that the lips are not rounded.

⇒ **For natural classes.** Remember that a natural class shares a feature or a group of features. Think about the features that the natural class shares. Include in the matrix only those features that all members of the natural class share.

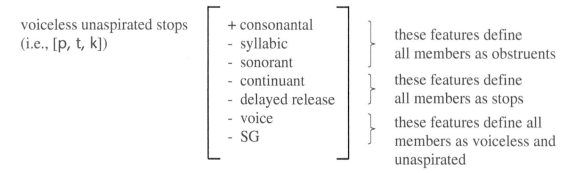

voiceless unaspirated stops
(i.e., [p, t, k])

+ consonantal
- syllabic
- sonorant       } these features define
                    all members as obstruents
- continuant
- delayed release } these features define
                    all members as stops
- voice
- SG             } these features define all
                    members as voiceless and
                    unaspirated

Note that place features have not been included in the matrix. This is because [p, t, k] each have a different place of articulation.

⇒ **For allophonic variation.** Remember that allophones are the predictable variants of phonemes and that their distribution can be described using a rule. Remember as well that rules have three parts: an individual phoneme or class of contrastive sounds, the allophone or change, and the environment in which the change occurs. Include features for each component of the rule. For the allophone, or change, only include the feature that changed from the contrastive sound(s). Some environments such as word- or syllable-initial, or word- or syllable-final, do not need features.

- For example, the rule (given here as a statement) "voiceless unaspirated stops become aspirated syllable initially" can be formulated using feature notation as shown below.

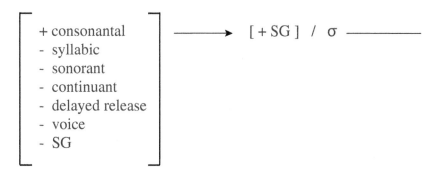

+ consonantal
- syllabic
- sonorant
- continuant          ⟶   [ + SG ]  /  σ  ————
- delayed release
- voice
- SG

**Try This!** In many dialects of Canadian English, [ʌj] and [ʌw] are allophones of /aj/ and /aw/, respectively. [ʌj] and [ʌw] occur before voiceless consonants and [aj] and [aw] occur elsewhere. This is called Canadian Raising. See table 3.10 on p. 64 for some examples of words containing the allophones. Put together a rule using features to capture how these sounds pattern in English. Remember that [a] is a low central unrounded vowel.

## FEATURE EXERCISES

1. State the feature that distinguishes each of the following pairs of sounds. (There may be more than one correct answer.)

a. [ θ ] / [ ð ]    _____

b. [ p ] / [ f ]    _____

c. [ s ] / [ θ ]  _____

d. [ b ] / [ m ]  _____

e. [ ʧ ] / [ ʃ ]  _____

2. Each of the following sets contains three sounds that belong to the same natural class. Add one other segment to each set, making sure that the natural class is preserved. Indicate the feature (including its value) that distinguishes the natural class.

|  | Segment Added | Distinguishing Feature |
|---|---|---|
| a. [ l̩  ə  n̩] | [    ] | _____ |
| b. [θ  s  f ] | [    ] | _____ |
| c. [i  e  u] | [    ] | _____ |
| d. [t  g  n] | [    ] | _____ |
| e. [j  r  n] | [    ] | _____ |
| f. [i  æ  ɛ ] | [    ] | _____ |

3. Name the natural class described by each of the following phonetic matrices.

a. $\begin{bmatrix} - \text{consonantal} \\ - \text{syllabic} \end{bmatrix}$

b. $\begin{bmatrix} + \text{consonantal} \\ - \text{syllabic} \\ - \text{sonorant} \\ + \text{continuant} \\ + \text{voice} \end{bmatrix}$

4. In each of the sets below, all the sounds except one constitute a natural class. Draw a circle around the sound that does not belong and state the feature that the remaining sounds share.

a. [ t  g  v  ʤ ]  _____

b. [ b  m  r  w ]  _____

c. [ n  t  g  j ]  _____

d. [ i  ɛ  u  æ ]  _____

5.  In each consonant system below, some segments are boxed. Determine if the boxed segments constitute a natural class. If they do, then state the feature(s) that make them a natural class.

a.

b.

c.

d.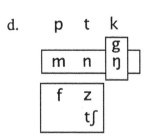

6.  Provide a feature matrix for each of the following groups of sounds.

a.  [ð θ f v]

c.  [u o]

b.  [g ʤ]

d.  [i ɪ e ɛ æ]

# DERIVATIONS

Derivations are a representation of how phonemes and allophones are related. Phonetic forms are derived from phonemic forms by applying processes in the form of a rule. There are three parts to a derivation. These parts are very similar to the components of a phonological rule.

⇒ **Underlying Representation (UR).** The underlying representation is a representation of native speaker knowledge and is always in phonemic transcription.

⇒ **Rules.** Remember that phonemes and allophones are linked by a rule. The rule applies to change the phoneme into the allophone. This, of course, only occurs when the structural description (environment) specified in the rule is found in the underlying representation.

⇒ **Phonetic Representation (PR).** The phonetic representation is also called the surface representation. Since the surface representation always represents pronunciation, it is in phonetic transcription.

**An example …**

In English, liquids become voiceless after a voiceless stop at the beginning of a syllable. This is an example of devoicing.

The derivation below illustrates how the phonetic form is derived from the phonological form using this rule.

| UR | /pliz/ | 'please' | /læf/ | 'laugh' |
|---|---|---|---|---|
| Liquid Devoicing | pl̥iz | | _____ | |
| PR | [ pl̥iz ] | | [ læf ] | |

- In the word *please*, Liquid Devoicing applies because [l] occurs after a voiceless consonant (i.e., [p]). The structural description of the rule has been met. Notice that after the rule has applied, [l] has become voiceless (i.e., [l̥] ).

- In the word *laugh*, the rule does not apply, as indicated by the dashed line, since the structural description necessary for the rule to apply was not met: [l] occurs at the beginning of the word and not after a voiceless consonant. The phonetic form, therefore, remains the same as the underlying form.

See figure 3.25 on p. 90 for an example of a derivation involving aspiration and vowel lengthening in English.

## RULE ORDERING

More than one rule can apply during the derivation of a particular form. Sometimes the order in which rules apply is crucial to deriving the appropriate phonetic form. That is, one rule must apply before another. An example involves the rule of liquid devoicing given above and a rule of schwa deletion. This rule deletes a schwa in an open syllable when it is followed by a stressed syllable.

**The Incorrect Order …** Schwa deletion must apply before liquid devoicing. If liquid devoicing is applied before schwa deletion, then liquids incorrectly remain voiced in the phonetic form. This is shown in the following derivation of the word 'police'.

| UR | / pə.lís /    'police' |
|---|---|
| Liquid Devoicing | ——— |
| Schwa Deletion | plís |
| PR | [ plís ] |

(**Note:** It is assumed that stress placement has already occurred. Normally, stress would not be present in the underlying form because it is predictable in English, and therefore would be applied using a stress rule.)

**The Correct Order ...**   Since liquids in English are produced without voice following a voiceless stop, schwa deletion must occur first so that in the resulting output, liquids occur after voiceless stops, creating the necessary environment for liquid devoicing to apply.

| UR | / pə.lís /    'police' |
|---|---|
| Schwa Deletion | plís |
| Liquid Devoicing | pl̥ís |
| PR | [ pl̥ís ] |

As shown in the above derivation, the phonetic form now contains, as it should in English, a voiceless liquid.

---

## QUICK REMINDER!

Underlying representations capture the phonological knowledge speakers have about the contrastive sounds of their language. Therefore, these representations are always in phonemic representation, which does not contain any predictable phonetic information.

Since surface representations capture actual phonetic outputs, they are always in phonetic representation. That is, they contain all of the predictable phonetic information not found in the underlying representation.

Processes, in the form of rules, apply to add predictable phonetic information to the underlying representation, thereby creating the surface representation.

# EVEN MORE PHONOLOGY PROBLEMS!

For each data set, do the following:

- Determine if the sounds are separate phonemes or allophones of the same phoneme. Remember to provide evidence in support of your conclusion, along with a representation of the phoneme(s).

- For all allophones of the same phoneme, provide a rule. Wherever possible, try to write one rule for all the sounds you have investigated. HINT … watch out for natural classes!

- For all allophones of the same phoneme involving natural classes, write a rule using feature notation.

- For all allophones of the same phoneme, identify the process that your rule describes.

- Provide derivations as indicated.

1. <u>Canadian French</u>:          [t] and [ts]

|  |  |
|---|---|
| [ts] | This symbol represents a voiceless alveolar affricate. |
| [y] | This symbol represents a high front tense rounded vowel. |
| [ʏ] | This symbol represents a high front lax rounded vowel. |

| | | | | | |
|---|---|---|---|---|---|
| 1. | [tu] | 'all' | 7. | [telegram] | 'telegram' |
| 2. | [abutsi] | 'ended' | 8. | [trɛ] | 'very' |
| 3. | [tɛl] | 'such' | 9. | [kyltsyr] | 'culture' |
| 4. | [tab] | 'stamp' | 10. | [minʏt] | 'minute' |
| 5. | [tsimɪd] | 'timid' | 11. | [tsy] | 'you' |
| 6. | [tsɪt] | 'title' | 12. | [tsʏb] | 'tube' |

- Provide a derivation for #5, #10, and #12.

2. <u>Burmese</u>:          [m] and [m̥],  [n] and [n̥],   [ŋ] and [ŋ̥]

Hint:  Given that you have been asked to investigate three sets of nasals, would you expect all the nasals to pattern in the same way?

| | | | | | |
|---|---|---|---|---|---|
| 1. | [mi] | 'five' | 8. | [hm̥i] | 'to lean against' |
| 2. | [mwej] | 'to give birth' | 9. | [hm̥wej] | 'fragrant' |
| 3. | [mji?] | 'river' | 10. | [hm̥jaj?] | 'to cure' |
| 4. | [ne] | 'small' | 11. | [hn̥ej] | 'slow' |
| 5. | [nwe] | 'to bend' | 12. | [hn̥a] | 'to lend property' |
| 6. | [ŋa] | 'five' | 13. | [hn̥wej] | 'to heat' |
| 7. | [ŋou?] | 'tree stump' | 14. | [hn̥e?] | 'bird' |

- Provide a derivation for #5, #11, and #14.

3. Malay:          [t] and [tʲ]

[ʲ]      This diacritic represents a sound that has been palatalized.

| | | | | | |
|---|---|---|---|---|---|
| 1. | [tarek] | 'pull' | 6. | [tʲampah] | 'tasteless' |
| 2. | [kətʲut] | 'shriveled' | 7. | [kətil] | 'pinch' |
| 3. | [pitər] | 'disk' | 8. | [tʲarek] | 'rip' |
| 4. | [tʃomel] | 'cute' | 9. | [lawat] | 'visit' |
| 5. | [batʲa] | 'steel' | 10. | [tʃampah] | 'tasteless' |

- Look at the Malay data again and examine [tʲ] and [tʃ]. What conclusion can you make about these two sounds? Give evidence to support your answer.

4. Tamil:     [p] and [b],  [k] and [g],  [ṭ] and [ḍ],  [t̪] and [d̪]

[ . ]   This diacritic means that a sound is retroflex.
[ ̪ ]   This diacritic means that a sound is dental.
[ ɨ ]   This symbol represents a high central unrounded vowel.

Remember:   When looking for complementary distribution, you must record the immediate surrounding phonetic environment around EACH OCCURRENCE of a sound.

| | | | | | |
|---|---|---|---|---|---|
| 1. | [pal] | 'tooth' | 11. | [id̪ɨ] | 'this' |
| 2. | [abayam] | 'refuge' | 12. | [ad̪ɨ] | 'that' |
| 3. | [kappal] | 'ship' | 13. | [kat̪t̪i] | 'knife' |
| 4. | [saabam] | 'curse' | 14. | [kud̪i] | 'jump' |
| 5. | [kaakkaaj] | 'crow' | 15. | [pat̪t̪i] | 'ten' |
| 6. | [mugil] | 'cloud' | 16. | [paaḍam] | 'foot' |
| 7. | [t̪ugil] | 'veil' | 17. | [iḍam] | 'place' |
| 8. | [t̪aṭṭɨ] | 'plate' | 18. | [kaaṭpaaḍi] | 'name of a town' |
| 9. | [padɨ] | 'lie down' | 19. | [paṭṭɨ] | 'silk' |
| 10. | [t̪uukkɨ] | 'carry' | | | |

- Provide a derivation for #3, #6, and #14.

5. Igbirra:    [e] and [a]

| | | | | | |
|---|---|---|---|---|---|
| 1. | [mezi] | 'I expect' | 5. | [mazɪ] | 'I am in pain' |
| 2. | [meze] | 'I am well' | 6. | [mazɛ] | 'I agree' |
| 3. | [meto] | 'I arrange' | 7. | [matɔ] | 'I pick' |
| 4. | [metu] | 'I beat' | 8. | [matʊ] | 'I send' |

- Are there minimal pairs?
- [e] and [a] both occur between m _ z and m _ t. What significance does this have for your analysis?

6.  Gascon:      [b] and [β],   [d] and [ð], [g] and [ɣ]

Hint:    Think about what process you would expect given pairs of stops and fricatives.

[ɣ]      This symbol represents a voiced velar fricative.

| | | | | |
|---|---|---|---|---|
| 1. | [brẽn] | 'endanger' | 10. | [ʒuɣɛt] | 'he played' |
| 2. | [dilys] | 'Monday' | 11. | [krãmbo] | 'room' |
| 3. | [taldepãn] | 'leftover bread' | 12. | [eʃaðo] | 'hoe' |
| 4. | [ʃiβaw] | 'horse' | 13. | [gat] | 'cat' |
| 5. | [pũnde] | 'to lay eggs' | 14. | [aβe] | 'to have' |
| 6. | [agro] | 'sour' | 15. | [biɣar] | 'mosquito' |
| 7. | [puðe] | 'to be able' | 16. | [ũmbro] | 'shadow' |
| 8. | [riɣut] | 'he laughed' | 17. | [dudze] | 'twelve' |
| 9. | [noβi] | 'husband' | 18. | [lũŋg] | 'long' |

- Examine the Gascon data again, paying attention to the oral and nasal
  vowels. Can you make any conclusions about nasalized vowels in this
  language? Write one statement involving classes of sounds, describing
  their behaviour.

- Provide a derivation for #5, #9, and #16. Do your rules need to be
  ordered? Why or why not?

---

## REMINDER ... REMINDER ...

To solve a phonology problem, you must have a firm grasp on minimal pairs, near minimal
pairs, complementary distribution, and phonemes and allophones. If you don't, then you
need to get some help!

**REVIEW! REVIEW!**   Make sure you can do the following:

- –   define phonemes and allophones
- –   spot minimal and near minimal pairs
- –   determine complementary distribution
- –   construct representations of phonemes
- –   construct syllable representations
- –   identify consonantal and vowel features
- –   put together feature matrices
- –   put together rules
- –   put together rules using feature notation
- –   construct derivations
- –   solve phonology problems

## QUESTIONS? PROBLEMS? DIFFICULTIES?

_____

_____

_____

_____

_____

_____

_____

_____

_____

_____

_____

_____

# CHAPTER 4. MORPHOLOGY: THE ANALYSIS OF WORD STRUCTURE

Morphology is the study of words: their categories, their internal structure, and the operations that form them. Important topics and concepts found in this chapter include the following:

1. Morphological terminology
2. Identifying morphemes
3. Identifying lexical categories
4. Analyzing word structure
5. Derivation
6. Compounding
7. Inflection
8. Morphological processes
9. Morphology problems
10. Morphophonemics

## MORPHOLOGICAL TERMINOLOGY

The following terms are crucial to understanding morphology. You should know them!

| TERM | DEFINITION |
|------|------------|
| Word | Words are the smallest free forms found in language. Free forms are elements that can appear in isolation or whose position is not fixed. Words can be simple or complex. See table 4.1 on p. 105 of the text for some examples. |
| Morpheme | A morpheme is the smallest meaning or functional unit found in language. Morphemes can be free or bound. |
| Allomorphs | Allomorphs are the different forms of a morpheme. |
| Root | A root is the core of a word. It is the portion of the word that carries most of the word's meaning. The majority of English words are built from roots that are free morphemes, making English a word-based language. Some English words, though, are built from roots that are bound morphemes. Think of some examples. |
| Affixes | Affixes are different types of bound morphemes. There are three types of affixes found in language: prefixes, suffixes, and infixes. See tables 4.3 and 4.4 on p. 108 for some examples. |
| Base | A base is any form to which an affix is added. The base may be the same as the root, but it can also be larger than the root. See figure 4.3 on p. 107 of the text for an illustration of the difference between roots and bases. |

# IDENTIFYING MORPHEMES

Morphemes are the building blocks of words. A word can contain only one morpheme, making it a simple word, or a word may contain more than one morpheme, making it a complex word. Below are some hints for determining the number of morphemes that a word contains.

⇒ A morpheme carries information about meaning or function. Think . . . can the word *haunt* be divided into the morphemes *h* and *aunt*? To do so, both *h* and *aunt* must have meaning. Do they? What about the word *bats*? What meaning does *s* have in this word?

⇒ The meanings of individual morphemes should contribute to the overall meaning of the word. Think . . . can the word *pumpkin* be divided into the morphemes *pump* and *kin*? To do so, the meaning of *pumpkin* must have something to do with the meaning of both *pump* and *kin*. Does it?

⇒ A morpheme is not the same as a syllable. A morpheme can consist of one or more syllables, but a morpheme does not have to be a syllable. Think . . . how many syllables are found in the morpheme *treat*? What about in the morpheme *Dracula*? What about the *s* found in *bats*? It is a morpheme, but is it a syllable?

⇒ Often as words are built, changes in pronunciation and/or spelling occur. These do not affect a morpheme's status as a morpheme. Think . . . when *y* is added to the morpheme *scare*, it becomes *scary*, and when *er* is added to *scary*, it becomes *scarier*. Is the root the same in both *scary* and *scarier*? Is the root *scare* or *scar*? What is the base for *scary*? What about for *scarier*? Is the base the same in both?

**Exercise!**   Identify the number of morphemes in each of the following words.

1. insert   _____        2. supply   _____

   memory   _____           supplies   _____

3. format   _____           supplier   _____

   flowchart_____        4. faster   _____

5. bug   _____              power   _____

   debug   _____            processor   _____

**Practice! Practice!**   For each of the following words, identify the number of morphemes and write the free and bound morphemes in the appropriate blanks. A free morpheme can be a word by itself, while a bound morpheme must be attached to another element. Remember, a word may have more than one bound morpheme. The first is done for you.

| WORD | TOTAL # OF MORPHEMES | FREE | BOUND |
|------|----------------------|------|-------|
| eraser | 2 | erase | -er |
| wicked | | | |
| invalid (A) | | | |
| invalid (N) | | | |
| Jack's | | | |
| optionality | | | |
| refurnish | | | |
| inabilities | | | |
| denationalize | | | |
| present | | | |
| activation | | | |
| rewinding | | | |

**Think . . .**   What type of bound morpheme is found in the complex words *optionality* and *activation*? Prefix? Suffix? Infix? Remember that for an affix to be an infix, it must be found inside another morpheme and not between two morphemes.

# IDENTIFYING LEXICAL CATEGORIES

In morphology, we are concerned with four lexical categories: nouns, verbs, adjectives, and prepositions. Nouns typically refer to people and things ( both concrete and abstract). Verbs typically denote actions, sensations, and states. Adjectives usually name properties. Prepositions generally encode spatial relations.

For each of the words below, state the number of morphemes found in the word, and identify the root, the lexical category of the root, and the lexical category of the entire word. Remember, the root is the core of the word and carries most of the word's meaning. Be careful: the root's lexical category and the word's lexical category may or may not be the same. The first is done for you.

| WORD | # OF MORPHS | ROOT | ROOT CATEGORY | WORD CATEGORY |
|------|-------------|------|---------------|---------------|
| healthiest | 3 | health | noun | adjective |
| amazement | | | | |
| reusable | | | | |
| dishonest | | | | |
| Calgary | | | | |
| lovelier | | | | |
| historical | | | | |
| uncontrolled | | | | |
| impersonal | | | | |
| trees | | | | |
| faster | | | | |
| rereads | | | | |
| beautiful | | | | |
| child | | | | |

# WORD TREES

A word tree is a representation of a word's internal structure. To put together a word tree, you need to be able to determine the number of morphemes in a word, identify roots and affixes, and assign lexical categories. Remember, prefixes are attached to the front of a base, while suffixes are attached to the end of a base. Infixes are affixes that occur inside another morpheme; they are not found in English.

Below are some examples of how to draw a word tree.

1. Words with a single affix

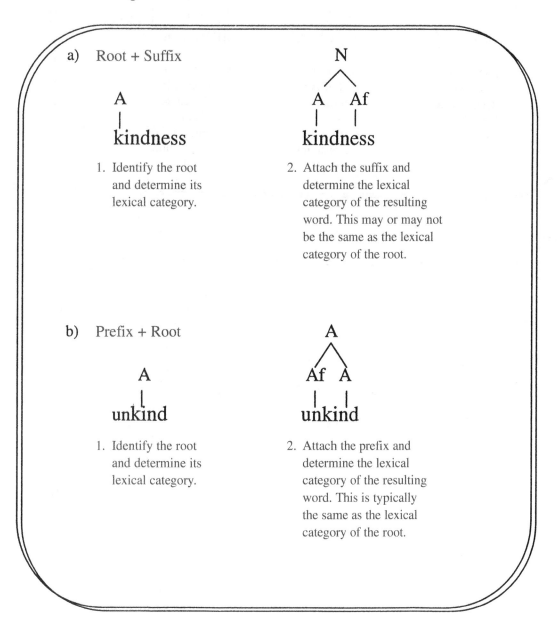

2. Words with multiple suffixes.

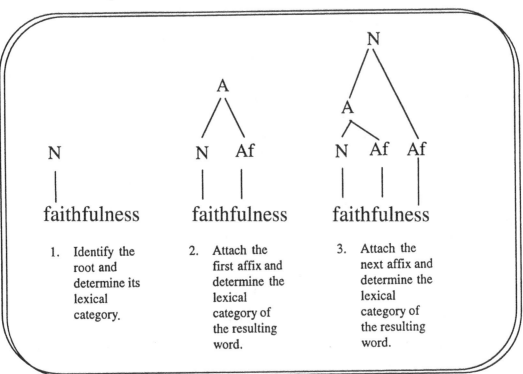

1. Identify the root and determine its lexical category.

2. Attach the first affix and determine the lexical category of the resulting word.

3. Attach the next affix and determine the lexical category of the resulting word.

3. Words with both a prefix and a suffix

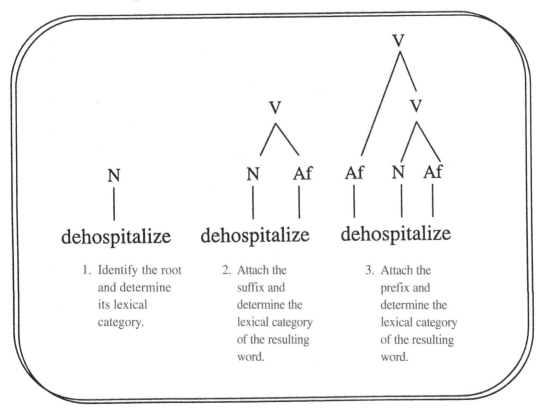

1. Identify the root and determine its lexical category.

2. Attach the suffix and determine the lexical category of the resulting word.

3. Attach the prefix and determine the lexical category of the resulting word.

4. Words that are structurally ambiguous

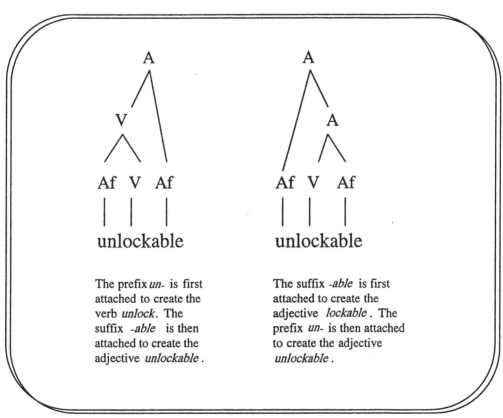

The prefix *un-* is first attached to create the verb *unlock*. The suffix *-able* is then attached to create the adjective *unlockable*.

The suffix *-able* is first attached to create the adjective *lockable*. The prefix *un-* is then attached to create the adjective *unlockable*.

**Exercise! Exercise!** To practice, draw trees for the following words:

- trees
- lovelier
- dishonest
- beautiful

- amazement
- reusable
- impersonal
- Calgary

---

### REMINDER! REMINDER!

To be able to draw word trees correctly, you need to be able to identify nouns, verbs, adjectives, and prepositions. If you are having difficulty with these, refer to Chapter 5 section 5.1 to get some help!

# DERIVATION

Derivation is a process of affixation. Affixation is a morphological process that adds affixes to words. Derivational affixes are affixes that build a word having a different (but usually related) meaning from that of the base. The resulting word may also belong to a different lexical category from its base.

⇒ English has many derivational suffixes. These suffixes typically cause both a meaning and category change to the base. For example:

* The suffix -*ity* combines with an adjective such as *stupid* to create the noun *stupidity*, meaning the result of being stupid.

* The suffix -*en* combines with an adjective such as *hard* to create the verb *harden*, meaning to become hard.

* The suffix -*ous* combines with a noun such as *poison* to create the adjective *poisonous*, meaning producing or possessing poison.

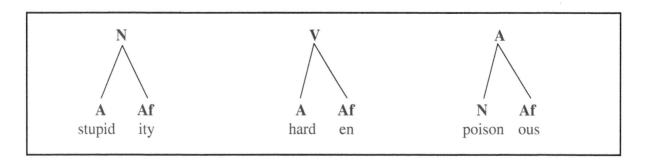

Think of some more derivational suffixes. What lexical category of words do they combine with? What lexical category of words do they create?

⇒ English also has many derivational prefixes. These cause a meaning change to the base, but usually do not change the lexical category of the base. It is the meaning change that makes them derivational. For example:

* The prefix *ex-* combines with a noun such as *friend* to create the noun *ex-friend*, meaning someone who is no longer a friend.

* The prefix *re-* combines with a verb such as *think* to create the verb *rethink*, meaning to think again.

* The prefix *in-* combines with an adjective such as *complete* to create the adjective *incomplete*, meaning not complete.

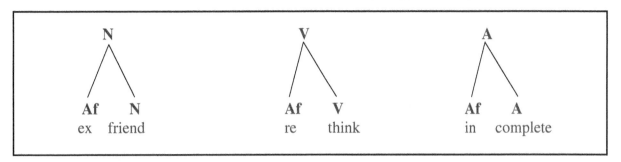

Think of some more derivational prefixes. What lexical category of words do they combine with and create? What meaning change occurs to the base when these are added?

More examples of English derivational prefixes and suffixes can be found in table 4.6 on p. 111.

⇒ Derivational affixes (including those found in English) are often subject to restrictions. For example:

- Derivational affixes combine with bases of particular lexical categories.
  e.g.,   -*ize* must be attached to a noun; -*er* must be attached to a verb

- Derivational affixes combine with bases having certain phonological properties.
  e.g.,   -*en* must be attached to a base having one syllable and ending in an obstruent

- Derivational affixes combine with bases of specific linguistic origin.
  e.g.,   -*ant* must be attached to a base of Latin origin

⇒ English has two types of derivational affixes. Class 1 affixes often cause changes to the consonant or vowel sounds in the base. Class 2 affixes do not. Class 1 affixes may also cause changes to which syllable is stressed. Class 2 affixes do not.  See tables 4.9 and 4.10 on p. 114 for examples of both types of English derivational affixes.

**Try This!**  Draw trees for the following words.  Remember that a word can contain more than one derivational affix.

- disappear
- homeless
- electricity
- unbreakable
- instructional
- lodger

**Now ...** Go back over the above words and identify which affixes are Class 1 affixes and which belong to Class 2.

# COMPOUNDING

Compounding is another process used to build words. Compounding involves the combination of two or more already existing words into a new word. Most English compounds are nouns, verbs, and adjectives. See figure 4.9 on p. 115 for some examples.

There are four important concepts about English compounds that you should know.

⇒ **Headedness.** The head of a compound is the morpheme that determines the category of the entire compound. Most English compounds are right-headed. That is, the category of the entire compound is the same as the category of the rightmost member of the compound. For example, since the rightmost member *board* is a noun, the compound *blackboard* is a noun. What is the head of *nation-wide*? (to) *dry-clean*?

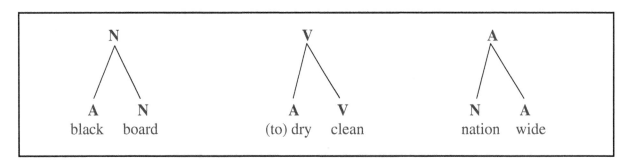

⇒ **Stress Patterns.** Even though compounds can be spelled as one word, two words, or with a hyphen separating the morphemes, a generalization can be made about the stress patterns found on them. Stress tends to be more prominent on the first member of the compound than on the second: for example, *greénhouse* (a garden centre) versus *green hoúse* (a house that is green).

⇒ **Tense/Plural.** Tense and plural markers are usually added to the compound as a whole and not to the first member of the compound. For example, the plural of *fire engine* is *fire engines* and not *fires engine*. What is the past tense of *drop kick*?

⇒ **Meaning Relationships.** Compounds can be classified as either endocentric or exocentric. This classification is based on the meaning relationship between the members of the compound. In an endocentric compound, the entire compound denotes a subtype of the head. For example, a *teacup* is a type of *cup*, and a *lunchroom* is a type of *room*. In an exocentric compound, the meaning of the compound does not come from the head. For example, a *redneck* is not a type of *neck*, but a type of person.

Compounds can be formed from smaller compounds. As well, compounding can be used in conjunction with derivation to build words. For example, the compound *blackboard* can combine with the derived word *eraser* to create the larger compound *blackboard eraser*.

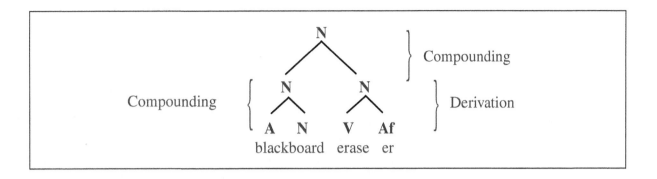

## Exercise!

For each compound below, state the lexical categories making it up and give another example of that type of compound. The first is done for you.

| COMPOUND | LEXICAL CATEGORIES | EXAMPLE |
|---|---|---|
| bathroom | Noun + Noun | movie star |
| scarecrow | _____ | _____ |
| skin deep | _____ | _____ |
| bittersweet | _____ | _____ |
| upstairs | _____ | _____ |

**Now ...** Go back and draw a word tree for each compound. **Then ...** Draw a word tree for each of the following compounds:

- (an) undertaking
- washer-dryer
- election night
- overgrown

# INFLECTION

Inflection involves modifying the form of a word to indicate grammatical information such as singular versus plural or past versus non-past.

Inflection is most commonly a process of affixation. Inflectional affixes do not change the lexical category of the base.

⇒ English has eight inflectional affixes. These are found on nouns, verbs, and adjectives, and provide the following grammatical information: plural (*-s*) and possessive (*-'s*); third person singular non-past tense (*-s*), past tense (*-ed*), progressive (*-ing*) and past participle (*-en/-ed*); comparative (*-er*) and superlative (*-est*).

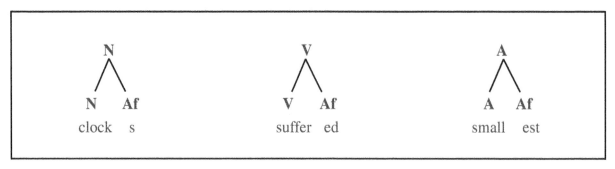

See table 4.14 on p. 118 for some examples of English inflectional affixes.

**Practice!**  For each of the following words, identify the lexical category of the root and the type of inflectional information found (i.e., past tense, superlative, plural, etc.). The first is done for you.

| WORD | LEXICAL CATEGORY | INFLECTIONAL INFORMATION |
|---|---|---|
| watched | verb | past tense |
| runs | | |
| sorriest | | |
| lamps | | |
| playing | | |
| driven | | |
| lovelier | | |

# INFLECTION VERSUS DERIVATION

It can sometimes be hard to determine whether an affix is an inflectional affix or a derivational affix. The boxes below provide some criteria for helping determine whether an affix is inflectional or derivational.

| Inflectional affixes … | Derivational affixes … |
|---|---|
| • do not change the lexical category or meaning of the base.<br>• occur after derivational affixes have been attached.<br>• are productive, meaning there are relatively few exceptions on the class of bases to which they can attach.<br>• are semantically transparent, meaning that it is easy to determine the contribution of the affix to the meaning of the resulting word. | • typically change both the lexical category and meaning of the base.<br>• occur closer to the root than inflectional affixes.<br>• are less productive than inflectional affixes, meaning there are restrictions on the class of bases to which they can attach.<br>• are less semantically transparent than inflectional affixes, meaning that it is not always easy to determine the contribution of the affix to the meaning of the resulting word. |

**Identify the Affix!** Each of the following English words contains at least one affix. For each word, identify all the affixes, and for each affix, state whether it is inflectional (IA) or derivational (DA). The first is done for you.

| WORD | AFFIX(ES) | IA / DA |
|---|---|---|
| trucks | -s | IA (plural) |
| insanity | | |
| reuse | | |
| girl's | | |
| smaller | | |
| delightful | | |
| nationalize | | |
| watched | | |
| mistreat | | |
| unhealthiest | | |

It can get even more complicated! Many affixes have the same form but can be either inflectional or derivational, or they can be different inflectional or different derivational affixes. To correctly identify an affix as inflectional or derivational, you need to pay attention to how the affix is functioning in the word rather than to its form. Use the four criteria outlined in this section to help you decide if an affix is functioning as an inflectional or a derivational affix.

**Form versus Function!**  In each group of four words below, two words have affixes of the same type, one word has a different affix, and one word has no affix at all. Next to each word, write S (same), D (different), or N (none) based on the other words in the data set. You may want to use a dictionary. The first is done for you.

1.  ovens        S

    lens         N

    hens         S

    listens      D


2.  greener      _____

    farmer       _____

    colder       _____

    water        _____


3.  greedy       _____

    ivory        _____

    jealousy     _____

    dirty        _____


4.  friendly     _____

    slowly       _____

    intelligently _____

    early        _____


5.  leaven       _____

    harden       _____

    spoken       _____

    thicken      _____


6.  intelligent  _____

    inhale       _____

    incongruous  _____

    inhuman      _____


7.  rider        _____

    colder       _____

    silver       _____

    actor        _____


8.  candied      _____

    shopped      _____

    cleaned      _____

    candid       _____

# PRACTICE WITH WORD TREES

Draw one tree for each of the words listed below and identify whether inflection, derivation, and/or compounding was used to build the word. Remember that more than one process can be used in a single word. Use the context sentence to help you determine the lexical category of the entire word!

For example, the word *creamiest* might be diagrammed as follows.

Creamiest chocolate tastes the best

| WORD | CONTEXT SENTENCE |
|---|---|
| 1.  taken | The baby has <u>taken</u> his first steps. |
| 2.  spoonfeeding | Mother is <u>spoonfeeding</u> the baby. |
| 3.  retry | She should <u>retry</u> the recipe. |
| 4.  silkiest | Sandra used the <u>silkiest</u> material. |
| 5.  introductions | Mary performed the <u>introductions</u>. |
| 6.  steps | John <u>steps</u> up the ladder. |
| 7.  steps | I hate those steep <u>steps</u>. |
| 8.  thickener | Flour is a type of <u>thickener</u>. |
| 9.  skiers | The <u>skiers</u> were rich. |
| 10.  insightful | Your answer is rather <u>insightful</u>. |
| 11.  stone-cold | Your french fries are <u>stone-cold</u>. |
| 12.  making | Jill is <u>making</u> candy. |
| 13.  boxing | We watched the <u>boxing</u>. |
| 14.  declaw | You should <u>declaw</u> that cat. |

15.  attractive                 That room is very <u>attractive</u>.

16.  moonrocks                  The astronauts collected many <u>moonrocks</u>.

17.  blessing                   Give me your <u>blessing</u>.

18.  blessing                   She is <u>blessing</u> the bread.

19.  school teacher             My mother was a <u>school teacher</u>.

20.  clumsiness                 I detest <u>clumsiness</u>.

21.  ex-Albertan                George is an <u>ex-Albertan</u>.

22.  hammered                   John <u>hammered</u> on the door.

23.  overthink                  Don't <u>overthink</u> the problem.

24.  unlocked                   We <u>unlocked</u> the door.

25.  impure                     <u>Impure</u> water is dangerous.

26.  criticize                  You <u>criticize</u> too much.

27.  treatment centre           He needs to go to a good <u>treatment centre</u>.

28.  defrosting                 The steaks are <u>defrosting</u>.

29.  stringier                  Her hair is <u>stringier</u> than yours.

30.  selfishness                <u>Selfishness</u> is not very attractive.

---

## QUICK REMINDER!

Remember that ALL English prefixes are derivational even though they do not cause a lexical category change!

# OTHER INFLECTIONAL PROCESSES

In addition to affixation, inflection can also be marked using internal change, suppletion, reduplication, and tone placement.

| PROCESS | DEFINITION |
|---------|------------|
| Internal Change | This process provides grammatical information by substituting a portion of the morpheme. In English, the tense of a word can be marked by replacing the vowel with another vowel (e.g., *run* → *ran*). See table 4.16 on p. 121 for more examples. |
| Suppletion | This process provides grammatical information by replacing one morpheme with an entirely different morpheme. In English, the tense of a word can be marked in this way (e.g., *go* → *went*). See table 4.17 on p. 122 of the text for more examples.<br><br>Partial suppletion is sometimes used to describe the change in words such as *think* → *thought*, in which more than a segment has been changed, but not the entire morpheme. |
| Reduplication | A process that repeats all (full) or a portion (partial) of the base to mark a semantic or grammatical contrast. This process is not productive in English. See tables 4.18 and 4.19 on p. 123 for some non-English examples. |
| Tone Placement | This process is found in tone languages where differences in tone can be used to mark grammatical information such as a change in tense or number. See table 4.20 on p. 124 for some examples from Mono-Bili (spoken in the Congo). |

**Exercise! Exercise!**   Each of the following words has been inflected. For each, identify the type of inflectional process that has been used to mark the grammatical contrast. The first has been done for you.

| WORD | TYPE OF INFLECTION |
|------|--------------------|
| drove | internal change |
| was | |
| (is) jumping | |

anak anak
'all sorts of children'

_____

better

_____

lovelier

_____

George's

_____

tatakbuh
'will run'

_____

mice

_____

**Reminder!** Many more inflectional phenomena, including case and agreement, are widely used in language. For more information on these and other inflectional phenomena, visit www.pearsoncanada.ca/ogrady.

## MORE MORPHOLOGICAL PROCESSES

| PROCESS | DEFINITION |
|---|---|
| Cliticization | Clitics are morphemes that behave like words in terms of meaning and function. Clitics differ, though, in that they cannot stand alone as a word. Cliticization attaches these elements to either the beginning of a following word or the end of a preceding word.<br>E.g., *re* from *are* is attached to *they*, as in *they're* |
| Conversion | A process that assigns an existing word to a different lexical category. The lexical category and meaning change that occur make this process a type of derivation.<br>E.g.,     *butter (N)* → *(to) butter (V)*<br>See table 4.21 on p. 125 for more examples. In two-syllable words, conversion can also be accompanied by a change in stress placement. See table 4.22 on p. 125  for some examples. |
| Clipping | A process that shortens a polysyllabic word by removing one or more syllables.   E.g., *condominium* → *condo* |
| Blends | A process that creates a new word by combining non-morphemic portions of two existing words.   E.g., *spiced* + *ham* → *spam* |

| Backformation | A process that creates a word by removing a real or supposed affix from an existing word in the language. <br> E.g., *enthuse ← enthusiasm* <br> See table 4.23 on p. 127 for more English examples. |
|---|---|
| Acronyms & Initialisms | A process that creates new words using the initial letters of the words in a phrase or title and pronouncing them as a word. <br> E.g., *scuba, UNICEF* <br> Acronyms are different from initialisms, in which each letter making up the word is pronounced. <br> E.g., *IBM, NHL* |
| Onomatopoeia | A process that creates new words that sound like the thing they name. <br> E.g., buzz, hiss, sizzle <br> See table 4.24 on p. 128 for some examples from various languages. |

Other ways to form new words include the following:

- Word manufacture (coinage), in which a totally new word is created. This process commonly occurs with product names.
- Creating words from names (called eponyms). See table 4.25 on p. 128 for some examples.
- Borrowing words from other languages.

**Practice! Practice!**   Identify the process responsible for the formation of each of the following English words. Choose any of the morphological phenomena from the above table, as well as inflection, derivation, and compounding. The first is done for you.

infomercial   _blending_____

(to) ship   _____

swam   _____

support-hose   _____

chirp   _____

MADD   _____

healthy        _____

demo           _____

éxport         _____

sadness        _____

he's           _____

headline       _____

beep           _____

ATM            _____

jumped         _____

There are many examples of different word formation processes in the following passage. Find all the examples of ACRONYM, BACKFORMATION, BLENDING, CLIPPING, COINAGE, COMPOUNDING, and INITIALISM.

> John didn't enthuse about UCLA, as he probably expected his profs to spoonfeed him. He preferred to avoid the smog by taking sandwiches to the beach where he would laze around and go scuba diving in his new dacron dry suit. One day he was suffering from a headache and dizziness, which he thought might be caused by sunstroke or the flu, so he went to the doctor. The doc sent him to the lab for a urinalysis and a blood test and suggested that he should see an ENT specialist as well. He is now OK, having returned from the USA, and he is learning about ohms, watts, and volts at MIT.

**Get ready for morphology problems ...**

# INTRODUCTION TO MORPHOLOGY PROBLEMS

The goal in morphology problems is to isolate and identify all the morphemes in the data given. To do this, you must identify recurring strings of sounds and match them with recurring meanings. Here are a few easy ones to try!

All data is given in phonetic transcription.

## 1. Mende (Sierra Leone)

| | | | | | |
|---|---|---|---|---|---|
| 1. | [pɛlɛ] | 'house' | 9. | [pɛlɛi] | 'the house' |
| 2. | [mɔm] | 'glass' | 10. | [mɔmi] | 'the glass' |
| 3. | [dɔmi] | 'story' | 11. | [dɔmii] | 'the story' |
| 4. | [kali] | 'hoe' | 12. | [kalii] | 'the hoe' |
| 5. | [hele] | 'elephant' | 13. | [helei] | 'the elephant' |
| 6. | [kaamɔ] | 'teacher' | 14. | [kaamɔi] | 'the teacher' |
| 7. | [navo] | 'boy' | 15. | [navoi] | 'the boy' |
| 8. | [numu] | 'person' | 16. | [numui] | 'the person' |

   a.   What is the morpheme meaning 'the'?

   b.   Given [sale] meaning 'proverb', what is the form for 'the proverb'?

   c.   If [kpindii] means 'the night', then what does [kpindi] mean?

## 2. Ganda (Uganda)

| | | | | | |
|---|---|---|---|---|---|
| 1. | [omukazi] | 'woman' | 6. | [abakazi] | 'women' |
| 2. | [omusawo] | 'doctor' | 7. | [abasawo] | 'doctors' |
| 3. | [omusika] | 'heir' | 8. | [abasika] | 'heirs' |
| 4. | [omuwala] | 'girl' | 9. | [abawala] | 'girls' |
| 5. | [omulenzi] | 'boy' | 10. | [abalenzi] | 'boys' |

   a.   What is the morpheme meaning 'singular'?

   b.   What is the morpheme meaning 'plural'?

   c.   Given [abalanga] meaning 'twins', what is the form for 'twin'?

### 3. Kanuri (Nigeria)

|   |   |   |    |   |   |
|---|---|---|----|---|---|
| 1. | [gana] | 'small' | 6. | [nəmgana] | 'smallness' |
| 2. | [kura] | 'big' | 7. | [nəmkura] | 'bigness' |
| 3. | [kurugu] | 'long' | 8. | [nəmkurugu] | 'length' |
| 4. | [karite] | 'excellent' | 9. | [nəmkarite] | 'excellence' |
| 5. | [dibi] | 'bad' | 10. | [nəmdibi] | 'badness' |

a.   What type of affix is shown (i.e., prefix, suffix, infix)?

b.   What is the affix?

c.   Given [kəji] meaning 'sweet', what is the form for 'sweetness'?

d.   Given [nəmgəla] meaning 'goodness', what is the form for 'good'?

e.   What morphological process was used to form the words in the second column?

f.   Draw a word-tree for [nəmkurugu] 'length'.

---

## REMINDER

For more tips on identifying morphemes in unfamiliar languages (i.e., solving morphology problems), see pp. 131 and 132.

# MORE MORPHOLOGY PROBLEMS

The following pages contain a number of data sets from different languages. These data sets are intended to give you practice in doing morphological analysis. Each contains sufficient data to make valid conclusions; however, the data may have been regularized somewhat. All data is in phonetic transcription.

## 1. Turkish

| | | | | | |
|---|---|---|---|---|---|
| 1. | [deniz] | 'an ocean' | 9. | [elim] | 'my hand' |
| 2. | [denize] | 'to an ocean' | 10. | [eller] | 'hands' |
| 3. | [denizin] | 'of an ocean' | 11. | [disler] | 'teeth' |
| 4. | [eve] | 'to a house' | 12. | [disimizin] | 'of our tooth' |
| 5. | [evden] | 'from a house' | 13. | [dislerimizin] | 'of our teeth' |
| 6. | [evcikden] | 'from a little house' | 14. | [elcike] | 'to a little hand' |
| 7. | [denizcikde] | 'in a little ocean' | 15. | [denizlerimizde] | 'in our oceans' |
| 8. | [elde] | 'in a hand' | 16. | [evciklerimizde] | 'in our little houses' |

Give the Turkish morpheme that corresponds to each of the following English translations.

| ocean | _____ | my | _____ |
|---|---|---|---|
| house | _____ | our | _____ |
| hand | _____ | of | _____ |
| tooth | _____ | little | _____ |
| plural | _____ | from | _____ |
| to | _____ | in | _____ |

What is the order of morphemes in a Turkish word in terms of noun, preposition, plural, possessive determiner and adjective? (Don't assume that this order will be the same as it is in English.)

What would be the Turkish word meaning 'of our little hands'? (HINT: Use the order you determined above.)

## 2. Bontoc (Philippines)

| | | | | | |
|---|---|---|---|---|---|
| 1. | [fikas] | 'strong' | 5. | [fumikas] | 'he is becoming strong' |
| 2. | [kilad] | 'red' | 6. | [kumilad] | 'he is becoming red' |
| 3. | [bato] | 'stone' | 7. | [bumato] | 'he is becoming stone' |
| 4. | [fusul] | 'enemy' | 8. | [fumusul] | 'he is becoming an enemy' |

What is the affix used to form the verbs?

What type of affix (i.e., prefix, suffix, infix) is used to form the verbs?

What morphological process is used to build the verbs?

## 3. Michoacan Aztec (also known as Nahuatl—Mexico)

| | | | | | |
|---|---|---|---|---|---|
| 1. | [nokali] | 'my house' | 8. | [mopelo] | 'your dog' |
| 2. | [nokalimes] | 'my houses' | 9. | [mopelomes] | 'your dogs' |
| 3. | [mokali] | 'your house' | 10. | [ipelo] | 'his dog' |
| 4. | [ikali] | 'his house' | 11. | [nokwahmili] | 'my cornfield' |
| 5. | [kali] | 'house' | 12. | [mokwahmili] | 'your cornfield' |
| 6. | [kalimes] | 'houses' | 13. | [ikwahmili] | 'his cornfield' |
| 7. | [nopelo] | 'my dog' | 14. | [ikwahmilimes] | 'his cornfields' |

Fill in the blanks with the corresponding Michoacan morphemes:

house _____          my _____

dog _____          your _____

cornfield _____          his _____

plural _____

What does [pelomes] mean in this language?

What would be the form for 'my cornfields' in this language? For 'his dogs'?

## 4. Isleta (a dialect of Southern Tiwa—New Mexico, USA)

1. [temiban]    'I went'          4. [mimiay]      'he was going'
2. [amiban]     'you went'        5. [tewanban]    'I came'
3. [temiwe]     'I am going'      6. [tewanhi]     'I will come'

List the morphemes corresponding to the following English translations:

I            _____          present progressive    _____

you          _____          past progressive       _____

he           _____          past                   _____

go           _____          future                 _____

come         _____

What type of affixes are the subject morphemes?

What type of affixes are the tense morphemes?

What is the order of morphemes in this language?

How would you say the following in this language?

he went          _____

I will go        _____

you were coming  _____

---

**HINT ...** The term 'progressive' refers to an ongoing action. In English, the progressive is formed by adding the inflectional affix -*ing* to a verb and adding the present (*am, are, is*) or past tense (*was, were*) of the auxiliary verb 'be'. So *I am going* is present progressive, and *he was going* is past progressive. Remember, the progressive may be formed differently in Isleta than in English. Remember as well that morphemes can have the same form but different functions!

**5.  Isthmus Zapoteco (Mexico)**      Note:    [ñ] is a palatal nasal

1.  [ñee]                'foot'
2.  [kañee]              'feet'
3.  [ñeebe]              'his foot'
4.  [kañeebe]            'his feet'
5.  [ñeeluʔ]             'your foot'
6.  [kañeetu]            'your (pl) feet'
7.  [kañeedu]            'our feet'
8.  [kazigi]             'chins'
9.  [zigibe]             'his chin'
10. [zigiluʔ]            'your chin'
11. [kazigitu]           'your (pl) chins'

12. [kazigidu]           'our chins'
13. [zike]               'shoulder'
14. [zikebe]             'his shoulder'
15. [kazikeluʔ]          'your shoulders'
16. [diaga]              'ear'
17. [kadiagatu]          'your (pl) ears'
18. [kadiagadu]          'our ears'
19. [bisozedu]           'our father'
20. [bisozetu]           'your (pl) father'
21. [kabisozetu]         'your (pl) fathers'

List the morphemes of Isthmus Zapoteco that correspond to each of the following words:

foot        _____        your        _____

shoulder    _____        our         _____

father      _____        his         _____

chin        _____        plural      _____

ear         _____

your (pl)   _____

What is the order of morphemes in Isthmus Zapoteco in terms of nouns, possessive determiners, and plural?

---

**TWO REMINDERS**

1.  An affix is an infix only when it is inserted inside a morpheme.
2.  Don't forget to use a hyphen to indicate that a morpheme is bound (i.e., an affix, either a prefix, suffix, or infix). Root words do not need a hyphen.

### 6. Fore (Papua New Guinea)

| | | | |
|---|---|---|---|
| 1. [natuwi] | 'I ate yesterday.' | 8. [natuni] | 'We ate yesterday.' |
| 2. [nagasuwi] | 'I ate today.' | 9. [nagasuni] | 'We ate today.' |
| 3. [nakuwi] | 'I will eat.' | 10. [nagasusi] | 'We (dual) ate today.' |
| 4. [nataːni] | 'You ate yesterday.' | 11. [nakuni] | 'We will eat.' |
| 5. [nataːnaw] | 'You ate yesterday?' | 12. [nakusi] | 'We (dual) will eat.' |
| 6. [nakiyi] | 'He will eat.' | 13. [nataːwi] | 'They ate yesterday.' |
| 7. [nakiyaw] | 'He will eat?' | 14. [nataːsi] | 'They (dual) ate' 'yesterday.' |

- Don't forget that what are inflectional affixes in many languages can be translated into separate words in English.

- In the glosses, 'yesterday', 'today', and 'tomorrow' are translations of the English past, present, and future tenses, respectively.

Identify the Fore morphemes that correspond to the following English words:

| | | | |
|---|---|---|---|
| I | _____ | eat | _____ |
| he | _____ | yesterday | _____ |
| we | _____ | today | _____ |
| they | _____ | will | _____ |
| we (dual) | _____ | question | _____ |
| they (dual) | _____ | statement | _____ |

Describe the order of the morphemes in terms of personal pronouns, question/statement markers, verbs, and adverbs.

Give the Fore words for the following:

He ate yesterday?   _____

They (dual) will eat?   _____

They ate today.   _____

# MORPHOPHONEMICS

Morphemes do not always have the same form. Allomorphs are the different forms of a morpheme. Consider the following English example.

⇒ **The Allomorphs ...** The English plural morpheme *-s* has three different phonetic forms:

> [-s] in words like *cats*
> [-z] in words like *dogs*
> [-əz] in words like *dishes*

⇒ **The Conditioning Environment ...** Which phonetic form is realized depends on the phonological characteristics of the final segment in the preceding word:

> [-s] occurs after a base ending in a voiceless consonant that is not strident
> [-z] occurs after a base ending in a voiced consonant that is not strident
> [-əz] occurs after a base ending in a strident consonant

The specific environment in which the different allomorphs occur is often referred to as the distribution of the allomorphs. This interaction between morphology and phonology is called **morphophonemics.**

For more information on morphophonemics, visit www.pearsoncanada.ca/ogrady and select Chapter 4, Morphophonemics.

**Practice!**   Identify morphemes in the following data from Luiseño. Watch out for allomorphs in the plural morpheme.

## Luiseño (Southern California)

| | | | | | |
|---|---|---|---|---|---|
| 1. | [nokaamay] | 'my son' | 13. | [pokaamay] | 'his son' |
| 2. | [ʔoki] | 'your house' | 14. | [poki] | 'his house' |
| 3. | [potaanat] | 'his blanket' | 15. | [notaanat] | 'my blanket' |
| 4. | [ʔohuukapi] | 'your pipe' | 16. | [pohuukapi] | 'his pipe' |
| 5. | [ʔotaanat] | 'your blanket' | 17. | [nohuukapi] | 'my pipe' |
| 6. | [noki] | 'my house' | 18. | [ʔokaamay] | 'your son' |
| 7. | [ʔokim] | 'your houses' | 19. | [pompeewum] | 'their wives' |
| 8. | [nokaamayum] | 'my sons' | 20. | [camhuukapim] | 'our pipes' |
| 9. | [popeew] | 'his wife' | 21. | [ʔotaanatum] | 'your blankets' |
| 10. | [ʔopeew] | 'your wife' | 22. | [pomkaamay] | 'their son' |
| 11. | [camtaanat] | 'our blanket' | 23. | [campeewum] | 'our wives' |
| 12. | [camhuukapi] | 'our pipe' | 24. | [pomkim] | 'their houses' |

List the Luiseño morphemes that correspond to the following English words:

| son | _____ | my | _____ |
| house | _____ | his | _____ |
| blanket | _____ | your | _____ |
| wife | _____ | their | _____ |
| pipe | _____ | our | _____ |

What are the two allomorphs of the Luiseño plural marker?

_____

State the conditioning environment that determines which allomorph occurs. Be very general!

a. _____

b. _____

**REVIEW! REVIEW!** Make sure you know how to do the following:

- define morphological terms
- divide a word into its morphemes
- assign lexical categories
- build word trees
- identify inflection and derivation
- construct compound words
- recognize endocentric and exocentric compounds
- recognize morphological processes used to build words
- do morphological analysis
- identify morphemes and morphological processes in unfamiliar languages
- find allomorphs

# QUESTIONS?  PROBLEMS?  DIFFICULTIES?

_____

_____

_____

_____

_____

_____

_____

_____

_____

_____

_____

# CHAPTER 5. SYNTAX:
# THE ANALYSIS OF SENTENCE STRUCTURE

Syntax is the study of how speakers of a language are able to combine words into sentences in order to convey any and all thoughts. Important topics and concepts found in this chapter include the following:

1. Lexical and non-lexical categories
2. Phrases
3. Phrase structure and phrase structure tests
4. Sentences
5. Complement clauses
6. Complement options
7. Syntactic operations
8. Deep and surface structure
9. *Yes/no* and *wh* questions
10. Inversion, *Wh* Movement and *Do* Insertion
11. Verb Raising
12. Relative clauses, modifiers, and passives

## WORDS

Words are an important part of a language's grammar. A speaker's lexicon (mental dictionary) contains information on the pronunciation and meaning of individual words. It also contains information on the syntactic category to which a word belongs.

There are two types of syntactic categories: lexical and non-lexical. Some of the major characteristics of each include the following:

**Lexical:**
- words that have meaning
- words that can be inflected
- includes nouns (N), verbs (V), adjectives (A), prepositions (P), and adverbs (Adv)

**Non-Lexical:**
- words whose meaning is harder to define
- words that have a grammatical function
- includes determiners (Det), auxiliary verbs (Aux), conjunctions (Con), and degree words (Deg)

See table 5.1 on p. 141 for some examples of lexical (content) and non-lexical (function) words.

The lexical category to which a word belongs can be determined by examining (1) its meaning, (2) the type of inflectional affixes that it can take, and (3) the non-lexical category words with which it can co-occur. Words can often belong to more than one category, so you also need to pay close attention to how the word is being used in a sentence.

**Practice!** Each sentence below contains some underlined words. Identify the category of each underlined word. Note that the underlined word can be either lexical or non-lexical.

1.  Pamela's heart <u>beat</u> <u>really</u> fast and her hands trembled as she <u>listened</u> to <u>the</u> <u>intermittent</u> <u>knocking</u> on the front <u>door</u> of her shanty located <u>near</u> the railroad <u>tracks</u> <u>beside</u> a hobo jungle, and she <u>thought</u>, "That's a <u>bum</u> rap, if ever I <u>heard</u> one."

2.  The railroad <u>agent</u> told the <u>Navajo</u>, "The <u>coming</u> of the Iron Horse <u>may</u> <u>bring</u> great <u>prosperity</u> to your people."

3.  "The <u>leg</u>, he is <u>fractured</u>," he <u>said</u> <u>in</u> broken English.

4.  The Great Barrier Reef is 900 miles <u>long</u>, <u>and</u> Wilmer Chanti, the <u>great</u> explorer, <u>says</u> it <u>could</u> <u>be</u> <u>circumnavigated</u> in forty days.

5.  When I <u>turned</u> the <u>key</u> to open <u>my</u> lab door, I thought that it <u>would</u> be a <u>very</u> <u>dull</u> day, until I noticed that my little cucaracha <u>had</u> <u>flopped</u> over on <u>his</u> back and <u>was</u> waving his <u>little</u> legs <u>frantically</u>, and I <u>realized</u> that someone had <u>bugged</u> my bug.

6.  It was <u>a</u> <u>rather</u> dark, <u>but</u> calm night, its <u>green</u> clarity <u>diluted</u> by my roommates, who, as usual, <u>were</u> <u>making</u> <u>cutting</u> remarks as they drank <u>that</u> bottle <u>of</u> old Scotch.

7.  "I <u>hate</u> <u>pineapples</u>," said Tom <u>dolefully</u>.

8.  Here's how to make a <u>fortune</u>. <u>Buy</u> fifty female <u>pigs</u> and fifty male deer. Then you <u>will</u> have a hundred sows and bucks.

---

**Reminder!**  There are two types of auxiliary verbs: modal and non-modal. Modal auxiliary verbs include *will, would, can, could, may, must, should, might*. Non-modal auxiliary verbs include all the different forms of *be* (*am, are, is, was, were, been, being*) and *have* (*has, had*).

Go back over the above exercise, and for any word that you identified as an auxiliary verb, determine if it is a modal or non-modal auxiliary verb.

# PHRASES

Words are grouped together to form phrases.  There are three important components to a phrase.

⇒ **Heads.**  A phrase must have a head. The head of a phrase is the obligatory nucleus around which the phrase is built. Four lexical categories usually function as the head of a phrase, thereby allowing for four types of phrases:

1. **NP** – noun phrase
2. **AP** – adjective phrase
3. **VP** – verb phrase
4. **PP** – prepositional phrase

The head of a noun phrase, of course, is a noun; the head of an adjective phrase, an adjective; the head of a verb phrase, a verb; and the head of a prepositional phrase, a preposition.

⇒ **Specifiers.**  A phrase can optionally contain a specifier.  Specifiers help to make the meaning of the head more precise.  Specifiers mark phrasal boundaries.  In English, specifiers occur before the head, thus marking the beginning of a phrase.

1. Determiners       – specify a noun
                                e.g., *the, a, these, that …*

2. Qualifiers         – specify a verb
                                e.g., *always, often, never …*

3. Degree words    – specify an adjective or a preposition
                                e.g., *very, quite, really …*

⇒ **Complements.**  A phrase can also optionally contain a complement. Complements provide more information about entities that are implied by the head of the phrase. Like specifiers, complements also provide information on the boundary of a phrase. In English, complements come after the head, thus marking the end of a phrase. Complements are typically other phrases.

---

### REMINDER! REMINDER!

Specifiers can help determine the category to which a word belongs. This is because the type of specifier found in a phrase depends on the category of the head. So if a word can occur with a determiner, it is a noun; if it can occur with an adverb, it is a verb; and if it can occur with a degree word, it is an adjective.

⇒ A phrase can consist of a single word or many words. If a phrase consists of a single word, that word must be the head of the phrase. If a phrase consists of many words, the phrase may consist of

- a specifier and a head,
- a head and a complement, or
- a specifier, a head, and a complement.

Below are some examples of the possibilities for each type of phrase.

## 1. Noun Phrase (NP)

    a.  *mud*         – contains only the head noun (*mud*)

    b.  *the mud*      – contains a specifier (*the*) and the head noun ( *mud*)

    c.  *mud*         – contains the head noun (*mud*) and a complement
        *on the floor*    prepositional phrase (*on the floor*)

    d.  *the mud*      – contains a specifier (*the*), the head noun (*mud*),
        *on the floor*    and a complement prepositional phrase (*on the floor*)

The prepositional phrase *on the floor* consists of a head preposition (*on*) and a complement noun phrase (*the floor*). The noun phrase *the floor* then consists of a specifier (*the*) and a head noun (*floor*).

## 2. Adjective Phrase (AP)

    a.  *happy*        – contains only the head adjective (*happy*)

    b.  *very happy*    – contains a specifier (*very*) and the head adjective (*happy*)

    c.  *happy with*   – contains the head adjective (*happy*) and a complement
        *the results*    prepositional phrase (*with the results*)

    d.  *very happy*   – contains a specifier (*very*), the head adjective (*happy*),
        *with the results*   and a complement prepositional phrase (*with the results*)

The prepositional phrase *with the results* consists of a head preposition (*with*) and a complement noun phrase (*the results*). The noun phrase *the results* then consists of a specifier (*the*) and a head noun (*results*).

### 3. Verb Phrase (VP)

    a. *sings*          – contains only the head verb (*sing*)

    b. *often sings*     – contains a specifier (*often*) and the head verb (*sings*)

    c. *sings a song*     – contains the head verb (*sing*) and a complement noun phrase (*a song*)

    d. *often sings a song*     – contains a specifier (*often*), the head verb (*sings*), and a a complement noun phrase (*a song*)

The complement noun phrase *a song* consists of a specifier (*a*) and a head noun (*song*).

### 4. Prepositional Phrase (PP)

    a. *in the car*     – contains the head preposition (*in*) and a complement noun phrase (*the car*)

    b. *almost in the car*     – contains a specifier (*almost*), the head preposition (*in*) and a complement noun phrase (*the car*)

The complement noun phrase *the car* contains a specifier (*the*) and a head noun (*car*).

**Now ...** Think of an example of each of the following:

⇒ a noun phrase containing a specifier, a head noun, and a complement
⇒ an adjective phrase containing a specifier and a head adjective
⇒ a verb phrase containing a head verb and a complement
⇒ a prepositional phrase containing a head preposition and a complement

---

## REMINDER!  REMINDER!

Prepositional phrases are different from the other three types of phrase in that prepositional phrases must always contain a complement, and this complement is always a noun phrase.

## Practice!

For each of the following phrases, determine the head of the phrase, the specifier, and the complement. Remember that every phrase must have a head but that specifiers and complements are optional! The first is done for you.

| | SPECIFIER | HEAD | COMPLEMENT |
|---|---|---|---|
| the rat | the | rat | none |
| men | | | |
| in the barn | | | |
| really mean | | | |
| worked | | | |
| worked at the station | | | |
| extremely boring | | | |
| that house on the corner | | | |
| never walks to the park | | | |
| very small | | | |
| in the room | | | |
| awfully cute | | | |
| seldom smiles | | | |
| swept the floor | | | |
| the poem about love | | | |
| pancakes | | | |

**Now ...** Go back and determine the type of each phrase. Remember: the lexical category of the head determines the type of phrase. If you're having trouble identifying the lexical category of the head, refer back to the Reminder box on p. 103 of this guide.

# PHRASE STRUCTURE TESTS

A number of tests can be done to determine whether a group of words is a phrase. Three frequently used tests are the Substitution Test, the Movement Test, and the Coordination Test. Be careful, though: not every test works for every phrase.

## Substitution Test

The Substitution Test states that a group of words is a phrase if you can substitute words such as *they*, *there*, or *do so*, and still be grammatical. The word used as a substitute also tells you the type of phrase you have.

**NP:**   A noun phrase can be substituted with a pronoun:
  e.g.,   **The boys** played in the mud. **They** played in the mud.
      (they = the boys)

**VP:**   A verb phrase can be substituted with *do so*:
  e.g.,   The girls will **play in the mud**, if the boys **do so**.
      (do so = play in the mud)

**PP:**   A prepositional phrase can often be substituted with *there*:
  e.g.,   The boys played **in the mud**. The boys played **there**.
      (there = in the mud)

## Movement Test

The Movement Test states that a group of words is a phrase if it can be moved to another position in the sentence and still be grammatical.

e.g.,   The children bought candy **at the store**. ⟶
      **At the store**, the children bought candy.

## Coordination Test

According to this test, a group of words is a phrase if it can be joined to another group of words using a conjunction (*and, but, or*) and still be grammatical.

e.g.,   The children **bought candy** and **left the store**.
      – two verb phrases joined with the conjunction *and*

## Try This!

1. Apply the Substitution Test to determine which of the bracketed sequences of words in the following sentences are phrases.

   a. [Juanita and Juan] arrived [in San Juan] [on Epiphany].
   b. The cabbage [rolls were] salty.
   c. They moved [the desk with the wooden top].
   d. Little Andrew swallowed [all the pills].
   e. The polar bears [were swimming across] the lake.
   f. Brendan [is writing a ballad about Canadian soldiers in Cyprus].

2. Apply the Movement Test to determine which of the bracketed sequences in the following sentences are phrases.

   a. The [army was surrounded] by the enemy.
   b. Leona likes [Viennese waltzes and Argentinian tangos].
   c. Jean ate his lunch [in the revolving restaurant].
   d. Eat, drink, and [be merry for] today will become yesterday.

3. Use a conjunction (*and, but, or*) to join each of the following phrases with a phrase of the same type. You might want to first use the Substitution Test to determine the type of phrase!

   a. the new desk
   b. assembled the new desk
   c. new
   d. in a hole
   e. rather huge
   f. worked on a movie
   g. beside the fence
   h. really lovely
   i. talked to the girls
   j. a dentist

# PHRASE STRUCTURE TREES

Specifiers, heads, and complements are arranged using the X' (X-bar) schema, in which X stands for any head.

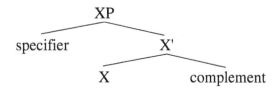

The representation of a phrase using the above schema is often referred to as a tree diagram.

⇒ Some things to remember about tree diagrams:

- All tree diagrams will have an XP, X', and X.
- All phrases have a head (X).
- If there is a specifier, it is attached at the XP level.
- If there is a complement, it is attached at the X' level.

The above conditions apply to all phrases (NP, VP, AP, and PP).

⇒ See figures 5.2 to 5.6 on pp. 145 to 147 for examples of tree diagrams of phrases containing only heads; specifiers and heads; specifiers, heads and complements; and heads and complements.

**Exercise!**   Draw tree diagrams for each of the following phrases. Remember that specifiers come before the head, and complements after the head.

1.  the rat
2.  men
3.  really mean
4.  ran
5.  in the barn
6.  ran into the shed
7.  rather boring
8.  many trucks
9.  the house on the corner
10. very small
11. under the stove
12. seldom smiles
13. swept the floor
14. fond of candy
15. the poem about love
16. silly
17. read the poem
18. really happy with George
19. usually eats lunch
20. looks good

---

# QUICK REMINDER

Use the Substitution Test to help you determine the type of phrase you are dealing with. Remember: the Substitution Test not only tells you if a group of words is or is not a phrase; it can also tell you the type of phrase you have. Refer back to pp. 107 and 108 in this guide for more information.

# SENTENCES

A sentence is the largest unit of syntactic analysis. Sentences have the same structure as do phrases in that they consist of a specifier, head, and complement.

⇒ **NP.** The noun phrase is typically referred to as the subject. See figures 5.2a, 5.3a, and 5.5a on pp. 145 to 147 for some examples of diagrammed NPs. The subject is the specifier of I.

⇒ **I (Infl).** This is the obligatory head of the sentence and is used to refer to inflection. There are two possibilities for I: +pst (past) and -pst (non-past), +pst is used for sentences in the past tense, and -pst is used for sentences in either the present or future tense.

Modal auxiliaries occur under I. This is because modals have an inherent tense (non-past), so I is a natural place for them to occur. I, then, has two possibilities:

- inflection alone (either +pst or -pst)
- inflection (-pst) and a modal auxiliary

⇒ **VP.** The verb phrase is typically referred to as the predicate. The VP is the complement of I. See figures 5.2b and 5.3b, on pp. 145 and 146 and figures 5.4 and 5.6a on p. 147 for some examples of diagrammed VPs.

Sentences, like phrases, are built according to the X' schema. Since I is the head of a sentence, IP is used to represent the syntactic unit of a sentence.

Below are two examples of fully diagrammed sentences, the first without a modal auxiliary and the second with a modal auxiliary. For another example of each possibility, see figures 5.8 and 5.9 on p. 149.

(1) *The children read a book.*

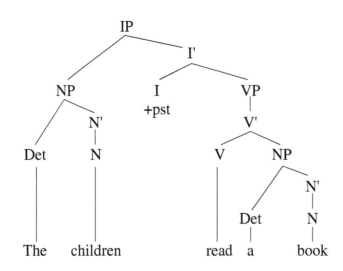

(2) *The children might read a book.*

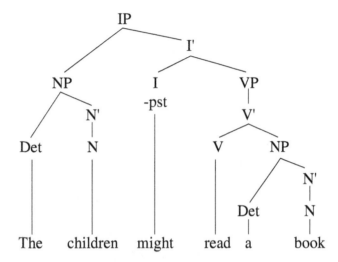

**Practice!** Draw a tree diagram for each of the following sentences.

1.  Abner should conceal the document.
2.  Marge usually watches the sunset.
3.  A penguin walked into the room.
4.  Carl might sell that car.
5.  The air smells really fresh.
6.  Grandparents may live in condominiums.
7.  The house across the street sold.
8.  Those monsters never hide under the bed.
9.  George may seem tired of studying.
10. Dogs will always hide in that park.

---

## QUICK REMINDER

A noun phrase (NP), a prepositional phrase (PP), or an adjective phrase (AP) are all potential complements of a verb. The particular complement that occurs depends on the verb. Some verbs can take more than one complement!

# COMPLEMENT CLAUSES

In addition to noun phrases, adjective phrases, and prepositional phrases, a sentence (IP) may also function as a complement. When a sentence functions as a complement, it can occur in the complement position of a verb phrase. The sentence contained within the verb phrase is called a complement clause (CP). The sentence within which the CP is found is called the matrix clause.

A CP is like any other type of phrase in that it consists of a specifier, a head, and a complement.

⇒ **Specifier.** The specifier position of a CP functions as a landing site for phrases undergoing the Move operation (see the section on Move beginning on p. 116 of this guide).

⇒ **Complementizer.** The head of a CP is a complementizer (C). Complementizers include words such as *that*, *if*, and *whether*.

⇒ **IP.** The complement of a complementizer is an IP (i.e., a sentence).

Below is a tree diagram of the sentence *John thinks that Mary will win*, which contains a CP inside the VP. See figures 5.11 and 5.12 on p. 154 for another example. See table 5.9 on p. 155 for examples of verbs that can have CP complements.

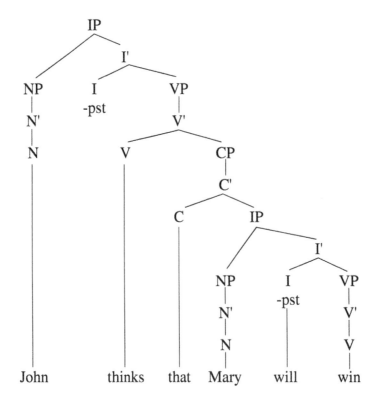

**Practice! Practice!** Draw a tree diagram for each of the following sentences.

1. Nancy hopes that Sean will become a pilot.
2. Kasey wondered whether aliens exist.
3. Sailors know that ships can sink at sea.
4. The passengers thought that the plane would never land.

---

### SOME HINTS FOR DRAWING PHRASE STRUCTURE TREES

1. Every sentence (IP) has the following structure.

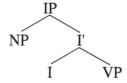

2. Every sentence contains I. Identify the tense of the sentence. Use +pst if a sentence is in the past tense, and -pst if the sentence is in either the present or future tense. If the sentence contains a modal auxiliary, this auxiliary occurs under I, and I will be -pst.

3. Every sentence has a verb. Identify the verb. Check if this verb has a specifier and/or a complement. Remember that the specifier of a verb is a preverbal adverb (qualifier) and marks the beginning of the phrase. If there is a complement, it can be either a phrase or a sentence.

   - If the complement is a phrase, identify the type of phrase and then diagram the phrase using the X' schema.
   - If the complement is a sentence, it will begin with the following structure.

   Identify the complementizer. Since a CP contains an IP, you will also need to identify and diagram the NP, I, and VP for this embedded IP.

4. Every sentence has a subject NP. Identify the noun. Check if this noun has a specifier and/or a complement. Remember that the specifier of a noun is a determiner and that this determiner marks the beginning of this noun phrase. If there is a complement, it will be a prepositional phrase. Diagram this phrase using the X' schema.

   For more hints on drawing tree diagrams of phrases and sentences, see the Appendix to Chapter 5 on pp. 175 to 177.

# MORE PRACTICE WITH SENTENCES

The following exercise contains many examples of sentences with and without complement clauses. Draw a tree diagram for each.

1. The repairman fixed the watch.

2. Neighbours can be unfriendly.

3. Nurses never complain.

4. The train often leaves on time.

5. The castle fell into the sea.

6. The rabbit might eat those lilies.

7. Children are very curious.

8. Sally lives in a house by the sea.

9. The secretary should mail the proposal.

10. This soup tastes really great.

11. The rabbit may sometimes hide under the bridge.

12. Sandra is almost at the restaurant.

13. Those men on the shore saw a signal.

14. The doctor was quite correct in his diagnosis.

15. The driver of that car sped through many streets.

16. George hoped that Fred would win a car.

17. The salesman wondered if those customers might buy that sofa.

18. Kayleigh usually thinks that playing at home is fun.

19. The media reported that no candidate won the election.

20. The captain hoped that the tourists would perhaps see a whale.

# MERGE

Merge is an operation contained within the computational system of the grammar. Merge is responsible for building the phrase structure in a manner compatible with the X' schema. Essentially, Merge combines words together to make phrases, phrases to make sentences, and sentences to make larger sentences.

⇒ The following example illustrates how Merge operates.

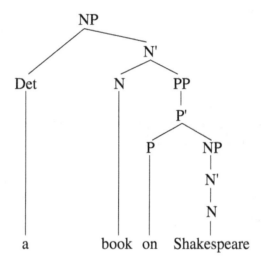

Merge created the above complex phrase by combining the noun phrase *Shakespeare* with the preposition *on* to create the prepositional phrase *on Shakespeare*. This phrase was then combined with the noun *book* and the specifier *a* to create the noun phrase *a book on Shakespeare*. Merge continues to operate in this way to create entire sentences.

## Complement Options

In addition to using the X' schema, Merge must combine words into phrases and sentences in a manner consistent with the complement options of the individual words. Essentially, individual words in a sentence must occur with complements of the right type for the sentence to be grammatical. The complement(s) with which a word can occur are called its complement options.

⇒ **Think ...** Does the verb *throw* require a complement or can it occur without a complement? If it requires a complement, what type of complement is needed? If it is used without this complement or with a complement of a different type, is the resulting sentence grammatical or ungrammatical? What about the verb *become*? What type of complement does it require? What about the verb *arrive*? Does it require a complement?

See table 5.5 on p. 151 for some examples of different verb complements in English. See tables 5.6, 5.7, and 5.8 on pp. 152 and 153 for some examples of complement options for nouns, adjectives, and prepositions.

Information on the complement options of words, along with the meaning and pronunciation of words, is found in a speaker's lexicon. Information about a word's complement options is often referred to as subcategorization.

**Try This!** Determine the complement options that the verbs listed below require. Do this by thinking of grammatical and ungrammatical sentences containing the verb.

- panic
- watch
- imagine

- write
- wonder
- play

Nouns, adjectives, and prepositions also have restrictions on the types of complements with which they can and cannot occur. Determine the complement options that the following words require. Start by identifying the lexical category of the word and then think of grammatical and ungrammatical sentences containing the word.

- pleasure
- with
- contribution

- intelligent
- out
- upset

## MOVE

Move is a second syntactic operation. Move transports elements from one position in a sentence to another. This is all that a Move operation can do: Move cannot change the categories of words, nor can it eliminate any part of the structure.

There are three important points to remember about how Move operates.

⇒ **CP.** Move transports elements to positions within a CP. For this to occur, every IP must be found within a larger CP. This CP is a 'shell' that contains an IP.

- Remember that a CP can function as a complement clause, in which case it is embedded in a larger sentence. When a CP is embedded within a larger sentence, C can contain a complementizer such as *that*, *if*, or *whether*. Refer to figure 5.12 on p. 154 for an example of a sentence with an embedded CP.

- For CP shells containing an IP (i.e., all other CPs), C contains information on whether the sentence is a question or a statement: if C contains +Q, the structure is a question, and if C is empty, it is a statement. It is the +Q that can trigger a Move operation. See figure 5.14 on p. 156 for an example of an IP within a CP shell.

⇒ **Trace.**  Moved elements leave behind a trace (*t*). A trace records (1) that a movement has occurred and (2) where in the structure the moved element originated. Leaving a trace is necessary, as Move cannot change the structure that Merge builds.

⇒ **Levels of Representation.**  Two levels of representation result: deep and surface structure.

- Merge occurs first to build the syntactic structure. The structure that Merge generates is called the deep structure (D-structure).

- Move may then apply. The surface structure (S-structure) is the result of applying Move.

If a Move operation has taken place, then the deep and surface structures are not the same. If no Move operation takes place, then the deep and surface structures are the same.

# QUESTIONS

Merge is responsible for building the structure of a sentence using both subcategorization information (i.e., complement options) and the X' schema.  However, Merge cannot create all the structures of a language. Some structures require a second operation.  Move transforms an existing structure (e.g., a statement) into another type of structure (e.g., a question) by transporting elements from one position in a sentence to another.

Move operates to create both *yes-no* and *wh* questions.

### *Yes-no* Questions

⇒ *Yes-no* questions are so named because the response to such a question is usually 'yes' or 'no'. *Yes-no* questions are formed by moving an auxiliary verb from its position in I to the complementizer position within a CP. This is informally called Inversion.

**Inversion:**  Move I to C.
E.g.,  Mary **will** leave  →  **Will** Mary *t* leave

**After Merge:**

**After Inversion:**

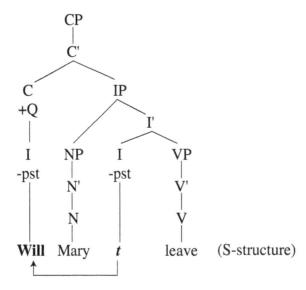

⇒ Many sentences do not contain an auxiliary verb. Yet these sentences can still be changed into a *yes-no* question. This is done by inserting the auxiliary verb *do* into the sentence. This is called *Do* Insertion and is an example of an operation that adds elements to a tree structure.

*Do* **Insertion:**   Insert interrogative *do* into an empty I position.

E.g.,   Mary left → Mary **did** leave → **Did** Mary *t* leave

**After Merge:**

(D-structure)

**After *Do* Insertion:**

**After Inversion:**

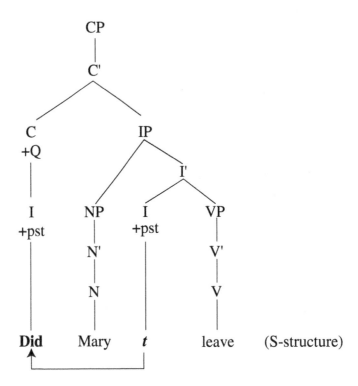

*Wh* **Questions**

⇒ *Wh* questions are so named because they begin with a *wh* word. *Who*, *what*, and *which* are all examples of *wh* words. *Who* and *what* are analyzed as nouns; *which* is a determiner. *Wh* questions are the result of *Wh* Movement. *Wh* Movement is normally followed by Inversion.

*Wh* **Movement:**  Move a *wh* phrase to the specifier position under CP.

E.g.,   George **should** buy *what*  →  *What* **should** George *t* buy *t*

**After Merge:**

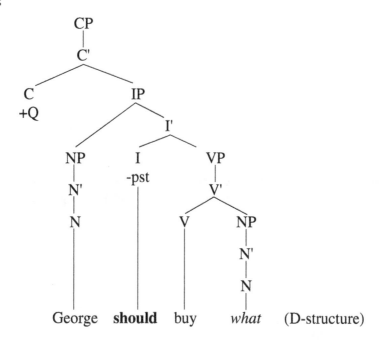

George **should** buy *what*    (D-structure)

**After *Wh* Movement and Inversion:**

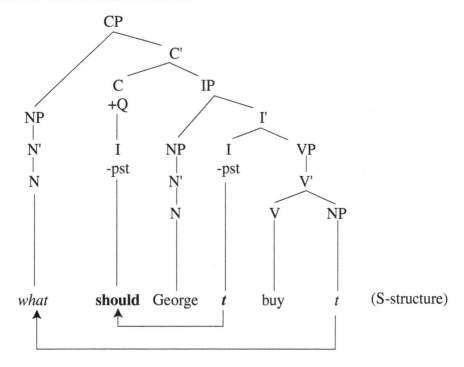

*what*    **should**  George    *t*    buy    *t*    (S-structure)

**Think!** *Do* Insertion can also occur during the formation of *wh* questions.

> E.g.,    George bought *what*  →  *What* George bought *t*  →
>
> *What* George **did** buy *t*  →  *What* **did** George *t* buy *t*

Try drawing a tree diagram of both the deep structure and surface structure for the above sentence. You do not need to draw any intermediate structures. Indicate with arrows all of the movements. Do this on the surface structure.

⇒ *Wh* Movement can move a *wh* phrase occurring as the complement of the verb (as in the previous example) or it can move a *wh* phrase occurring in the subject position.

> E.g.,    *Who* broke the lamp  →  *Who t* broke the lamp

**After Merge:**

(D-structure)

**After *Wh* Movement:**

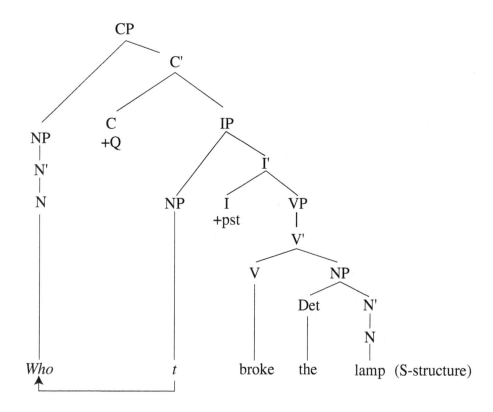

**Think ...** Compare the above deep and surface structures. Is the word order in the deep and surface structure the same? Is *Do* Insertion required when *Wh* Movement moves a subject NP?

See figures 5.15 and 5.17 to 5.21 on pp. 157 to 164 for more examples of tree diagrams of the deep and surface structures of sentences in which Inversion, *Do* Insertion, and *Wh* Movement have taken place.

**Try This!** For each of the following sentences, draw a tree diagram for both the deep and surface structures. On the surface structure, indicate with arrows the elements that have moved and where they have moved.

1. Will Paul enjoy the trip?
2. What can Joan eat?
3. What did the spy uncover?
4. Who saw the lion?
5. Do beagles always bark?

# VERB RAISING

Move can also transport a verb to a new position in the sentence. This is often called Verb Raising. In English, Verb Raising affects auxiliary verbs.

⇒ There are two types of auxiliary verbs:

- Modal auxiliaries (e.g., *will, could, should, would,* etc.) occur in I.

- Non-modal auxiliaries (*have* and *be*) are a special type of verb. As such, they occur in V and they take a verb phrase as a complement.

Below is a tree diagram of a sentence containing a non-modal auxiliary verb.

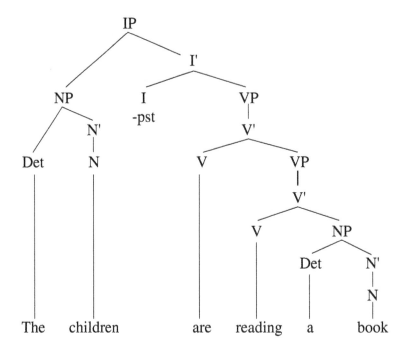

**Think ...** A sentence can have more than one auxiliary. For example, the sentence *The children have been reading a book* contains two non-modal auxiliaries. How would you diagram the verb phrase of this sentence? What about the sentence *The children will be reading a book*, which contains both a modal and a non-modal auxiliary? How would you diagram the verb phrase for this sentence?

**Remember ...** Non-modal auxiliaries can also occur as the only verb in the sentence. They still occur in V, but they take a noun phrase, adjective phrase, or prepositional phrase rather than a verb phrase as a complement.

⇒ Both modal and non-modal auxiliaries can be inverted to create a *yes-no* question:

- Modal auxiliaries occur in I and are moved from I to C using Inversion.

- Non-modal auxiliaries occur in V. Before moving from I to C, they must first be moved from V to I. The move from V to I is called Verb Raising. See figure 5.22 on p. 165 for another example of V to I movement.

**Verb Raising:**   Move V to I.

E.g.,   Mary **is** leaving  →  Mary **is** *t* leaving

**After Merge:**

(D-structure)

**After Verb Raising:**

**After Inversion:**

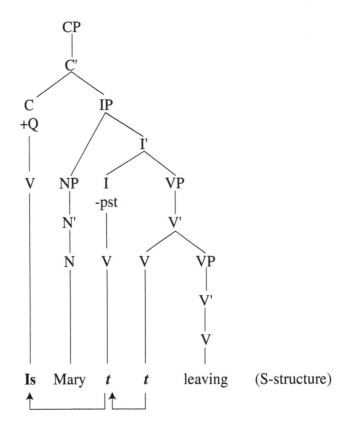

**Think!**   Verb Raising can also occur during the formation of *wh* questions.

E.g., Sylvia **was** thinking *what*  →  *What* Sylvia **was** thinking *t*  →

*What* Sylvia **was** *t* thinking *t*  →  *What* **was** Sylvia *t t* thinking *t*

Does moving an auxiliary verb from V to I change the word order of the sentence? Does Verb Raising take place if *Wh* Movement moves a subject NP? Why or why not? Think about *Do* Insertion. If this takes place, is Verb Raising needed? Why or why not?

Try drawing a tree diagram of both the deep structure and surface structure for the above sentence. You do not need to draw trees for any intermediate structures. Indicate with arrows all of the movements. Do this on the surface structure.

**Try This!**   For each of the following sentences, draw a tree diagram of both the deep and surface structures.

1.  Had the elves washed in the tub?
2.  Are the neighbours moving?
3.  What was Sally painting?
4.  Which restaurant is the city closing?

---

### REMINDER! REMINDER!

Verb Raising is a good example of the variation that occurs across languages. In English, only auxiliary (non-modal) verbs can move to I; regular (main) verbs cannot move. What this means is that only auxiliary verbs (both modal and non-modal) can be inverted to create questions. This is not true of all languages. For example, in French, any type of verb can move into I. This means that both regular (main) verbs and auxiliary verbs can be inverted in French. The idea is that all languages use the Move operation, but how this operation is instantiated can vary from language to language!

See figures 5.22 and 5.23 on pp. 165 and 166 of the text for tree diagrams illustrating Verb Raising in French.

---

## Some Hints ...

You need to be able to determine the deep structure for any sentence you are given, and to do so, you need to be able to identify any of the movements that have occurred. Remember, Inversion, *Wh* Movement, and Verb Raising are all applications of the Move operation. *Do* Insertion is also a syntactic operation.  You may also have to construct a tree diagram of the deep and surface structures.

Here are some clues to help you identify which movements have occurred and to put surface structure sentences back into their deep structure:

| YOU SEE: | YOU THINK: | YOU DO: |
|---|---|---|
| A modal auxiliary verb before the subject | Inversion has taken place. | Put the modal auxiliary back into its deep structure position (I). |
| A non-modal auxiliary verb before the subject | Inversion has taken place. Verb Raising has taken place. | Put the non-modal auxiliary back into its deep structure position (V). |
| A *wh* word or phrase | *Wh* Movement has taken place. | Examine each verb in the sentence. Determine if a verb is missing either a subject or an object.  Put the *wh* word or phrase into that position. |
| *Do, did,* or *does* at the beginning of a sentence, or after a *wh* word or phrase | *Do* Insertion has taken place. | Remove *do, did,* or *does* from the sentence. |

**Remember ...**   To include a trace (*t*) for each movement!

See the Appendix to Chapter 5 on pp. 177 to 179 for more hints on how to analyze sentences involving the Move operation.

# TRANSFORMATION WORKSHEET

Draw a tree diagram of both the deep and surface structure for each of the following sentences. Identify any movements that have occurred to derive the surface structure. Be careful: for some sentences, the deep structure and surface structure will be the same.

1.  Can the clown amuse that boy?
2.  Which coat should Hilary wear?
3.  Did Bill sell the house?
4.  Who does the jury blame?
5.  Margo dreamt that Frances flew to England.
6.  Has the player left the team?
7.  What was Joanne eating?
8.  Could the vandals destroy the billboard?
9.  Christopher has drawn a picture.
10. Who might these clothes fit?
11. Were the maids cleaning the house?
12. Will the winner be claiming the prize?
13. Does Henry think that Harry might survive in the jungle?
14. What does Mary want?
15. The jury believed that the prisoner was guilty.
16. Do children like cake?
17. Who prepared the meal?
18. Colin was wondering whether George would order pizza.

---

## TWO IMPORTANT REMINDERS

1. You are trying to determine which elements have already been moved; therefore, you must **never** move any additional words or phrases!
2. No movements may have occurred, only one movement may have occurred, or more than one movement may have occurred. To find the deep structure, you need to (1) find all instances of Move, and (2) determine if *Do* Insertion has occurred.

# OTHER SYNTACTIC PHENOMENA

Some other syntactic structures include modifiers, relative clauses, and passives. Each of these structures builds on the basic syntactic system (i.e., Merge and Move) for forming sentences.

**Modifiers**

Modifiers are words and phrases that denote properties of heads. There are two main types of modifiers.

⇒ Adjective phrases modify nouns in that they indicate a property of the noun.

   E.g., A **very cold** wind is blowing.

⇒ Adverb phrases modify verbs in that they can provide information on the manner (for example) of the verb.

   E.g., The ballerina danced **gracefully**.

   Modifiers attach at the XP level. See figure 5.26 on p. 169 of the text for some examples of diagrams of phrases containing modifiers.

A relative clause is a special type of CP that modifies nouns. That is, it is a clause that provides more information about a noun. A relative clause occurs after the noun that it modifies.

A relative clause is like a *wh* question in two ways:

⇒ It begins with a *wh* word (e.g., *who* or *which*) called a relative pronoun.

   E.g., The house [**which** Jerry designed]<sub>CP</sub> won an award.

⇒ The *wh* word occurs within the sentence and is moved to the specifier position of C, leaving a trace behind. This is *Wh* Movement.

   E.g., The house [**which** Jerry  designed *t* ]<sub>CP</sub> won an award.
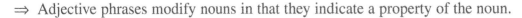

See figures 5.28 and 5.29 on pp. 170 and 171 for tree diagrams of the deep and surface structures of a relative clause.

**Think ...** The presence of +Q in C triggers *Wh* Movement during the formation of *wh* questions. What triggers *Wh* Movement during the formation of relative clauses? What feature must be present in C?

**Passives**

A sentence may be either active or passive. Active and passive sentences differ in the following ways:

⇒ In an active sentence, the agent (doer of the action) occurs in the subject position. In a passive sentence, this agent is often absent. If the agent is present, it is found within a prepositional phrase that occurs after the verb and contains the preposition *by*.

⇒ In a passive sentence, the direct object of the corresponding active sentence usually functions as the subject of the sentence. Verbs that cannot occur with a direct object in an active sentence can also not occur in passive sentences.

> E.g.,   **Active:**      The chef prepared the meal.
>
> > **Passive:**     The meal was prepared. / The meal was prepared by the chef.

Passive sentences are formed using NP Movement, another type of Move. NP Movement transports an object from its deep structure position as a complement of the verb to an empty subject position.

> E.g.,   **D-structure:**     was prepared *the meal*
>
> > **S-structure:**     *The meal* was prepared *t*

See figure 5.31 on p. 173 for an example of a tree diagram of the D-structure of a passive sentence. See figure 5.32 on p. 173 for an example of a tree diagram of the S-structure of a passive sentence.

**Exercise!**  The following exercises will give you some practice with identifying relative clauses, modifiers, and passives.

1.  Each of the following sentences contains at least one modifier. Identify all the modifiers. For each modifier, determine if it is modifying a noun or a verb. Identify the noun or verb that is being modified.

    a.   The musicians often play music loudly.
    b.   The really awful movie won top prize.
    c.   The undercover police car drove away speedily.

2.  Each of the following phrases contains a relative clause. Identify the relative clause and determine its deep structure.

    a.   the roads which the snowplows have finished clearing
    b.   the roads which were plowed yesterday
    c.   the trucks which the city uses

**Think ...** The *wh* word can sometimes be deleted from relative clauses. Can the *wh* word be deleted (if it has not yet been deleted) from any of the above sentences?

3. Decide if each of the following sentences is active or passive. Remember: a passive sentence does not necessarily include an agent.

a.  Those tigers were trained.
b.  The company should make a donation.
c.  That lamp could be fixed.

For each passive sentence, determine what the deep structure would be.

---

**REVIEW! REVIEW!** If you can do the following, then you've conquered syntax:

 – describe the differences between lexical and non-lexical categories
 – assign words to their syntactic category
 – determine if a group of words is or is not a phrase
 – identify and diagram phrases
 – diagram sentences, including those with complement clauses
 – determine complement options
 – understand the Merge and Move operations
 – spot *yes-no* and *wh* questions
 – spot Inversion, *Wh* Movement, Verb Raising, and *Do* Insertion
 – find the deep structure of a sentence
 – recognize relative clauses, modifiers, and passives

---

# QUESTIONS?  PROBLEMS?  DIFFICULTIES?

_____

_____

_____

_____

_____

_____

_____

_____

# CHAPTER 6. SEMANTICS: THE ANALYSIS OF MEANING

Semantics is the study of meaning in human language. Meaning refers, very generally, to the content of an utterance.

Important concepts and topics in this chapter include the following:

1.  Semantic relations
2.  Theories of meaning
3.  Concepts
4.  Lexicalization
5.  Grammaticalization
6.  Lexical and structural ambiguity
7.  Thematic roles
8.  Pronoun interpretation
9.  Role of pragmatics
10. Conversation

## SEMANTIC RELATIONS

Determining the semantic relations that exist between words, phrases, and sentences constitutes one of the basic notions used in evaluating meaning.

⇒ **Between words**

- Synonymy: Words that have similar meanings
- Antonymy: Words that have opposite meanings
- Polysemy: One word with two or more related meanings
- Homophony: Two words with the same pronunciation, but different meanings

See tables 6.1 to 6.4 on pp. 184 and 185 of the text for some English examples of the above relations.

**Think ...** Polysemy and homophony can result in lexical ambiguity—a single form that has two or more meanings. Think of some examples. Keep in mind ...

- Different words with the same spelling are called homographs.
- Homophones may or may not have the same spelling.
- Homographs, therefore, may or may not be homophones.

⇒ **Between sentences**

- Paraphrase: Two sentences that have very similar meanings
  - e.g.,  The cat ate the mouse.
    - The mouse was eaten by the cat.
- Entailment: Two sentences in which the truth of the first implies the truth of the second, but the truth of the second does not necessarily imply the truth of the first
  - e.g.,  George killed the burglar.
    - The burglar is dead.
- Contradiction: Two sentences such that if one is true, then the second must be false
  - e.g.,  George is rich.
    - George lives in a shelter.

**Try This!** For each of the following, identify the relation that exists between either the words or the sentences. The first is done for you.

1. test
   exam                                    synonyms
   _____

2. Mary sang a solo.
   A solo was sung by Mary.
   _____

3. bug (insect)
   bug (microphone)
   _____

4. Sam is a widower.
   Sam's wife is alive.
   _____

5. The bear attacked a camper.
   The camper is injured.
   _____

6. parent
   offspring
   _____

7. George gave Sally the book.
   George gave the book to Sally.
   _____

8. Nancy brought salmon for dinner.
   There is nothing to eat for dinner.
   _____

9. hungry
   famished
   _____

10. steak (a piece of meat)
    stake (a sharp piece of wood)
    _____

# THEORIES OF MEANING

As native speakers of a language, we all know the meaning of a great many words in our language. It is actually difficult to determine the precise meaning of a word. Without using a dictionary, try and determine the meaning of the words *spring, bridge,* and *Hawaii*. Some of the theories of meaning outlined below might help.

⇒ **Connotation.** This theory states that the meaning of a word is simply the set of associations that the word evokes. Think about what connotations the words *spring, bridge,* and *Hawaii* evoke.

⇒ **Denotation.** This theory states that the meaning of a word is not the set of associations it evokes, but rather the entity to which it refers: that is, its denotation or referent. Think about what denotation the words *spring, bridge,* and *Hawaii* have.

⇒ **Extension and Intension.** This theory attempts to combine the first two. Extension refers to the referent of a word, and intension to the associations it evokes. Thus, the meaning of a word includes both its extension and its intension. What is the extension and intension of *spring, bridge,* and *Hawaii*?

⇒ **Componential Analysis.** This theory is based on the idea that meaning can be decomposed into smaller semantic units. These units of meaning are called features. Semantic features can be combined to group entities into classes. For example, the semantic features [+living, +human, -adult] give us the category of children. Think about how you might decompose the meaning of the words *spring, bridge,* and *Hawaii* into semantic features.

Componential analysis allows us to make generalizations. For example, features of a verb's meaning can be relevant when it comes to choosing the phrases to go along with that verb to form a verb phrase.

**Think ...** What difficulties do connotation, denotation, extension, intension, and componential analysis have in determining the meaning of the words *spring, bridge,* and *Hawaii*?

## Practice! Practice!

1. For each of the following words, attempt to define their meaning according to the theories of connotation, denotation, and extension and intension.

   a. summer
   b. a linguistics instructor
   c. grass

2. Identify the types of phrases with which the verbs in A and B can occur. What difference in meaning between the verbs in A and the verbs in B determines the type of complement the verbs require?

| **A** | **B** |
|-------|-------|
| sweep | crawl |
| kick  | fell  |

3. Examine the following two groups of words and determine the semantic feature(s) each group has in common. What semantic feature(s) are different between members of each group? What about between the two groups?

Group A:      grandmother   / mother / daughter /   widow
Group B:      grandfather   /  father  /    son    /   widower

**Now ...** Try doing a componential analysis for   ⇒ ewe and lamb
                                                     ⇒ mare, filly, and colt

What difficulties did you have in decomposing the meanings of the nouns?

## CONCEPTS

Linguists use the term 'concepts' to refer to the system we use to identify, classify, and organize all elements of our many and varied experiences. Our conceptual system reveals how meaning is expressed through language.

⇒ **Fuzzy Concepts.** Fuzzy concepts are concepts that can differ from person to person. They have no clear boundaries. Think about how much something has to cost before you would consider it expensive.

⇒ **Graded Membership.** Concepts have internal structure. The members of a concept can be graded according to how typical they are within that concept. The most typical member is selected as the prototype. Other members are arranged around the prototype with members sharing more properties closer to the prototype. Members sharing fewer properties are farther from the prototype. Think ... Does the concept of *house* have a graded membership? If so, what might the prototype be? Could this prototype vary from person to person?

⇒ **Metaphor.** The concepts expressed by language do not exist in isolation but are interconnected and associated. Metaphors, the understanding of one concept in terms of another, can be used to make these connections. Metaphors can be based on perceptions, physical experiences, culture, and shared feelings. Think of a metaphor that attributes animal-like properties to people. What might be the basis of such a metaphor?

**Exercise! Exercise!** For each of the following concepts, determine whether they are fuzzy or graded.

1. cats
2. mountains
3. time
4. vegetables

For any of the above that exhibit a graded membership, determine the member that is prototypical for you. How might this differ from person to person?

Languages can differ in terms of how they express different concepts. This can be done using processes of lexicalization and grammaticalization.

⇒ **Lexicalization.** Lexicalization refers to the process whereby concepts (e.g., snow, light) are encoded into the meanings of words. Languages may differ in terms of how many words they use to convey a concept. How concepts are encoded also varies from language to language. See tables 6.9, 6.10, and 6.11 on pp. 196 to 198 for some examples of systematic differences in how motion is encoded into English, French, and Atsugewi verbs.

⇒ **Grammaticalization.** Grammaticalization refers to concepts that are expressed as affixes or functional categories. See table 6.12 on p. 199 for some examples of concepts in English that have been grammaticalized. Concepts that are grammaticalized can vary from language to language. See table 6.13 on p. 199 for an example in Hidatsa in which evidence for the truth of a statement has been grammaticalized. Think about the different ways in which negation has been grammaticalized in English.

## Try This!

1. Quite often, languages contain different forms of grammaticalized affixes or functional categories. Consider the data below from Cree involving possession and answer the questions that follow.

|   | Noun | My Noun | Gloss |
|---|------|---------|-------|
| 1. | mispiton | nispiton | 'arm' |
| 2. | tʃima:n | nitʃima:n | 'canoe' |
| 3. | miski:sik | niski:sik | 'eye' |
| 4. | mo:htawiya | no:htawiya | 'father' |
| 5. | mo:ka:wiya | no:ka:wiya | 'mother' |
| 6. | astotin | nitastotin | 'cap' |

What are the two different (morphological) ways of indicating possession? What is the semantic basis for this difference? Try to relate it to different kinds of possession: which of the above could you give away and which couldn't you?

2.  The language data below illustrates differences in the use of singular and plural prefixes in Swahili. Group the nouns into classes based on their use of the different prefixes. What is the semantic basis for your grouping?

| | Sg. | Pl. | Gloss |
|---|---|---|---|
| 1. | mtoto | watoto | 'child' |
| 2. | mhindi | mihindi | 'corn' |
| 3. | kikombe | vikombe | 'hair' |
| 4. | mkindu | mikindu | 'date palm' |
| 5. | mfigili | mifigili | 'radish' |
| 6. | mwalimu | wawalimu | 'teacher' |
| 7. | kioo | vioo | 'mirror' |
| 8. | mume | waume | 'husband' |
| 9. | kikapu | vikapu | 'basket' |
| 10. | mboga | miboga | 'pumpkin' |

3.  German neuter nouns can occur in a prepositional phrase in either the dative case (definite article *dem*) or the accusative case (definite article *das*). Examine the following sentences and determine the semantic basis for the choice of either the dative or accusative case.

1.  Monika arbeitet in dem Kaffeehaus. (Monika works in the coffeehouse.)
    Stefan kommt in das Kaffeehaus. (Stefan comes into the coffeehouse.)

2.  Ritas Stuhl steht neben dem Fenster. (Rita's stool stands next to the window.)
    Jan stellt seinen Stuhl neben das Fenster. (Jan puts his chair next to the window.)

3.  Ein Schuh steht unter dem Bett. (A shoe is under the bed.)
    Kurt stellt den anderen Schuh unter das Bett. (Kurt puts the other shoe under the bed.)

4.  Ilsa ist in dem Wohnzimmer. (Ilsa is in the living room.)
    Armin geht in das Wohnzimmer. (Armin goes into the living room.)

What concept is contained in the German articles that is not found in English articles?

## THE ROLE OF SYNTAX

Not only do the words and phrases that make up a sentence contribute to its meaning, but the position of words and phrases in the syntactic structure also has a role.

The contribution of syntax to sentence interpretation includes constructional meaning, structural ambiguity, thematic roles, and pronoun interpretation.

## Constructional Meaning

⇒ The meaning of a sentence goes beyond the meaning of the individual words and phrases that it is composed of. The syntactic structure, or construction, also contributes to the meaning of the sentence.

⇒ Two common constructions are the following:

- The caused-motion construction: X causes Y to go somewhere
- The ditransitive construction: X causes Y to have Z

**Think ...**   What construction is found in the sentence *Joe sold Sabrina a car*? What about in the sentence *Joe flew the airplane to Red Deer*? Is there anything in the verb that implies 'caused motion'? What about 'causes another person to have something'? If not, then where do these meanings come from?

## Structural Ambiguity

Structural ambiguity occurs when a group of words in a sentence can be combined in more than one way. Each different combination is associated with a different meaning. Ambiguity can be found in both noun and verb phrases.

⇒ **Noun Phrases.**  In the sentence *The surface was painted with red flowers and leaves*, the noun phrase *red flowers and leaves* can be combined in two ways. Each combination corresponds to a particular grouping of words in syntactic structure. Each grouping has its own meaning.

Meaning One:   red [flowers and leaves]
          —Both the flowers and the leaves are red.

Meaning Two:   [red flowers] and [leaves]
          —Only the flowers are red.

⇒ **Verb Phrases.**  In the sentence *Sam ate the cake in the kitchen,* the verb phrase *ate the cake in the kitchen* can be grouped together in two ways. As with noun phrases, each grouping corresponds to a particular syntactic structure and meaning.

Meaning One:   [ate [the cake in the kitchen]]
          —Sam ate the cake that was in the kitchen.

Meaning Two:   [ate [the cake] [in the kitchen]]
          —Sam was in the kitchen eating cake.

**Remember ...**    A sentence can also be lexically ambiguous. This type of ambiguity results from one word in the sentence having more than one meaning. Think about the ambiguity in the sentence *The glasses are on the table.* Which word has more than one meaning? What are the two different meanings? Why would we typically not notice this ambiguity during a conversation?

Each of the sentences below is either lexically or structurally ambiguous. Remember that lexical ambiguity comes from a single word, while structural ambiguity comes from more than one possible combination of a group of words.

## Try This!

1.  Cool beer and wine are what we want.
2.  Fred was lost.
3.  I met the woman standing by the water cooler.
4.  Parliament passed a dangerous drug bill.
5.  George saw the light.
6.  George and Harry or Fred will draw the picture.
7.  I want to look at the pictures in the attic.
8.  The instructor left his key in the office.

**Now ...**    Go back over the sentences, and for all those that are structurally ambiguous, determine which words need to be grouped together for each possible interpretation or meaning. You might want to start by first identifying which phrase (noun or verb) contains the ambiguity. Remember that each interpretation will have a different grouping!

### Thematic Roles

To interpret sentences, we need to know who is doing the action, what is undergoing the action, the starting point of the action, etc. Thematic, or theta, roles capture the relations between a sentence and the event it describes.

There are three important properties of thematic roles.

⇒ **Common Thematic Roles.**  Some of the common thematic roles include the following:

- agent (the entity performing the action)
- theme (the entity undergoing the action or movement)
- source (the starting point of a movement)
- goal (the end point of a movement)
- location (the place where an action occurs)

**Think ...**   What thematic role would be assigned to the noun phrases in the sentence *The gardener planted flowers by the front door*? What about the noun phrases in the sentence *John drove the car to Vancouver*? Does a sentence have to contain all the thematic roles outlined above?

⇒ **Thematic Role Assignment.**   Thematic roles are assigned to noun phrases based on their position within the sentence. Typically, verbs and prepositions assign thematic roles.

- A verb assigns the agent role (if it has one) to its subject noun phrase.
- A verb assigns the theme role (if it has one) to its complement noun phrase.
- A preposition assigns a thematic role to its complement noun phrases. The specific role that is assigned depends on the specific preposition.

Knowledge of the thematic roles that individual verbs and prepositions assign is stored in our mental lexicon.

See figures 6.4, 6.5, and 6.6 on pp. 204 and 205 for examples of thematic role assignment by prepositions and verbs.

**Think ...**   How do the noun phrases in the sentences *The gardener planted flowers by the front door* and *John drove the car to Vancouver* receive their thematic roles?

⇒ **Thematic Roles and Deep Structure.**   Thematic roles are assigned at deep structure.

- The Merge operation determines the position of the noun phrase within the syntactic structure (i.e., the D-structure). It is the noun phrase's position as a result of Merge that determines its thematic role.
- The operation Move can move noun phrases to other positions in the structure.
- If Move has transported the noun phrase to another position in the structure, this operation must be undone to determine how the noun phrase received its thematic role. That is, the noun phrase must be returned to its originating position.
- The sentence *What should George buy at the store?* has the D-structure *George should buy what at the store.* In the D-structure, the verb *buy* assigns the agent role to *George* and the theme role to *what*.

**Think ...**   Does *what* retain its role after Move changes the position of *what* in the sentence? How does *the store* receive its thematic role and what role does *the store* receive?

**Exercise!**  For each of the following sentences, identify all the noun phrases and the thematic role assigned to each noun phrase.

1.  Sarah drove that bus from Toronto to St. John's.
2.  The children are eating their ice cream with spoons.
3.  Which shoes did you buy at the store?
4.  Alyssa came from work.
5.  The boys walked to the park.
6.  Sally mailed a parcel to her nephew.
7.  What did Bill leave at your house?
8.  The letter was sent.
9.  Ginger scribbled her address on the paper with a pen.
10.  The designer turned that ugly room into a masterpiece.

**Now ...**  Go back through each sentence and for each thematic role, determine the verb or preposition that assigned the role. Make sure you put any sentences in which Move has applied into the deep structure first. Remember: the deep structure is the result of Merge.

### Pronoun Interpretation

Pronouns replace, or stand for, a noun phrase. This noun phrase is called the antecedent, and it is this antecedent that determines how the pronoun is interpreted.

## Think ...

- What is the antecedent of the pronoun *she* in the sentence *Janice's sister bought the dress that she liked*? Could *she* refer to Janice? Janice's sister? Could it refer to someone else not mentioned in the sentence?
- Consider the pronoun *herself* in the sentence *Janice's sister wondered if Fiona liked herself*. Does *herself* refer to Fiona, Janice, or Janice's sister? Can *herself* refer to someone not mentioned in the sentence?

It is the syntactic structure of the sentence that helps determine which noun phrase can or cannot function as the antecedent of a pronoun. The following concepts are important in understanding how the syntactic structure does this for pronominals and reflexive pronouns.

⇒ **Pronominals and Reflexives.**  English pronominals and reflexives vary in terms of number (singular and plural), person (1st, 2nd, and 3rd), and gender (masculine, feminine, and neuter) in the 3rd person. See table 6.16 on p. 207 for a complete list of the pronominals and reflexives found in English. For example, *she* is a pronominal (3rd person, singular, feminine) and *herself* is a reflexive (3rd person, singular, feminine).

⇒ **C-Command.** The interpretation of pronominals and reflexive pronouns is based on the idea of c-command. A noun phrase c-commands another noun phrase if it is found in the following structure:

NP$_a$ c-commands NP$_b$ since the first category above NP$_a$ (as indicated by the branching structure) contains NP$_b$.

⇒ **Principles.** Two principles of interpretation are relevant. The first applies to reflexive pronouns and the second to pronominals. Notice that these principles are opposite to each other.

- Principle A. This principle applies to reflexive pronouns and states that a reflexive pronoun must have an antecedent that c-commands it in the same minimal IP. A minimal IP is simply the smallest IP containing the pronoun.

See figure 6.9 on p. 208 for an illustration of how this principle determines which NPs can and cannot serve as an antecedent for a reflexive pronoun. Essentially, if an NP c-commands a reflexive, the NP can serve as the reflexive's antecedent. Conversely, if an NP does not c-command a reflexive, the NP cannot serve as the reflexive's antecedent.

- Principle B. This principle applies to pronominals and states that a pronominal cannot have an antecedent that c-commands it in the same minimal IP. Again, a minimal IP is simply the smallest IP containing the pronoun.

See figure 6.10 on p. 209 for an illustration of how this principle determines which NPs can and cannot serve as antecedents for a pronominal. Essentially, if an NP c-commands a pronominal, the NP cannot serve as the pronominal's antecedent. If an NP does not c-command a pronominal, the NP can serve as the pronominal's antecedent.

**Try This!** Using Principles A and B, determine the antecedent of either the pronominal or the reflexive in the sentences *Janice bought the dress that she liked, Janice wondered if Fiona liked herself, Janice's sister liked herself*, and *Janice's sister liked her*. It might be useful to draw a tree diagram of the IP containing either the pronominal or reflexive. When doing so, use the following structure for the NP *Janice's sister*.

**Now ...** In the sentence *Janice's sister bought the dress that she liked,* determine whether *she* can refer to either Janice or Janice's sister. In the sentence *Janice's sister wondered if Fiona liked herself,* determine why *herself* must refer to Fiona and not to either Janice or Janice's sister.

# ROLE OF PRAGMATICS

Besides the structure of a sentence and the thematic roles assigned to the noun phrases within a sentence, there are many other factors involved in sentence interpretation. Pragmatics is the study of the role that other necessary information has in sentence interpretation.

⇒ **Beliefs and Attitudes.** Non-linguistic knowledge can be used to interpret elements within a sentence. Think about the sentence *City Council denied the demonstrators a permit because they advocated violence.* Does the pronoun *they* refer to the demonstrators or the council members? Think about how the pronoun reference changes if we change the verb from *advocate* to *abhor.* Who does the pronoun refer to now? How is this difference in pronoun reference related to our beliefs about demonstrators and council members?

⇒ **Presupposition.** Presupposition refers to the assumption or belief implied by the use of a particular word. Think about the meaning of the sentence *John admitted that the soccer team had won the game* in relation to the meaning of the sentence *John said that the soccer team had won the game.* Which verb, *admitted* or *said,* indicates that the speaker is presupposing the truth of the claim being made?

⇒ **Setting / Deictics.** The form and interpretation of some words depends on the location of the speaker and listener within a particular setting. These words are called deictics. Some examples of English deictics include *here / there* and *this / that. Here* and *this* are used to refer to items close to the speaker, while *there* and *that* are used to refer to words close to the listener. See table 6.17 on p. 211 for some examples of how deictic distinctions can vary across languages.

⇒ **Discourse / Topic.**   Many sentences can only be interpreted in reference to information contained in preceding sentences. **Discourse** is the term used to describe the connected series of utterances. Old (given) information refers to knowledge that speakers assume addressees know, while new information refers to knowledge that is being introduced into the discourse for the first time. **Topic** refers to what a sentence or portion of the discourse is about. Some languages (e.g., Japanese) use a marker to indicate the topic of the discourse.

**Practice! Practice!**   Sentences can be difficult to interpret because they are ungrammatical, because they violate our knowledge of the world, or because they contain words that have no known referent. For each of the following sentences, identify why it is hard to interpret.

1. Our ten-month-old son is six feet tall.
2. Mike red bought car a.
3. Palm trees grow vigorously at the North Pole.
4. Radiculus glautons are found in the soil.
5. The bumblebee picked up the cat and flew back to the hive with it.

**Now ...**   Reconsider sentence 4. What meaning might you assign to the unknown words in this sentence? What might be the meaning of the overall sentence?

Why might the sentence *His mother wants you to be a doctor* be difficult to interpret if it is not part of a discourse (i.e., as a stand-alone sentence)?

# CONVERSATION

We use words and sentences to convey messages. And we often do this by having a conversation with someone. Conversations have rules. These rules refer to our understanding of how language is used to convey messages. Our knowledge of these rules also contributes to our interpretation of utterances.

⇒ **Cooperative Principle.**   This is the general principle guiding all conversations. It requires participants (speakers and addressees) to make their contributions to the conversation appropriate to the conversation.

⇒ **Specific Maxims.**   Conversations also have more specific guidelines. These guidelines are called specific maxims, and if we follow these maxims, then we have adhered to the Cooperative Principle.

- Maxim of Relevance (Make your contribution relevant)
- Maxim of Quality (Make your contribution truthful)
- Maxim of Quantity (Make your contribution only as informative as required)
- Maxim of Manner (Make your contribution unambiguous, clear, and logical)

⇒ **Conversational Implicature.**    During the course of a conversation, we are often able to make inferences about what is meant but was not actually said. Consider, for example, the following interaction:

Mike:        How did you do on the last exam?
Jim:         Want to come with me to the Registrar's Office?

Think about which conversational maxim Jim has violated. What can you infer about how Jim did on the exam even though he doesn't actually tell Mike how he did?

## Try This!!

You've just missed your bus and are standing at the bus stop waiting for the next bus. The time is 2 PM and the next bus is due at 2:15 PM, but you don't know that. You ask someone at the bus stop when the next bus is due and receive several replies. Each reply you receive may or may not violate one or more conversational maxims. For each reply, identify which maxim(s), if any, has/ have been violated.

1.  When's the next bus?
    At 2:30. (He's lying.)

    _____

2.  When's the next bus?
    When I was little I was obsessed with buses. I wanted to be a bus driver. I had hundreds of different kinds of buses. Little buses, big buses, red buses, blue buses and even double-decker buses. Did you know that in England, many buses are double-decker? I have made a study of buses. I think the next bus will be here in 15 minutes. Did you know that in India there are no buses?  Did you know I wanted to be a bus driver? Did you know …

    _____

3.  When's the next bus?
    Let me think! If the last bus was here at 1:50 and if they run every 20 minutes or so, then the next bus should be here at 2:10. (He has no idea.)

    _____

4.  When's the next bus?
    At 2:15, but if we were in Newfoundland that would be 2:45.

    _____

5.  When's the next bus?
    I don't know. (He's telling the truth.)

    _____

**REVIEW! REVIEW!** Make sure you can do the following:

- identify the semantic relations between words (4)
- identify the semantic relations between sentences (3)
- define connotation, denotation, extension, and intension
- do componential analysis
- spot fuzzy concepts, grammaticalized concepts, and lexicalized concepts
- spot the semantic basis for different word classes
- spot lexical ambiguity
- spot and represent structural ambiguity
- identify noun phrases and their thematic roles
- identify the effect of world knowledge on sentence interpretation
- identify when presupposition occurs in sentence interpretation
- spot the different forms of deictic terms
- identify conversational principles and maxims

## QUESTIONS?  PROBLEMS?  DIFFICULTIES?

# CHAPTER 7. HISTORICAL LINGUISTICS: THE STUDY OF LANGUAGE CHANGE

Historical linguistics studies the principles governing language change, including both its description and explanation. Important topics and concepts in this chapter include the following:

1. Phonetic sound change
2. Phonological change
3. Morphological change
4. Syntactic change
5. Lexical change
6. Semantic change
7. Language reconstruction
8. The discovery of Indo-European
9. Naturalness and typology

## LANGUAGE CHANGE

Consider the following important points concerning language change:

⇒ Language is always changing. However, for a particular change to take hold, it must be accepted by the language community as a whole.

⇒ Language change is regular and systematic. Some changes affect all words without exception. Other changes begin in a small number of words in the speech of a small number of speakers. These changes may gradually spread through both the vocabulary and the population.

⇒ Languages change because of the way language is acquired. Children are not born with a complete grammar but must construct a grammar based on the language they are exposed to. Therefore, changes will occur from one generation to the next, and because all children have the same genetic capabilities for language and construct their grammars in similar fashions, the same patterns of change repeat both within and across languages.

⇒ Causes of language change include articulatory simplification (see table 7.2 on p. 223 of the text for some examples), spelling pronunciation, reanalysis, analogy, and borrowing as a result of language contact. Hypercorrections (overgeneralizations about a particular rule) can also cause languages to change.

# SEQUENTIAL SOUND CHANGE

While all aspects of a language's structure can change, sound change is often the most noticeable. There are many types of sound change that can occur; however, most sound changes involve sequences of segments. The major types of sequential sound changes are outlined in the boxes below.

⇒ **Assimilation.**  Assimilation involves sounds changing to become more like the nearby sounds. Assimilation increases the efficiency of the articulations involved in producing the sequence of sounds. Such an increase in efficiency results from simplifying articulatory movements.

Some common examples include the following:

---

**Assimilation Processes**

a.  Place of Articulation Assimilation
    A sound becomes similar to a nearby sound in terms of place of articulation. See table 7.4 on p. 226 for some examples.

b.  Voicing Assimilation
    A consonant changes its voicing to be like a nearby sound. See the first example in table 7.5 on p. 226.

c.  Total Assimilation
    A sound assimilates totally to a following sound. See table 7.6 on p. 226 for some examples.

d.  Palatalization
    A non-palatal sound becomes or moves toward a palatal sound. This usually occurs near a sound that is made with the tongue at or near the hard palate— usually [y] or [i]. Palatalization is often the first step in the process of creating an affricate (called affrication) from a stop. See table 7.7 on p. 227 for some examples.

e.  Nasalization
    A vowel becomes nasal near a nasal sound. See table 7.8 on p. 227 for some examples.

---

**Remember ...**  Assimilation most often affects adjacent segments. It can, however, apply at a distance. Umlaut, which is responsible for irregular plurals such as *goose/geese,* is an example of such an assimilatory process. See table 7.9 on p. 228 for some more examples.

⇒ **Weakening and Deletion.** Sounds, both vowels and consonants, tend to weaken over time. They can also delete. Deletion is often the end result of the weakening process.

- Full vowels have a tendency to weaken, or reduce, to a schwa-like vowel. Vowels are often subject to deletion when they occur in unstressed syllables.

  Vowel weakening and deletion processes include the following:

| **Vowel Weakening** | **Vowel Deletion** |
|---|---|
| a. Vowel Reduction<br>A full vowel reduces to schwa. This process typically affects short vowels in unstressed syllables. | a. Apocope<br>The deletion of a word-final vowel<br><br>b. Syncope<br>The deletion of a word-internal vowel |

  See table 7.14 on p. 230 and table 7.15 on p. 231 for some examples of the above processes.

- Consonants tend to weaken along a path determined by the hierarchy shown below.

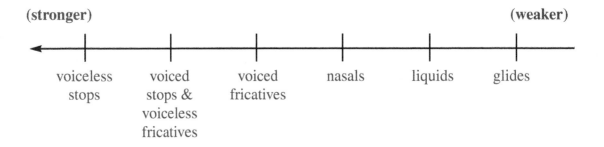

**Think ...** Which is stronger? [t] or [s]? [t] or [d]? [tt] or [t]? [s] or [z]? [s] or [ss]? [v] or [f]? Remember, geminate (long) consonants are stronger than their non-geminate counterparts.

Consonantal weakening and deletion processes include the following:

| **Consonantal Weakening** | **Consonantal Deletion** |
|---|---|
| a. Degemination<br>    A long sound becomes short.<br>    This is usually the first step in<br>    the weakening of consonants.<br><br>b. Frication<br>    A stop weakens to a fricative.<br>    This often occurs between vowels.<br><br>c. Voicing<br>    Voiceless stops or fricatives<br>    weaken to voiced stops or<br>    fricatives.<br><br>d. Rhotacism<br>    This is a fairly common type of<br>    weakening in which [z] weakens<br>    to [r]. | a. Consonantal Deletion<br>    Consonants often delete when<br>    they occur as part of a<br>    consonant cluster, or as the<br>    final consonant in a word, or<br>    as the last step after several<br>    weakening processes. See<br>    table 7.16 on p. 231 for some<br>    examples. |

See table 7.17 on p. 232 for an example of Degemination, Frication, and Voicing in Romance and table 7.18 on p. 233 for some examples of Rhotacism.

**Remember ...** It is most common for consonants to weaken over time. However, consonants can also strengthen. For example, glides often strengthen to affricates. This process is called Glide Strengthening and is common in word-initial position. See table 7.19 on p. 233 of the text for some examples.

⇒ **Others.** There are other types of sound changes as well, many of which will be familiar to you from the phonology chapter! These types of sound changes are not as frequent as those already presented, but like assimilation, they tend to have the overall effect of making sequences of sounds easier to articulate. Like assimilation, these changes can also affect adjacent segments or segments at a distance.

Here are some common examples:

---

**<u>Other Processes</u>**

a.  Dissimilation
    A sound becomes less like a nearby sound. This often occurs so that a
    sequence of sounds is easier to articulate or perceive.

b.  Epenthesis
    A sound is inserted. This usually occurs to break up a consonant cluster
    that is hard to pronounce. See table 7.10 on p. 228 for some examples
    from Old English and table 7.12 on p. 229 for some examples from
    the development of the Romance language.

c.  Metathesis
    The position of two sounds changes relative to each other. See table 7.13
    on p. 229 of the text for some examples from Old English.

---

# OTHER TYPES OF SOUND CHANGE

The changes considered so far all involve segments changing under the influence of nearby,
although not necessarily adjacent, segments. There are two other common types of sound
change: segmental and auditory.

⇒ **Segmental Change.**   Segmental change involves a change within the segment itself.
   Segmental change often involves affricates. Affricates are considered a complex segment,
   since they consist of a stop and a fricative. Complex segments often simplify over time.

   One common example is given below:

---

**<u>Segmental Change Processes</u>**

Deaffrication
    An affricate becomes a fricative by eliminating the stop portion of the affricate.
    See tables 7.20 and 7.21 on p. 233 for an example of this process in the change from
    Old French to French and how this process influenced the pronunciation of French
    words borrowed into English.

---

⇒ **Auditory Change.**  In addition to the articulatory considerations typically involved in sound change, auditory factors can also have an influence.

One common example is given below:

---

**Auditory Change Processes**

Substitution
 One segment is replaced with a similar sounding segment. See table 7.22 on p. 234 of the text for an example in the change from Middle English to English.

---

## NAME THAT SOUND CHANGE

Each of the following exemplifies one or more sound changes. The older form is on the left, and the more recent form on the right. Identify the sound change that has taken place for each of the underlined sound(s).

1.  Proto-Quechua   [cum<u>p</u>i]   >   Tena   [cum<u>b</u>i]

    _____

2.  Old English   [<u>hl</u>af]   >   Modern English   [<u>l</u>of]

    _____

3.  Latin   [mar<u>e</u>]   >   Portuguese   [mar]

    _____

4.  Proto-Slavic   [<u>k</u>emerai]   >   Russian   [<u>tʃ</u>emer]

    _____

5.  Proto-Tupi-Guaraní   [puʔ<u>am</u>]   >   Guaraní   [puʔ<u>ã</u>]

    _____

6. Latin   [ornamentum]   >   Old French   [ornəment]

_____

7. Old English   [knotta]   >   Mod. English   [nɑt]

_____

8. Proto-Germanic   [doːmaz]   >   Old Icelandic   [doːmr̩]

_____

9. Latin   [venre]   >   Spanish   [vendre]

_____

10. Early Latin   [inpossiliss]   >   Latin   [impossibilis]

_____

11. Proto-Bantu   [mukiːpa]   >   Swahili   [mʃipa]

_____

12. Proto-Romance   [sekuru]   >   Spanish   [seɡuru]

_____

13. Latin   [pekkatum]   >   [pekaθo]   >   [pekaðo]

_____

14. Proto-Romance   [biskɔktu]   >   Latin   [biskotto]

_____

**Think ...** Sound change tends to occur in a step-by-step fashion, so a single sound can often be subject to a number of different sound changes. But these multiple sound changes are often not visible in the resulting form.

**Now ...** Examine the change below that affected the word meaning 'good' in the development from Proto-Germanic to Old Icelandic, and see if you can identify all the changes, including any intermediate but not visible changes that have affected the underlined sounds.

Proto-Germanic   [goːdas]   Old Icelandic   [goːðr̩]

# PHONOLOGICAL SOUND CHANGE

The sound changes described in the previous sections can influence a language's phonological inventory. That is, they can add, eliminate, or rearrange the phonemes within a language.

⇒ **Phonological Splits.**   A phonological split adds phonemes to a language's phonological inventory. In a phonological split, allophones of the same phoneme come to contrast with each other. This is often caused by a loss of the conditioning environment. That is, sounds that were once predictable are no longer predictable and are therefore phonemic.

Consider the following example in the development of English.

Old English:   In Old English, /n/ had two allophones:
– [ŋ] occurred before velar stops
– [n] occurred elsewhere

So ... a word like *sing* was pronounced as [sɪŋg].

Middle English:   Consonant Deletion applied to remove [g] at the end of a word (after a nasal consonant). This created a minimal pair between *sing*, now pronounced as [sɪŋ], and *sin*, pronounced as [sɪn]. And minimal pairs tell us that sounds contrast.

This split can be diagrammed as follows:

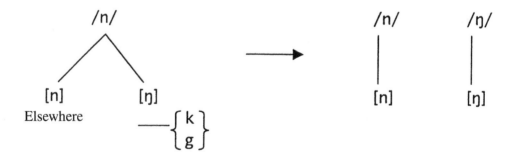

What phoneme was added to the language?

**Think ...**   Spelling often lags behind sound change. We still spell *sing* with the final *g* even though it is now silent. Many silent letters in our English spelling system are a reflection of older pronunciations!

⇒ **Phonological Mergers.** While a phonological split adds phonemes to a language, a phonological merger reduces the number of contrasts.

A good example of a phonological merger comes from Cockney English. In Cockney English, the interdental and labiodental fricatives have merged. That is, all instances of [θ] and [ð] have become [f] and [v], respectively. This merger can be diagrammed as follows (for the voiceless fricatives):

Put together a similar diagram for the voiced fricatives. **Think ...** What phonemes have been lost from the phonemic inventory?

⇒ **Phonological Shifts.** A phonological shift does not add to or diminish a language's phonemic inventory. Rather, some of the phonemes are reorganized with respect to each other.

The Great English Vowel Shift, beginning in Middle English, is a well-known example of a phonological shift affecting vowels. The chart below shows the Middle English long vowels before the vowel shift occurred.

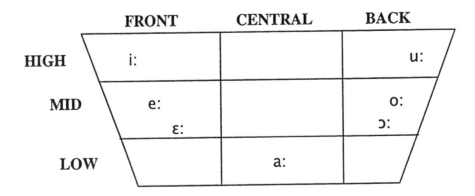

The Great English Vowel Shift affected only the long vowels. It probably began with the diphthongization of [i] and [u]. The creation of the diphthongs [aj] and [aw] reduced the number of simple vowels from seven to five. The remaining vowels then shifted upwards in their articulation.

The vowel shifts are summarized below.

1. Long [i] became the diphthong [aj]
2. Long [u] became the diphthong [aw]

3. Long [e] became [i]
4. Long [ɛ] became [i]
5. Long [a] became [e]
6. Long [o] became [u]
7. Long [ɔ] became [o]

See figure 7.8 on p. 237 for a diagram outlining how the vowels shifted.

As the vowels shifted, length was lost. After the Great English Vowel Shift, the long vowels now looked like this:

|  | FRONT | CENTRAL | BACK |
|---|---|---|---|
| HIGH | i |  | u |
| MID | e |  | o |
|  |  | aj   aw |  |
| LOW |  |  |  |

Compare the two vowel charts. What was the overall effect of the vowel shift in terms of the number of vowels?

**Think ...** Many of our vowel spellings reflect Middle English pronunciation. For example, the word *goose* is spelled with *oo* because this orthographic symbol represented [o:]. *Goose* continues to be spelled this way, even though as a result of the Great English Vowel Shift, [o:] became [u], changing the pronunciation of *goose* to [gus]. One reason for this mismatch between spelling and pronunciation is that spelling was standardized before the vowels had finished shifting.

**Try This!**  For each of the Middle English words below, state the vowel change that would have occurred as a result of the Great English Vowel Shift, and then give the spelling of the corresponding Modern English word.

| Middle English | Vowel Change | Modern English Word |
|---|---|---|
| [no:n] | _____ | _____ |
| [li:fə] | _____ | _____ |
| [swe:t] | _____ | _____ |
| [bɔ:st] | _____ | _____ |
| [gu:n] | _____ | _____ |

# GRIMM'S LAW

Phonological shifts can also affect consonants. One famous example is Grimm's Law, named for Jacob Grimm (of Grimm's Fairy Tables). In 1822, Jacob Grimm noticed some regular correspondences between the Germanic languages and the non-Germanic Indo-European languages. The correspondences he noticed are listed below:

| Non-Germanic Consonant | As in these Non-Germanic Words | Corresponding Germanic Consonant | As in these Germanic Cognates |
|---|---|---|---|
| [p] | **p**ater (Latin) | [f] | **f**ather (German – **V**ater) |
| [t] | **t**onare (Latin) | [θ] | **th**under |
| [k] | **c**anis (Latin) | [x] → [h] | **h**ound (German – **H**und) |
| [b] | kanna**b**is (Greek) | [p] | hem**p** |
| [d] | **d**uo (Latin) | [t] | **t**wo |
| [g] | a**g**er (Latin) | [k] | a**c**re |
| [bh] | **bh**rata (Sanskrit) | [b] | **b**rother (German – **B**ruder) |
| [dh] | vi**dh**ava (Sanskrit) | [d] | wi**d**ow |
| [gh] | **gh**ansas (Sanskrit) | [g] | **g**oose (German – **G**ans) |

Grimm explained these correspondences using three sound changes.

**(1) Voiceless stops became voiceless fricatives (i.e., weakening – frication).**

| PIE | | Proto-Germanic (PG) |
|---|---|---|
| [p] | > | [f] |
| [t] | > | [θ] |
| [k] | > | [x] → [h] |

**(2) Voiced stops became voiceless stops.**

| PIE | | PG |
|---|---|---|
| [b] | > | [p] |
| [d] | > | [t] |
| [g] | > | [k] |

**(3) Voiced aspirated stops became voiced unaspirated stops.**

| PIE | | PG |
|---|---|---|
| [bh] | > | [b] |
| [dh] | > | [d] |
| [gh] | > | [g] |

The first of Grimm's rules involves the weakening of stops to fricatives. This, of course, is a phonetically plausible sound change. The result of this weakening process left Proto-Germanic without voiceless stops. Since it is rare for a language to completely lack voiceless stops, this gap was filled by devoicing the voiced stops. The reintroduction of voiceless stops in turn created a lack of voiced stops. This new gap was filled by deaspirating the voiced aspirated stops. This, of course, created yet another gap: a lack of voiced aspirated stops. This gap was not filled!

There are exceptions to Grimm's Law. Some exceptions can be traced back to borrowings from Latin and French. Such borrowings did not undergo Grimm's Law, since these words entered the language long after the sound shift had occurred.

**Try This!**   For each bolded sound in the reconstructed Proto-Indo-European (PIE) word, give the Germanic sound that resulted from Grimm's Law. Then give the Modern English equivalent of the proto-form.

| PIE WORD | GERMANIC SOUND (IN IPA) | ENGLISH WORD IN REGULAR SPELLING |
|---|---|---|
| 1.  *g**el | _____ | _____ool |
| 2.  *le**b | _____ | li_____ |
| 3.  *g**re**bh | _____ | _____ra_____ |
| 4.  *g**hrei**b | _____ | _____ri_____ |
| 5.  *pulo | _____ | _____oul |
| 6.  *koimo | _____ | _____ome |
| 7.  *swad | _____ | swee_____ |

# MORPHOLOGICAL CHANGE

Morphological change affects the structure of words within a language. Morphological change involves either the addition or the loss of affixes. Recall from morphology that affixes are bound morphemes that attach to a base. Affixes provide grammatical information (inflection) or are used to create new words (derivation).

⇒ **The addition of affixes.**  Affixes can be added to a language through

- borrowing
- grammaticalization (creating new grammatical forms from lexical forms)
- fusion (developing an affix from two words that are frequently adjacent to each other). See table 7.28 on p. 239 for some examples from English, and table 7.29 on p. 239 for some examples from Italian.

⇒ **The loss of affixes.**   Affixes can also be lost through

- lack of use. See table 7.30 on p. 240 for some English examples.
- sound change. See tables 7.31 and 7.32 on pp. 240 and 241 for an example of how sound changes caused the loss of Old English case affixes.

**The effect of adding or losing affixes.**   The loss of affixes can result in a synthetic morphological system becoming analytic, while the addition of affixes can result in an analytic morphological system gradually becoming synthetic. An analytic language has very few inflectional affixes (e.g., Modern English). In contrast, a synthetic language has many inflectional affixes (e.g., Old English).

**Reanalysis and Analogy.**  Reanalysis and analogy can also affect the morphological structure of a language. Reanalysis adds new morphemes to a language, while analogy can change an existing morphological pattern. See table 7.35 on p. 243 for an example of reanalysis in the development of English.

**Try This!**  Folk etymology refers to the analysis of a word based on an incorrect historical division of that word into its apparent morphemes. This is usually done without reference to the word's origins. Hence the use of the word 'folk'! See table 7.34 on p. 242 for some English examples.

Identify the base and affix for each of the following words:

- yearling
- duckling
- gosling

- underling
- hireling
- nursling

Are the words in the second column as common as those in the first? Do they have the same meaning?

Historically, each of the above words consists of a base plus the affix -ling. This German affix has the meaning 'having the quality of'. What has happened to this affix in terms of its form? Why would such a reanalysis occur? What happened to the affix in terms of its meaning? What might have caused this shift?

What about the word *earthling*? How does this relate to the original German affix as well as the above words? What about the word *darling*?

## SYNTACTIC CHANGE

Change can also affect the syntactic component of a language's grammar. Change often affects the word order patterns and the movement operations (transformations) found within a language.

⇒ **Word Order.**   Languages can change their basic word order pattern. One common change involves the change from an SOV (subject-object-verb) order to an SVO (subject-verb-object) order. This is a change that happened in the development of English. English descended from a Germanic language having an SOV order.

⇒ **Movement Operations (transformations).**  *Yes-no* questions in English are formed using Inversion. In Old English, both main verbs and auxiliary verbs could be inverted. In Modern English, though, only auxiliary verbs can be inverted. Now, any sentence that does not contain an auxiliary must be made into a *yes-no* question by inserting *do*.

**Try This!** Below are some sentences from sixteenth-century English along with their modern counterparts. Examine the sentences, and determine how negatives were formed. How does this differ from today's English?

1. A kinder gentleman treads not the Earth.
   A kinder gentleman doesn't tread the Earth.
2. Hate counsels not in such a quantity.
   Hate doesn't counsel in such a quantity.
3. Clamber not you up to the casement then.
   Don't climb up to the casement then.

## CONNECTIONS

Changes can have far-reaching effects. A change that affects the phonology of a language can eventually affect the morphology, which in turn can affect the syntax of a language.

Consider an example (somewhat simplified) from the development of English.

⇒ Old English was a highly inflected language. Old English inflectional affixes included the following:

1. Case:     Nominative, Accusative, Dative, Genitive
2. Number:  Singular, Dual, Plural
3. Person:   First, Second, Third
4. Gender:  Masculine, Feminine, Neuter
5. Tense:    Past, Present

Inflectional affixes were found on pronouns, nouns, articles, adjectives, verbs, etc. As in many highly inflected languages, Old English had a fairly free word order. Sentences with SVO, VSO, and SOV orders could all be found.

⇒ During Middle English, sound changes started happening in unstressed syllables. These sound changes included the following three:

- m → n / _____#           (a bilabial nasal became alveolar at the end of a word)
- n → Ø / _____#           (alveolar nasals were deleted at the end of words)
- a, o, u, i, e → ə / _____#   (short vowels reduced to schwa at the end of words)

These three sound changes affected the inflectional system since inflectional affixes in Old English were suffixes, and suffixes are typically not stressed.

The following two examples illustrate the application of the above rules:

**Old English**                                              **Middle English**

foxum   >   foxun   >   foxu   >   foxə
helpan  >   helpan  >   helpa  >   helpə

As a result of these sound changes, all the affixes became the same: 'ə'. Since it was now impossible to tell what information was contained in an affix, the Old English affixes were dropped. The language's morphology became more analytic!

⇒ But speakers still needed to know what the subject of a sentence was, what the object of a sentence was, and what noun an adjective referred to. To get this information, speakers of English began to …

1. Rely on prepositions.
2. Rely on fixed word order (SVO).

So sound change can have a drastic effect on the structure of a language over time!

## QUICK REMINDER!

Just like with phonological rules, sound changes also often require an order to their application. For example, the three sound changes presented in the last section occurred in a certain order. [m] had to first change to [n] before it could be deleted. If this change had not occured first, then [n] would not have deleted and the affixes would not have all become [ə]. Note that it doesn't matter when the vowel reduction change occurred.

## LEXICAL CHANGE

Lexical change involves modifications to the lexicon. There are two main types of lexical change: addition and loss.

### Addition of Lexical Items ...

New lexical items are typically added to a language's vocabulary in one of two ways.

⇒ **Word Formation.** Some of the morphological phenomena found in the morphology chapter are frequently used to add new words to a language. These new words often fill a lexical gap resulting from technological innovations. Compounding, derivation, acronyms, backformation, blending, clipping, and conversion can all be used to add new words to a language. See table 7.38 on p. 247 for some Old English examples of compounding and derivation.

⇒ **Borrowing.** As languages come into contact, they often borrow words from each other. Borrowed words are often called loan words. There are three types of influences that languages can have on each other.

- *Substratum Influence.* This type of influence results in the borrowing of place names as well as names for unfamiliar objects or items. For example, English borrowed place names such as Thames, London, and Dover from the Celtic language.

- *Superstratum Influence.* This type of influence often results in borrowings related to all things official. For example, English borrowed many words from the French language during the Middle English period. French loan words are typically found in relation to government, religion, the judiciary, science, culture, and warfare. See table 7.40 on p. 249 for some examples.

- *Adstratum Influence.* Adstratum influence often results in the borrowing of common, everyday words. For example, English borrowed many Scandinavian words, including *cake, egg, husband, score, window,* and *ugly.* See table 7.42 on p. 250 for some examples of the French influnce on Montreal English.

**Loss of Lexical Items ...**

Words can also be lost from the vocabulary of a language. Loan words, non-loan words, compounds, and derived words can all be lost. The most common reason for the loss of a lexical item is some societal change that has rendered an object, and therefore its name, obsolete. See table 7.46 on p. 251 for some words no longer used in English. See table 7.39 on p. 248 for some Old English compounds and derived forms that are no longer used.

# SEMANTIC CHANGE

In addition to the addition and loss of lexical items, the meanings of existing words can also change over time. There are seven main types of semantic change.

| TYPE | DEFINITION |
|---|---|
| Broadening | The meaning of a word becomes more general or inclusive over time. See table 7.47 on p. 252 for some examples. |
| Narrowing | The meaning of a word becomes less general or inclusive over time. See table 7.48 on p. 252 for some examples. |
| Amelioration | The meaning of a word changes to become more positive or favourable. See table 7.49 on p. 253 for some examples. |
| Pejoration | The meaning of a word changes to become less positive or favourable. See table 7.50 on p. 253 for some examples. |
| Weakening | The meaning of a word weakens over time. See table 7.51 on p. 253 for some examples. |
| Semantic Shift | A word loses its former meaning and takes on a new, but related, meaning. See table 7.52 on p. 253 for some examples. |
| Metaphor | A word with a concrete meaning takes on a more abstract meaning, without losing the original meaning. See table 7.53 on p. 255 for some examples. |

**Practice! Practice!** For each of the following words, identify which of the processes in the above table best captures the semantic change that has occurred.

| Word | Earlier Meaning | Later Meaning | Semantic Change |
|------|-----------------|---------------|-----------------|
| 1. aisle | passage between pews of a church | passage between rows of seats | _____ |
| 2. mischievous | disastrous | playfully annoying | _____ |
| 3. blue | a colour | being melancholy | _____ |
| 4. spill | shed blood | waste of liquid | _____ |
| 5. fond | foolish | affectionate | _____ |
| 6. butler | male servant in charge of the wine cellar | male servant in charge of a household | _____ |
| 7. passenger | traveller | one who travels by vehicle or vessel | _____ |
| 8. wretch | exile | unhappy person | _____ |
| 9. notorious | widely known | widely and unfavourably known | _____ |
| 10. chair | a seat | head of a university or college department | _____ |

# COMPARATIVE RECONSTRUCTION

By comparing languages with each other, it can be determined if they are or are not genetically related. Genetically related languages are languages that have descended from a common ancestor. Using the comparative method, this ancestor can be reconstructed. This is typically done by comparing later forms to determine what the earlier form must have looked like. Although it is possible to reconstruct all aspects of a language's grammar, the focus here is on phonological reconstruction.

**Some important terms ...**

⇒ **Cognates** are phonetically and semantically similar words that have descended from a common source. Cognates are compared to reconstruct what this common source must have looked like.

⇒ A **proto-language** is a language that has been reconstructed using a comparative method. Written evidence of what this language actually looked like typically doesn't exist.

⇒ A proto-language consists of **proto-forms**. These are the individual reconstructed words of the proto-language. Proto-forms are usually indicated with an asterisk ( * ).

**Some important strategies ...**

⇒ **The Phonetic Plausibility Strategy** requires that any change posited to account for the differences between the proto-form (the ancestor) and the cognates must be phonetically plausible. That is, a sound change that has been found to occur in the course of language development must be able to account for these differences. For our purposes, the sound changes listed under the heading **sequential change**, as well as under **segmental** and **auditory change**, are all plausible.

⇒ **The Majority Rules Strategy** operates in the absence of a phonetically plausible sound change. This strategy states that when no phonetically plausible sound change can be determined, we may reconstruct the segment that occurs in the majority of the cognates. This strategy should only be used as a last resort.

**An example ...**

Reconstruct the proto-forms for the data below.

|    | **Lang A** | **Lang B** | **Lang C** |
|----|-----------|-----------|-----------|
| 1. | [hauda]   | [hauta]   | [hauta]   |
| 2. | [sav]     | [ʃive]    | [sav]     |

⇒ **First.** Determine the number of sounds that need to be reconstructed. This is straightforward for (1) in that all the cognates have the same number of sounds: five. The situation is different in (2). In (2), two of the cognates contain three sounds, and one contains four. If four sounds are reconstructed, then deletion must have occurred in Lang A and C. If three sounds are reconstructed, then epenthesis must have occurred in Lang B. It is more plausible for deletion rather than epenthesis to occur at the end of words. (2), therefore, requires the reconstruction of four sounds.

⇒ **Second.** Look for any total correspondences. These are sounds that have not changed; they are the same for all the cognates. Reconstruct these sounds. The proto-forms after this step are *hau?a and *??v?.

⇒ **Third.** Examine alternations between the different languages and determine phonetic plausibility.

- (1) exhibits an alternation between [t] and [d]. Either [t] or [d] can be reconstructed in the proto-form.

    - If [d] is reconstructed, then the change from the proto-form to the form in Lang B and C ([d] > [t]) does not correspond to a sound change. Therefore, this has a low phonetic plausibility.
    - If [t] is reconstructed, then the change from the proto-form to Lang A ([t] > [d]) can be explained as an instance of weakening (a voiceless stop weakens to a voiced stop). This has a high phonetic plausibility.

Reconstruct the change that has the highest phonetic plausibility. The proto-form therefore becomes *hauta.

- (2) exhibits three alternations. First, consider the alternation between [s] and [ʃ].

    - If [ʃ] is reconstructed, then the change [ʃ] > [s] in Lang A and C has low phonetic plausibility, since it does not correspond to a sound change.
    - If [s] is reconstructed, then the change [s] > [ʃ] in Lang B can be explained as palatalization. Therefore, [s] is reconstructed.

Second, consider the presence or absence of a word-final vowel in the cognates. Recall from above that it is more plausible for a sound to delete than to be epenthesized in this position. Therefore, [e] is reconstructed.

Third, consider the vowel alternation between [a] and [i].

    - If [a] is reconstructed then the change [a] > [i] occurs in Lang B.
    - If [i] is reconstructed, then the opposite change ([i] > [a]) occurs in Lang A and C.

Neither one corresponds to a sound change, and so both have a low phonetic plausibility. This strategy, therefore, cannot be used to reconstruct this segment. The proto-form, after this step, is *s?ve.

⇒ **Fourth.** Any sounds for which no phonetically plausible sound change could be identified require using the Majority Rules Strategy. In (2), the alternation between [a] and [i] cannot be accounted for using a sound change; therefore, [a] is reconstructed since it occurs in the majority of the cognates. The proto-form becomes \*save. Notice that this proto-form does not correspond to any of the cognates. This is okay!

⇒ **Fifth.** Put together a summary of the sound changes that have occurred since the different languages split from the proto-language. Remember that the proto-form you have just reconstructed is older than the cognates from the descendant languages. Voicing and Apocope have occurred in the development of Lang A, while only Apocope occurred in the development of Lang C. Palatalization occurred in the development of Lang B.

**Something to think about ...**

⇒ Sound changes that tend to occur across languages are often referred to as natural. Sound changes that are phonetically plausible are more natural than those that are not. **Naturalness** is important to think about when doing reconstruction, since language change is regular and systematic.

⇒ It is also important to think about universal properties of language when doing reconstruction. This is often referred to as **typological plausibility**. Think about the change from voiced stops to voiceless stops in Grimm's Law (see pp. 158–159 in this guide). This change has a low phonetic plausibility and is therefore not a natural sound change. However, this change occurred because weakening (frication) left the language without voiceless stops, which are found in virtually every language. The change from voiced to voiceless stops, therefore, happened for typological reasons.

---

### REMINDER!  REMINDER!

In order to do language reconstruction, you need to be able to identify phonetically plausible sound changes. And in order to do this, you need to know the different types of sequential, segmental, and auditory sound changes. Make sure you are very familiar with them!

---

**Practice!** Each data group below contains some cognate sets. Assume that all the cognates are in phonetic transcription and that all members of the cognate set have the same meaning. Reconstruct the proto-forms and list all the sound changes that have taken place in each language. Remember: for some languages there may be no sound changes, while for others there may be multiple sound changes.

While the data are hypothetical or highly regularized, they exemplify processes found in actual languages.

<u>GROUP ONE</u>

|     | <u>Lang A</u> | <u>Lang B</u> | **Proto-Form** |
|-----|---------------|---------------|----------------|
| 1.  | [mũtə]        | [muθo]        | * _____ |
| 2.  | [fumə]        | [vumo]        | * _____ |
| 3.  | [pippon]      | [bipona]      | * _____ |
| 4.  | [nõk]         | [noga]        | * _____ |
| 5.  | [wus]         | [juza]        | * _____ |
| 6.  | [fitə]        | [vido]        | * _____ |

Summary of Sound Changes:

| Lang A | |
|--------|--|
| Lang B | |

**Remember ... the reconstructed form does not have to be the same as any of the forms found in the descendant languages!**

## GROUP TWO

|     | Lang A | Lang B | Lang C | Lang D | Proto-Form |
|-----|--------|--------|--------|--------|------------|
| 1.  | [puxa] | [buga] | [puka] | [puk]  | *_____ |
| 2.  | [nizudz] | [nizuz] | [nizu] | [nir] | *_____ |

Summary of Sound Changes:

| Lang A | |
|--------|--|
| Lang B | |
| Lang C | |
| Lang D | |

## GROUP THREE

|     | Lang A | Lang B | Lang C | Lang D | Proto-Form |
|-----|--------|--------|--------|--------|------------|
| 1.  | [pika] | [big]  | [pik]  | [biha] | *_____ |
| 2.  | [wira] | [wiz]  | [wir]  | [wira] | *_____ |
| 3.  | [vida] | [bita] | [vit]  | [viθa] | *_____ |

Summary of Sound Changes:

| Lang A | |
|--------|--|
| Lang B | |
| Lang C | |
| Lang D | |

GROUP FOUR

| | Lang A | Lang B | Lang C | Proto-Form |
|---|---|---|---|---|
| 1. | [tuhu] | [tuu] | [tuhu] | *_____ |
| 2. | [nika] | [nika] | [nika] | *_____ |
| 3. | [kaza] | [kasa] | [kaʃa] | *_____ |
| 4. | [tuku] | [tuku] | [tuku] | *_____ |
| 5. | [juhu] | [juu] | [juhu] | *_____ |
| 6. | [pida] | [piθa] | [pita] | *_____ |
| 7. | [kadi] | [kaθi] | [kati] | *_____ |
| 8. | [kwazi] | [kwasi] | [kwaʃi] | *_____ |

Summary of Sound Changes:

| Lang A | |
|---|---|
| Lang B | |
| Lang C | |

**Reminder ... Always look for a plausible sound change first.**
**Only use majority rules as a last resort.**

## GROUP FIVE

|     | Lang A | Lang B | Lang C | Lang D | Proto-Form |
|-----|--------|--------|--------|--------|------------|
| 1.  | [puxə] | [buga] | [pukka] | [puk] | * _____ |
| 2.  | [lirə] | [liza] | [litsu] | [wis] | * _____ |
| 3.  | [mani] | [mani] | [mãnni] | [mã] | * _____ |
| 4.  | [wanə] | [jana] | [wãnna] | [wã] | * _____ |
| 5.  | [kaxə] | [gaga] | [kakka] | [kak] | * _____ |
| 6.  | [tupi] | [dubi] | [tubi] | [tup] | * _____ |
| 7.  | [samu] | [samu] | [sãmmu] | [sã] | * _____ |
| 8.  | [matu] | [madu] | [madu] | [mat] | * _____ |

Summary of Sound Changes:

| Lang A | |
|--------|--|
| Lang B | |
| Lang C | |
| Lang D | |

## Now try this one!

<u>Proto-Middle Indic</u>    (Note: The data has been modified.)

| | Magadhi Prakrit | Pali Prakrit | Maharastri | Gloss |
|---|---|---|---|---|
| 1. | [abala] | [apara] | [avara] | 'other' |
| 2. | [diba] | [dipa] | [diva] | 'lamp' |
| 3. | [hasta] | [hatta] | [hatta] | 'hand' |
| 4. | [loga] | [loka] | [loa] | 'world' |
| 5. | [nala] | [nara] | [nara] | 'man' |
| 6. | [nispʰala] | [nippʰala] | [nippʰala] | 'fruitless' |
| 7. | [paskʰaladi] | [pakkʰalati] | [pakkʰalai] | '(he) stumbles' |
| 8. | [pidi] | [pita] | [pia] | 'father' |
| 9. | [puspa] | [puppa] | [puppa] | 'flower' |
| 10. | [ʃuska] | [sukka] | [sukka] | 'dry' |

Proto-forms:

| | |
|---|---|
| 1. | 6. |
| 2. | 7. |
| 3. | 8. |
| 4. | 9. |
| 5. | 10. |

Sound Changes:

| Magadhi Prakrit | Pali Prakrit | Maharastri |
|---|---|---|
| | | |
| | | |
| | | |
| | | |

**REVIEW! REVIEW!** Make sure you know about the following:

- the nature of language change
- the causes of language change (five)
- how change spreads through a language and its population
- the different types of sequential, segmental, and auditory sound changes
- how to identify sound changes
- the difference between phonological splits, mergers, and shifts
- the sound changes making up the Great English Vowel Shift
- the three sound changes making up Grimm's Law
- the different types of morphological and syntactic change
- the different types of lexical and semantic change
- how to reconstruct proto-forms and summarize sound changes
- the role of naturalness and typology in language reconstruction

## QUESTIONS?  PROBLEMS?  DIFFICULTIES?

_____

_____

_____

_____

_____

_____

_____

_____

_____

_____

_____

# CHAPTER 8.
# THE CLASSIFICATION OF LANGUAGES

Language classification involves arranging languages into groups based on shared characteristics. Important topics and concepts found in this chapter include the following:

1. Language universals
2. Markedness theory
3. Structural classification
4. Phonological classification
5. Morphological classification
6. Syntactic classification
7. Genetic classification
8. The Indo-European family of languages

## TERMS AND CONCEPTS

The following terms and concepts are important in understanding how linguists classify languages:

| TERM | DEFINITION |
|------|-----------|
| mutual intelligibility | Mutual intelligibility is a criterion used to determine whether language varieties are dialects of the same language or are different languages altogether. Essentially, if speakers can understand each other, the varieties are considered dialects of the same language and if the speakers cannot understand each other, they are considered different languages. |
| language loss | Languages can be lost (become extinct) over time. An extinct language is not a language that evolves over time into one or more languages (e.g., Latin), but a language that ceases to be spoken altogether. For example, Manx and Ubykh disappeared completely: they have no speakers and no descendant languages. |
| classic pattern of language loss | Language loss typically takes three generations. Parents are monolingual speakers of a language; their children adopt a new language and become bilingual speakers; and their children's children grow up monolingual in the new language. |

# TYPOLOGICAL CLASSIFICATION

Linguistic typology classifies languages, grouping them together based on their structural characteristics. This type of classification can be done using phonological properties, morphological systems, and grammatical structures. Typological studies are done with the purpose of uncovering universal characteristics of language.

⇒ **Linguistic Universals.** Linguistic universals are structural characteristics that occur in all or most languages.

- An absolute universal is a structural characteristic that is found in all languages.
- A universal tendency is a structural characteristic that is found in most languages.
- An implicational universal outlines a particular relationship between two structural characteristics: namely, the presence of characteristic A in a language implies that the language will also have characteristic B.

**Think ...** The vowel phoneme /a/ is found in almost all of the world's languages. What type of universal does this statement represent? What about this statement: All of the world's languages have stops?

⇒ **Markedness Theory.** Markedness theory provides another way to analyze linguistic universals. Structural characteristics can be identified as being more or less marked in relation to each other.

- Unmarked characteristics are characteristics that are considered to be less complex and/or more common across languages (e.g., stops).
- Marked characteristics are characteristics that are considered to be more complex and/or less common across languages (e.g., fricatives and affricates).

Markedness is closely related to implicational universals. If the presence of A implies the presences of B, this means that a language cannot have A unless it also has B. B is therefore more common than A in languages of the world, making it less marked than A. The markedness (implicational) relationship between A and B can be represented as "B > A," which is read as "B is less marked than (implied by) A."

Since a language will typically not have a more marked characteristic (A) unless it also has its less marked counterpart (B), implicational universals and markedness theory can be used to determine the possible and impossible characteristics of language. If A implies B, then

- it is possible for a language to have both B and A, and
- it is possible for a language to have B without having A, but
- it is not possible for a language to have A without having B. This is because if a language has A, it also has to have B.

**Try This!** Consider the following statement: If a language has derivational affixes, it will also have inflectional affixes. What type of universal does this statement represent? Which would be the more marked type of affix, derivational or inflectional? Which would be the less marked type of affix? Is it possible for a language to have both inflectional and derivational affixes? Only inflectional affixes? Only derivational affixes?

# PHONOLOGICAL CLASSIFICATION

Phonological classification can be based on the different types of vowel systems, consonant systems, and suprasegmentals found across languages. Phonological classification is done using the phonemes of a language.

⇒ **Vowel Systems.** Languages can be classified according to the size and pattern of their vowel system. The most common system has five vowels: /i, u, e, o, a/. Approximately half of the world's languages have this system. Other common vowel systems have three, four, six, seven, eight, or nine different vowels. See figure 8.2 on p. 285 of the text for examples of some of the common vowel systems.

Here are some universal tendencies:

- /a/ is the most commonly occurring vowel phoneme. /i/ and /u/ are almost as common.
- Front vowels such as /i, e, æ/ are generally unrounded, while non-low back vowels such as /u, o, ɔ/ are generally rounded.
- Low back vowels such as /a/ are generally unrounded.

**Think ...** How many vowel phonemes are found in English? Is this more or less than the average number found across languages? Does English follow each of the universal tendencies shown above?

Here are some implicational universals pertaining to vowels:

- If a language has contrastive nasal vowels, then it will also have contrastive oral vowels.
- If a language has contrastive long vowels, then it will also have contrastive short vowels. See table 8.4 on p. 286 of the text for some examples of contrastive long and short vowels in Finnish.

**Think ...** Which vowels are more marked? Nasal or oral vowels? Long or short vowels? What are the possible and impossible combinations of sounds that these implicational universals predict? See tables 8.3 and 8.5 on pp. 284 and 286 if you are having difficulty.

⇒ **Consonant Systems.** There is a great deal of variation in the number of consonant phonemes found in languages. Some languages (e.g., Rotokas, spoken in Papua New Guinea) have as few as six, while others (e.g., !Kung, spoken in Namibia and Angola) have as many as ninety-six.

Some well-established universals include:

* All languages have stops. Not all languages have fricatives.
* The most common stop phonemes are /p, t, k/, with /t/ being the most common.
* The most commonly occurring fricative is /s/, followed by /f/.
* Most languages have at least one nasal phoneme.
* If a language has only one nasal phoneme, it is most likely /n/. If a language has contrasting nasal phonemes, they are most likely /m/ and /n/.
* Most languages have at least one phonemic liquid. (Some languages have none.)

**Think ...** How many consonant phonemes are found in English? Does English conform to the universal tendencies outlined above?

Here are some universal implications pertaining to consonants:

* If a language has voiced obstruent phonemes, then it will also have the corresponding voiceless obstruent phonemes.
* If a language has voiceless sonorant phonemes, then it will also have the corresponding voiced sonorant phonemes.
* If a language has fricative phonemes, then it will also have stop phonemes.
* If a language has affricate phonemes, then it will also have fricative and stop phonemes.

**Think ...** Which is more marked? Voiced or voiceless obstruent phonemes? Voiced or voiceless sonorant phonemes? Remember that obstruents are stops, fricatives, and affricates, while sonorants are nasals, liquids, and glides. Is the markedness relationship the same for obstruents and sonorants? What are the possible and impossible combinations of sounds that these implicational universals predict? See tables 8.6 and 8.7 on p. 287 if you are having difficulty.

**Now ...** Think about the relationship between stops, fricatives, and affricates. Which is the least marked of the three? Which is the most marked? Why? What are the possible and impossible combinations of these three sounds in language? See table 8.9 on p. 288 if you are having difficulty.

⇒ **Suprasegmentals.** Suprasegmentals are prosodic characteristics of a sound independent of the sound's individual articulation. Generalizations can be made about the use of tone, stress, and syllable structure in the world's languages.

**Tone**

* Tone languages (languages in which differences in pitch are used to indicate differences in meaning) can have two, three, or four contrastive register tones. A register tone is a level tone. Most tone languages have two.

- If a tone language has contrastive contour tones, then it will also have contrastive register tones. A contour tone is a tone that involves moving pitch.

**Think ...** Which are more marked, register or contour tones? Can a language have contour tones without also having register tones?

### Stress

- In a fixed stress system, the stress is predictable: for example, always on the first syllable, like Hungarian, or always on the last syllable, like Modern Hebrew.
- In a free stress system, stress is not predictable; it must be learned for every word. In these languages (e.g., Russian), a difference in stress placement can cause a meaning difference. See table 8.13 on p. 289 for some examples of the relationship between stress and meaning in Russian.

### Syllable Structure

- All languages have CV and V syllable types. This means that all languages allow syllables that begin with an onset but not all languages have syllables with codas.
- If a language has syllables with branching, or complex, onsets (an onset with more than one member), then it will have syllables with simple onsets (an onset with only one member). Similarly, if a language has syllables with branching, or complex, codas, then it will also have languages with simple codas.

**Think ...** Can a language have complex onsets without having simple onsets? Can a language have complex codas without simple codas? Which are more marked, simple onsets and codas or complex onsets and codas?

## Exercise!

1. For each of the following pairs, circle the more marked item of the two.
   - a. fricatives               affricates
   - b. VC                       VCC
   - c. voiced obstruents        voiceless obstruents
   - d. register tones           contour tones
   - e. short vowels             long vowels
   - f. CCV                      CV

2.  Complete the following statements.

    a.  The most common vowel system has _____ vowels, which are _____.
    b.  The three most common stops are _____, with _____ being the most common.
    c.  The two most common fricatives are _____ and _____.
    d.  The two most common nasals are _____ and _____.
    e.  Front vowels are generally _____ while back vowels are generally _____ _____.
    f.  Low vowels are generally _____.

3.  Assume that a language contains the following consonants: /p, b, g, z, pf, n, m, r̥/. Use your knowledge of implicational universals to predict which other consonants might be found in this language. Note: /pf/ is a labial affricate.

4.  Assume that a language contains the following vowels: /eː, oː, uː, iː, aː, ã/. Use your knowledge of implicational universals to predict which other vowels might be found in this language.

5.  Examine the data below and answer the questions that follow. (Note: The data is from a hypothetical language.)

    | /droŋ/ | 'basket' | /sas.gnu/ | 'foot' |
    |---|---|---|---|
    | /ben/ | 'stove' | /gle/ | 'sun' |
    | /a.dupt/ | 'chicken' | /brit.e.aks/ | 'chair' |

    a.  Identify the syllable types present in each of the words. Remember that a period indicates a syllable boundary.
    b.  Does this language have complex onsets? Complex codas?
    c.  Which other syllable type would be found in this language.
    d.  Which syllable structure universals (including implicational universals) are evident in the data?

6.  Examine the following data and answer the questions below. (Note: The data is from a hypothetical language.)

    | H  M | H  LH | HL M |
    |---|---|---|
    |  | ∨ | ∨  | |
    | /t i k u/ 'man' | /t i k u/ 'woman' | /t i k u/ 'child' |

    a.  Identify the tones as either register or contour.
    b.  Use your knowledge of implicational universals to predict which other tones the language might have.

7. Using your knowledge of implicational universals, decide whether each of the following corresponds to a possible or impossible combination of sounds in language.

    a. contrastive long vowels without contrastive short vowels    _____

    b. voiced sonorants without voiceless sonorant phonemes    _____

    c. affricates without fricatives    _____

    d. contrastive oral vowels without contrastive nasal vowels    _____

    e. voiceless obstruents without voiced obstruent phonemes    _____

    f. register tones without contour tones    _____

# MORPHOLOGICAL CLASSIFICATION

Morphological classification is based on the different ways in which languages combine morphemes to form words. There are four types of morphological systems.

⇒ **Isolating.**  In an isolating language, words consist only of free morphemes. There are no affixes. Information such as tense or plural is contained within separate free morphemes.

- Mandarin is an example of a language with an isolating morphology.

⇒ **Agglutinating.**  In an agglutinating language, words contain many affixes. Each affix typically corresponds to a single piece of grammatical information (e.g., number, tense, possession, etc.).

- Turkish is an example of a language with an agglutinating morphology.

⇒ **Fusional.**  In a fusional (or inflectional) language, words also contain many affixes. However, each affix may contain several pieces of grammatical information at the same time. That is, one affix may contain information on gender, number, case, and so on.

- Russian is a good example of a language with a fusional morphology.

⇒ **Polysynthetic.**  In a polysynthetic language, a single word consists of a number of roots and affixes. These words often express meanings that are associated with entire sentences in other languages.

- Inuktitut is a good example of a language with a polysynthetic morphology.

**Think ...** What type of morphological system does English have? Think about the information found in pronouns such as *he, she, him,* and *her;* in derived words such as *activation, optionality,* and *denationalize;* and in phrases such as *John will sing.* What type of system do each of these correspond to? Remember that many languages have a mix of the different types of systems. This means that the type of system found in English pronouns does not have to be the same as that found in English derived words.

Some universal generalizations can be made about word structure:
⇒ If a language has derivational affixes, then it will also have inflectional affixes.

⇒ If a word has both a derivational and an inflectional affix, the derivational affix will be closer to the root.

- See table 8.16 on p. 293 for some examples of the ordering of inflectional and derivational affixes in English and Turkish.

⇒ If a language has only suffixes, it will only have postpositions. A postposition is the equivalent of a preposition. The difference between the two is that a preposition occurs before its noun phrase complement, while a postposition occurs after its noun phrase complement.

- Turkish is an example of a language that has only suffixes and postpositions rather than prepositions.

**Try This!**  Identify the morphological system evident in each of these words. Note that the words are divided into their morphemes (indicated with a hyphen). The meaning of each morpheme is given in English directly underneath. The equivalent English translation is given on the third line.

a. Blackfoot:  maːt-jaːk-waːxkaji-waːtsiksi
not-will-go home-he
'He is not going home.'

b. Italian:  parl-av-o        port-av-ano      trov-av-i
speak-past-I     carry-past-they  find-past-you
'I spoke'         'they carried'    'you found'

**Now ...** Which implicational universal related to affixes is evident in the following Latvian words?

lidot-aj-s                        rakstit-aj-a
to fly-one who flies-nominative    to write-one who writes-genitive
'aviator (subject)'                'writer's (possessive)'

# SYNTACTIC CLASSIFICATION

Syntactic classification is typically restricted to the study of word order patterns. Ninety-five percent of the world's languages use one of three word order patterns in basic declarative sentences (e.g., *The boy kicked the ball*). These patterns are described below.

⇒ **SOV.** In this word order pattern, the subject (S) comes first, followed by the object (O) and then the verb (V). Using this pattern, the English sentence *The boy kicked the ball* would have the order *The boy the ball kicked*.

- Turkish and Japanese are examples of languages that follow this pattern.

⇒ **SVO.** In this word order pattern, the subject (S) comes first, followed by the verb (V) and then the object (O). This pattern corresponds to the English sentence *The boy kicked the ball*.

- English and French are examples of languages that follow this pattern.

⇒ **VSO.** In this word order pattern, the verb (V) comes first, followed by the subject (S) and then the object (O). Using this pattern, the English sentence *The boy kicked the ball* would have the order *Kicked the boy the ball*.

- Welsh is an example of a language using this pattern.

**Think ...** What do the three word order patterns have in common? Why might this be so? Are there other word order patterns found in the world's languages that do not follow this generalization? Which word order pattern is the most common?

There are also some universal generalizations that can be made regarding word order. These are related to whether a language places the verb before the object (VO) or after the object (OV).

⇒ VO languages
- have prepositions (e.g., *in* the park, *with* his foot)
- place prepositional phrases after the verb (e.g., The boy <u>ran</u> *in the park*)
- generally place adverbs after the verb (e.g., The boy <u>ran</u> *quickly*)

⇒ OV languages
- have postpositions (e.g., the park *in*, his foot *with*)
- place prepositional phrases before the verb (e.g., The boy *the park in* <u>ran</u>)
- place adverbs before the verb (e.g., The boy *quickly* <u>ran</u>)

## Practice!

1. Determine the word order in each of the following sentences. The English translation for each word is given on the line underneath. The equivalent English sentence is given on the third line. (Yuwaalaraay is an Australian language.)

a. Spanish:
Los soldados quebraron  las ventanas.
the soldiers broke       the windows
'The soldiers broke the windows.'

b. Yuwaalaraay:
duyugu nama dayn yiy
snake  that  man  bit
'The snake bit that man.'

2. Would you expect Spanish to have prepositions or postpositions? What about Yuwaalaraay? Would the phrase containing the preposition or postposition come before or after the verb in Spanish? What about in Yuwaalaraay?

3. What is the difference in the ordering of nouns and demonstratives in the following phrases? (Tinrin is an Austronesian language; Limbu is a Sino-Tibetan language spoken in Nepal.)

Tinrin:    moo horro ha
           Det   prayer this
           'this prayer (going on right now)'

Limbu:    khɛy nɛpphu cum   ha
          that  two     friend plural
          'those two friends'

---

## WHY? WHY?

Why are some patterns found in language? Why are other patterns not found in language? Why are some structural characteristics more common than others? There are no definitive answers to such questions, although some possible explanations have been given:

- Some phonological universals may have a perceptual basis. Others may be motivated by articulatory constraints (e.g., the greater number of obstruents in comparison to sonorants).
- Some morphological universals may be linked to language change (see Chapter 7). Others may be related to the internal structure of words (see Chapter 3).
- Syntactic patterns may be linked to how we process language (see Chapter 14).

---

## GENETIC CLASSIFICATION

Genetic classification groups languages together based on common ancestry. These groups of languages are called "families," since all members of the group are descended from the same ancestor. This common ancestor is usually found using the comparative method of reconstruction discussed in Chapter 7.

There can be many difficulties in doing genetic classification. One is the amount of data that is needed to be sure of the genetic status of a language. Some others are given below.

⇒ **Language Contact.** When languages come into contact with each other, they often borrow sounds, words, morphemes, and syntactic structures from one another. The result is that languages that are unrelated may end up being similar in many ways.

⇒ **Sound Change.** Sound changes can make it difficult to find relationships between languages, since sound changes may render words in related languages very different from one another. The result is that languages that are related may not look similar.

⇒ **Vocabulary Change.** Words that are often good indicators of a genetic relationship between two languages may be lost from the lexicon over time.

# THE INDO-EUROPEAN FAMILY

English belongs to the Indo-European family of languages. These languages are found in Europe as well as in the Middle East and India. The Indo-European language family currently has nine branches.

⇒ **Albanian.** Albanian, the only member of this family, is spoken in Albania and in parts of the former Yugoslavia, Greece, and Italy.

⇒ **Armenian.** Armenian, the only member of this family, is spoken in the Republic of Armenia as well as in Turkey, Iran, Syria, Lebanon, and Egypt.

⇒ **Baltic.** Latvian and Lithuanian are the two Baltic languages. They are spoken in Latvia and Lithuania (west of Russia and northeast of Poland).

⇒ **Celtic.** The Celtic languages are divided into the Insular and Continental branches. The Insular branch is further divided into the Brythonic and Goidelic (or Gaelic) sub-branches. Celtic languages are spoken in the British Isles as well as in northwestern France.

⇒ **Germanic.** The Germanic languages are divided into East, North, and West branches. North Germanic languages are spoken in Scandinavia, while the West Germanic languages are spoken in Germany, the Netherlands, Belgium, South Africa, England, and of course, North America.

⇒ **Hellenic.** This branch has only one member: Greek.

⇒ **Indo-Iranian.** This branch is divided into Indic and Iranian languages. Iranian languages are spoken in Iran, Afghanistan, Iraq, Turkey, the former Yugoslavia, and China. Indic languages are spoken in northern India, Pakistan, and Bangladesh.

⇒ **Italic.** The Italic languages are divided into four branches: Ibero-Romance, Gallo-Romance, Italo-Romance, and Balkano-Romance.

⇒ **Slavic.** The Slavic languages are divided into East, West, and South branches. These languages are spoken in Russia, the Ukraine, Belarus, and the former Yugolsavia.

See figure 8.8 on p. 305 of the text for the approximate locations of the different Indo-European languages.

**Now ...** Using tables 8.20 to 8.25 on pp. 301 to 305, construct a diagram of the Indo-European language family by filling in the chart below. Provide (1) the names of the sub-branches in the different branches and (2) the languages of each branch or sub-branch. Extinct languages and their branches have been omitted from the diagram.

**DID YOU KNOW ...**

- The ancestor of the Indo-European language family is a reconstructed language called Proto-Indo-European (PIE).
- The reconstruction of PIE is based on Old English, Old Norse, Latin, Sanskrit, and Attic Greek, among other languages.
- Lithuanian has a case system thought to be similar to that found in PIE.
- English descended from the languages spoken by the Germanic tribes: the Angles, Jutes, and Saxons.
- Frisian is the closest relative to English.
- Some Indo-European languages are extinct. For example, Gothic is an extinct East Germanic language and Cornish is an extinct Celtic (Continental) language.

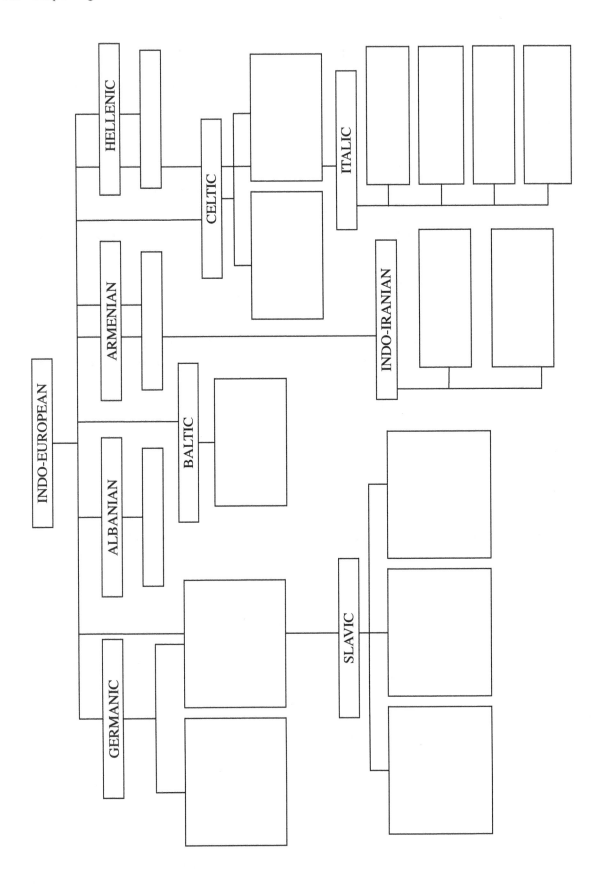

# PRACTICE! PRACTICE!

1.  Name a language that is a sister (i.e., a member of the sub-branch, or branch if the language has no sub-branch) to each of the following languages.

| LANG | SISTER | LANG | SISTER |
|------|--------|------|--------|
| Italian | _____ | Polish | _____ |
| Swedish | _____ | Russian | _____ |
| Yiddish | _____ | Latvian | _____ |
| Catalan | _____ | Bulgarian | _____ |

2.  Circle the language that does not fit.

| a. Greek | Danish | Frisian |
|----------|--------|---------|
| b. Russian | Hungarian | Polish |
| c. Persian | Bengali | Romany |
| d. Portuguese | Macedonian | Sardinian |
| e. Albanian | Romanian | Catalan |
| f. Italian | German | Spanish |

3.  Give the sub-branch (and branch if applicable) for each of the following languages.

a. Danish _____

b. Scots Gaelic _____

c. Sardinian _____

d. Kurdish _____

e. Bengali _____

f. Slovene _____

g. Bulgarian _____

h. Czech _____

i. Greek _____

j. Yiddish _____

4. Determine whether each of the following statements is true or false.

a. The genetic relationship between Norwegian and Swedish is the same as that between Latvian and Lithuanian.

TRUE               FALSE

b. The genetic relationship between Spanish and French is the same as that between Czech and Polish.

TRUE               FALSE

c. The genetic relationship between Swedish and Slovene is the same as that between Norwegian and German.

TRUE               FALSE

d. The genetic relationship between Frisian and Danish is the same as the genetic relationship between Italian and Romanian.

TRUE               FALSE

---

**REVIEW! REVIEW!**   Make sure you know ...

- what mutual intelligibility means
- the different types of language universals
- how to determine marked and unmarked traits
- how to determine possible and impossible phonological, morphological, and syntactic systems
- the common phonological systems found across the world's languages
- the four types of morphological systems found across the world's languages
- the three most common word order patterns found across the world's languages
- phonological, morphological, and syntactic universals
- the branches of the Indo-European language family
- the languages of each branch of the Indo-European language family

# QUESTIONS? PROBLEMS? DIFFICULTIES?

_____

_____

_____

_____

_____

_____

_____

_____

_____

_____

_____

# CHAPTER 9.
# ABORIGINAL LANGUAGES OF CANADA

The study of the Aboriginal languages of North America is valuable for both historical and theoretical reasons. Important concepts found in this chapter include the following:

1. Genetic classification
2. Stocks and phyla
3. Isolates
4. Contact languages
5. Language decline
6. Structural diversity
7. Polysynthesis

## STUDYING ABORIGINAL LANGUAGES

Consider the following points concerning the study of Aboriginal languages:

⇒ It is a myth that Aboriginal languages are 'primitive' in any way. Aboriginal languages display significant structural diversity, and certain structural and semantic properties of these languages are not found in languages that have received more attention from linguists (such as English).

⇒ The study of Aboriginal languages has revealed important new insights into the nature of human language.

⇒ Aboriginal languages provide linguists with the opportunity to test principles and theoretical concepts. Concepts and principles developed by studying other languages can be reconsidered in light of new data.

⇒ The study of Aboriginal languages can lead to important insights in anthropology and archaeology: languages can provide valuable clues about the origin and migration patterns of the indigenous peoples of North America.

⇒ The Aboriginal languages are in a state of decline. Many Aboriginal languages became extinct in the past several centuries, and others face extinction today. More recently, many Aboriginal communities have been working to preserve their languages and cultures.

# GENETIC CLASSIFICATION: TERMINOLOGY

The following concepts, which were introduced in Chapter 8, are important in order to understand how linguists arrive at the genetic classification of the Aboriginal languages of Canada. Make sure you are familiar with the meanings of these terms.

| TERM | DEFINITION |
|---|---|
| genetic classification | A genetic classification groups languages according to their development from a shared ancestry. |
| family | Languages believed to be related and thus descended from a common language are said to make up a language family. |
| stock | Language families that are believed to be related are placed into a larger group called a language stock. |
| phylum | Language stocks that are believed to be related are placed into a larger group called a superstock or phylum. The plural of *phylum* is *phyla*. Another term for phylum is *macrofamily*. |
| isolate | An isolate is a language that appears to have no known relatives. In other words, it cannot be shown that the language shares a common ancestor with any other language or languages that linguists have studied. |
| dialect | A dialect is a variety that can be shown to be different in systematic ways from another variety of the same language (for example, English as spoken in Vancouver compared to English as spoken in London, England). It is not always a straightforward task to classify a particular variety as a language or a dialect since non-linguistic factors (political, socio-cultural, socio-historical, religious, etc.) often play a significant role in shaping people's perceptions of the difference between a dialect and a language. |

# ABORIGINAL LANGUAGES OF CANADA

Linguists generally recognize the following language families and isolates, organized according to the three political groupings of Canada's indigenous peoples:

⇒ First Nations

- Algonquian
- Athabaskan-Eyak-Tlingit
- Haida (isolate)
- Iroquoian
- Ktunaxa/Kootenay-Kinbasket (isolate)
- Salish
- Siouan-Catawban

- Tsimshian
- Wakashan

⇒ Inuit

- Eskimo-Aleut

⇒ Métis

- Michif (unique mixed language)

**Practice! Practice!** Many of the names of languages and language families introduced in this chapter will be new to you. Try the following exercises, which will provide you with an opportunity to become more familiar with these new languages and groups.

**Try This!** Below is a map of Canada with numbers. Study figure 9.1 on p. 312 and see how many language families and isolates you can identify. Provide the name of the language or family next to the appropriate number. Here are the names of the language families and isolates:

| | | | |
|---|---|---|---|
| Algonquian | Athabaskan | Eskimo-Aleut | Haida |
| Iroquoian | Kutenai | Salish | Siouan |
| Tlingit | Tsimshian | Wakashan | |

1. _____  2. _____

3. _____  4. _____

5. _____  6. _____

7. _____  8. _____

9. _____  10. _____

11. _____

**Now ...** Study the tables on pp. 313 to 317. Try to name the language family of which each language below is a member. Write *isolate* if the language given is an isolate. See how many you can identify without looking up the answer!

1.   Slave                              _____

2.   Inuktitut                          _____

3.   Ktunaxa/Kootenay-Kinbasket         _____

4.   Ojibwe                             _____

5.   Okanagan                           _____

6.   Gitksan                            _____

7.   Nuu-chah-nulth                     _____

8.   Cayuga                             _____

9.   Haida                              _____

10.  Mohawk                             _____

11.  Stoney (Nakoda)                    _____

12.  Bella Coola/Nuxalk                 _____

13.  Mi'kmaq                            _____

14.  Dëne Sųłine                        _____

15.  Cree                               _____

**Exercise!** See how many details about Canada's Aboriginal languages you can recall. Indicate whether the following statements, based on the discussion on pp. 312 to 317, are true or false.

1. Tuscarora and Seneca are two members of the Iroquian family.
2. The Wakashan languages are spoken principally in Quebec and Ontario.
3. There are approximately a hundred speakers of Eyak today.
4. Mi'kmaq is spoken in the Maritime Provinces.
5. An Inuktitut syllabary is used in Nunavut.
6. The Salish family contains Canada's two most widely spoken Aboriginal languages.
7. Dialects of Cree and Ojibwe are spoken in several Canadian provinces, including British Columbia and Ontario.
8. Haida, an isolate, is spoken in Labrador.
9. Ojibwe is the only Algonquian language widely spoken outside of Canada.
10. The greatest linguistic diversity in any Aboriginal language family in Canada is found in the Athabaskan-Eyak-Tlingit family.

## CONTACT LANGUAGES

Contact languages emerge in contexts where speakers of two or more varieties interact closely. There are different types of contact languages, and a more detailed discussion is found in Chapter 14. You should be familiar with the following concepts and terms.

| TERM | DEFINITION |
|---|---|
| contact language | A contact language is a language that results from the interaction of two or more languages in a community. Contact situations can result in the formation of pidgins, creoles, and mixed languages, all of which are difficult to classify genetically because they are not derived from a single source language. |
| lingua franca | A lingua franca is a language adopted as a means of communication among speakers of different languages. Typically, the lingua franca is the second (or third) language of the speakers who use it. Today, English is the international lingua franca of technology, science, and business. |
| trade language | A lingua franca used predominantly for the purpose of trade is a trade language. Often, a pidgin is a trade langauge. |
| pidgin | Pidgin languages emerge when there is a need for speakers of different languages to communicate (for trade purposes, for example). In comparison to non-pidgins, they are generally characterized by a limited vocabulary and a reduced grammar. A pidgin is usually not the native language of the speakers who use it. |

mixed language

A mixed language is a language with features clearly drawn from two distinct sources. Mixed languages are believed to be quite rare. An often-cited example is Michif, the mixed language of the Métis, in which the nominal morphology is based on Métis French and the verbal morphology of Cree.

**Try This!**   Below are some phrases (not in phonetic transcription) from Chinook Jargon, a trade language widely used in the nineteenth and early twentieth centuries in the Pacific Northwest, including British Columbia. Chinook Jargon has a simplified or reduced grammar. Its vocabulary comes predominantly from Chinook, Nuu-chah-nulth (Wakashan), French, and English. Try to identify the words from French and English.

Source: Thomas, E.H. *Chinook: A History and a Dictionary of the Northwest Coast Trade Jargon*. Portland: Binfords & Mort, 1935 (reprinted 1970).

1. tenas cosho
2. tahtlum cole
3. mamook bloom
4. doctin kopa letah
5. tenas pish
6. mamook piah
7. klatawa kopa saghalie lamontay
8. potlatch lamah
9. poolie lapome
10. mamook le pan

**Now ...** Here is some information that will help you analyze the Chinook Jargon expressions. The meanings of some Chinook and Nuu-chah-nulth terms that appear in the expressions are the following:

kopa (Chinook) 'of, about'
klatawa (Nuu-chah-nulth) 'to go, to travel'
mamook (Nuu-chah-nulth) 'to make'
potlatch (Nuu-chah-nulth) 'to give'
saghalie (Chinook) 'up, above'
tahtlum (Chinook) 'ten'
tenas (Nuu-chah-nulth) 'little, small'

**Also, keep in mind ...**

⇒ In contact situations, words that are taken from one language into another often undergo phonological adaptation (i.e., sounds in the borrowed words are altered or substituted so that they conform to the phonology of the borrowing language). For example, if the borrowing language does not have labiodental fricatives [f v], speakers may substitute a stop that is close in place of articulation [p b] for the labiodental fricative in words of the source language.

⇒ Words that are taken from one of the languages in a contact environment may also undergo morphological reanalysis (see Chapter 7): speakers interpret the morpheme boundaries differently from how they are interepreted in the source language. Reanalysis can also happen independently of contact. For example, in English, the earlier determiner + noun sequence *a napron* was later reinterpreted as *an apron*.

**Think ...** Here are the translations for the above exercises. After matching them to the original phrases in Chinook Jargon, consider whether there are any other observations you can make about the Chinook Jargon examples.

Match these English translations to the above Chinook Jargon examples.

1. to make/build fire
2. shake hands (i.e., 'give' one's hand)
3. to go to the top of the mountain
4. rotten apple
5. knead (make) bread
6. minnow (i.e., small fish)
7. to sweep
8. ten years (winters)
9. piglet
10. dentist

# DECLINE OF ABORIGINAL LANGUAGES

Many factors contribute to language decline, a situation in which the functions and number of speakers of a language decrease. Language decline can lead, of course, to language death or extinction (when there are no more speakers of a language). Many Aboriginal languages have become extinct, and many face extinction today.

**Think ...** Identify at least three different factors that have led to the decline of Aboriginal languages in Canada.

**Exercise!**   From the group of Aboriginal languages below, identify three languages that are extinct; three languages that face imminent extinction because they have fewer than a dozen speakers left; and three languages that have recently had an orthography established.

| Dogrib | Okanagan | Secwepemctsín |
| Ktunaxa | Pentlatch | Tagish |
| Laurentian | Plains Cree | Tuscarora |
| Nicola | Squamish | Tsilhqut'in |

1. Three languages that are exinct:
2. Three languages facing extinction:
3. Three languages with recent establishment of orthography:

# STRUCTURAL FEATURES OF ABORIGINAL LANGUAGES

The Aboriginal languages of Canada are structurally very diverse. Some salient typological features of Canadian Aboriginal languages are discussed in the chapter. To understand these characteristics, you should be familiar with the following terms:

⇒ **Polysynthesis**. Polysynthetic languages are languages that are morphologically very rich. Typically, words consist of many morphemes, and linguists have often observed that what can be expressed in a word in a polysynthetic language can require a sentence in other types of languages. Recall the Inuktitut example given on p. 321: the English sentence *He has a good house* is expressed by the polymorphemic word *Iglugiktuq* (*Iglu-gik-tuq*). Languages in which each word can only have one morpheme are said to be **isolating** or **analytic**. Isolating and polysynthetic languages represent the extreme ends of a continuum of morphological systems (see the discussion in Chapter 8 for more details).

⇒ **Inclusive-Exclusive**. Languages that have an inclusive-exclusive contrast make a distinction regarding whether or not the addressee is included in the interpretation of the first person plural morpheme; such languages make distinctions that are not captured by English *we*. In the inclusive form, the addressee is included in the meaning of the first person plural (*you and I*); in the exclusive form, the addressee is excluded, so that the equivalent of *we* refers only to the speaker and others (*I and others*).

⇒ **Proximate-Obviative**. Languages that have the proximate-obviative contrast are able to select verb forms that indicate whether the referent of the subject (a third person) of the verb is and remains the focus of the conversation (proximate), or whether the referent is different from that of the previous focus (i.e., a different third person). One way to think about this is to imagine that in English you could indicate through the verb that the second 'he' is a different person from the first 'he' in the following example: *John phoned. He told me that he will help me with that.* In English we cannot mark the verb 'will' so that it tells us that the referent of the subject in this case is different from that of 'phoned' and 'told'. This is the type of contrast that is possible in languages with proximate and obviative verb forms.

**Exercise!**  See how much you can recall about some of the striking structural characteristics of Canada's Aboriginal languages. Indicate whether the following statements, based on the discussion on pp. 319 to 325, are true or false.

1.   Most Canadian Aboriginal languages have a strict VSO word order.
2.   Many Aboriginal languages have greater number distinctions than English.
3.   Canadian Aboriginal languages are largely isolating languages.
4.   Most Aboriginal languages have over thirty consonantal phonemes.
5.   Many Aboriginal languages mark nouns for animacy and inanimacy.
6.   The inclusive-exclusive contrast is found in Algonquian and other families.
7.   Word order is not fixed in many Aboriginal languages.
8.   The distinction between a noun and a verb is said to be weak in many Aboriginal languages.

**Try This!**   Consider the following data, based on the Mohawk examples presented on p. 324. The statements corresponding to 'Sak likes her dress' on p. 324 have been converted here to questions of the type 'Does Sak like her dress?' (a yes-no question).

| | |
|---|---|
| Sak ken ra-nuhwe'-s ako-atya'tawi | 'Sak does like her-dress?' |
| Sak ken ako-atya'tawi ra-nuhwe'-s | 'Sak does her-dress like?' |
| Ra-nuhwe'-s ken Sak ako-atya'tawi | 'Like does Sak her-dress?' |
| Ra-nuhwe'-s ken ako-atya'tawi ne Sak | 'Like does her-dress Sak?' |
| Ako-atya'tawi ken ra-nuhwe'-s ne Sak | 'Her-dress does like Sak?' |
| Ako-atya'tawi ken Sak ra-nuhwe'-s | 'Her-dress does Sak like?' |

Describe the morpheme that is required to form a *yes-no* question in Mohawk? Discuss word order in relation to this morpheme in Mohawk.

**Now ...**   Consider the following. Although all of the above questions correspond roughly to English 'Does Sak like her dress?', more precise interpretations would be as follows:

| | |
|---|---|
| Sak ken ra-nuhwe'-s ako-atya'tawi | 'Does <u>Sak</u> like her-dress (as opposed to Sose)?' |
| Sak ken ako-atya'tawi ra-nuhwe'-s | 'Does <u>Sak</u> like her-dress (as opposed to Sose)?' |
| Ra-nuhwe'-s ken Sak ako-atya'tawi | 'Does Sak <u>like</u> her-dress (as opposed to wear/dislike)?' |
| Ra-nuhwe'-s ken ako-atya'tawi ne | 'Does Sak <u>like</u> her-dress (as opposed to wear/dislike)?' |
| Ako-atya'tawi ken ra-nuhwe'-s ne | 'Does Sak like <u>her-dress</u> (as opposed to her hat)?' |
| Ako-atya'tawi ken Sak ra-nuhwe'-s | 'Does Sak like <u>her-dress</u> (as opposed to her hat)?' |

What observations can you make about word order flexibility in *yes-no* questions in Mohawk? How does word order relate to interrogative placement and interpretation?

**Exercise!**   Consider the following data from Plains Cree, as spoken near James Bay (Kashechewan, Ontario). The examples have been adapted from C. Douglas Ellis, *Spoken Cree* (Winnipeg: Pica Pica Press, 1983). Examine the data; then answer the questions that follow. As discussed on p. 323, Cree distinguishes between animate and inanimate nouns; only animacy and third person forms are demonstrated in these examples.

| | |
|---|---|
| tʃa:n itohte:w | 'John goes/is going (there).' |
| pimohte:w | 'He/She walks/is walking.' |
| tʃa:n kihtohte:w | 'John goes/is going away.' |
| takihtohte:w | 'He will go away.' |
| tʃa:n o:hta:wija itohte:liwa | 'John's father goes/is going (there).' |
| ki:te:pwe:w ka:kih tʃipahta:li tʃi atimwa | 'He shouted when the dog ran away.' |
| tʃa:n ki:kihtohte:w ne:sta ma:tjiw ki:kihtohte:w | 'John went away, and Matthew went away too.' |

| | |
|---|---|
| atim wa:pame:w tʃa:na | 'The dog sees John.' |
| tʃa:n wa:pame:w me:ri:wa e:kihtohte:t | 'John sees Mary as John is going away.' |
| tʃa:n wa:pame:w me:ri:wa e:kihtohte:li tʃi | 'John sees Mary as Mary is going away.' |
| a:lik ki:wa:pame:w tʃa:na e:pimohte:t | 'Alex saw John as Alex was walking.' |
| a:lik ki:wa:pame:w tʃa:na e:pimohte:li tʃi | 'Alex saw John as John was walking.' |

1.  Identify the Plains Cree morphemes that correspond to each of the following meanings:

| | |
|---|---|
| his father | and/too |
| dog | when (relative marker) |
| future | as (dependent clause marker) |
| past (completed action marker) | shout |

2.  Two types of verbs are used in the examples. What are these two types?

3.  What are the third person singular (proximate) verbal endings?

4.  What are the third person singular (obviative) verbal endings?

5.  How is the obviative marked on nouns?

**Try This!**   Consider the following additional data from Plains Cree. The possessive of nouns is formed by adding a prefix to a stem. In this exercise, you are given the form that corresponds to the first person singular possessive ('my') + noun, as well as the noun stem to which the prefix is added. Identify the forms of the prefix meaning 'my' and explain the allomorphic variation.

| | | | |
|---|---|---|---|
| nita:ʃokan | 'my wharf' | a:ʃokan | 'wharf' |
| nimaskisin | 'my shoe' | maskisin | 'shoe' |
| nitʃi:ma:n | 'my canoe' | tʃi:ma:n | 'canoe' |
| nite:htapiwin | 'my chair' | te:htapiwin | 'chair' |
| nitastotin | 'my hat' | astotin | 'hat' |
| nitamisk | 'my beaver' | amisk | 'beaver' |
| nime:skanaw | 'my path' | me:skanaw | 'path' |

**Think ...**   Now look at the following examples, which also contain forms corresponding to 'my' + noun, as in the previous exercise. As occurs in other Algonquian languages, some noun stems cannot appear as free morphemes (they are bound or dependent stems): they must always be accompanied by a possessive prefix (whether the one corresponding to 'my' or a different one). Compare the examples below to those in the previous exercise. The distinction between the two groups of nouns is a semantic one. What is the semantic motivation for the distinction?

| | | | |
|---|---|---|---|
| nikosis | 'my son' | *kosis | 'son' |
| nitoːn | 'my mouth' | *toːn | 'mouth' |
| nispiton | 'my arm' | *spiton | 'arm' |
| nimoʃoːm | 'my grandfather' | *moʃoːm | 'grandfather' |
| niteːhi | 'my heart' | *teːhi | 'heart' |
| nitoːteːm | 'my friend' | *toːteːm | 'friend' |
| nikaːwij | 'my mother' | *kaːwij | 'mother' |

## QUESTIONS? PROBLEMS? DIFFICULTIES?

_____

_____

_____

_____

_____

_____

_____

_____

_____

_____

_____

_____

# CHAPTER 10.
# FIRST LANGUAGE ACQUISITION

The study of first language acquisition examines how children come to know language. Important topics and concepts found in this chapter include the following:

1. Studying first language acquisition
2. Phonological development
3. Children's phonetic processes
4. Vocabulary development
5. Morphological development
6. Syntactic development
7. Critical period hypothesis
8. How language acquisition occurs

## STUDYING FIRST LANGUAGE ACQUISITION

Linguists attempt to understand exactly how it is that children come to master sounds, vocabulary, meaning, word formation, and sentence structure of language. Of course, this can only be done by studying children's language. The following concepts are important in understanding how linguists study first language acquisition.

⇒ What do children acquire when they acquire language?

- Children acquire a grammar. This grammar is a mental system of knowledge that allows them to speak and understand language (see Chapter 1).

⇒ Why do linguists believe that children acquire a grammar?

- First, language is creative (see Chapter 1). Speakers of a language can understand and produce an unlimited number of novel sentences on any topic. Children would never be able to do this if they simply memorized and imitated the sentences that they hear.

- Second, errors that children make (such as *worser* instead of *worse* and *gooder* instead of *good*) indicate that they have formulated a rule. They could not simply be imitating adults, since adults don't normally produce such words.

⇒ How do linguists study the development of language in children?

- Linguists sometimes take a naturalistic approach to studying children's language development. Naturalistic studies often involve keeping a record of a child's utterances from birth until approximately age four. For this reason, such studies are typically referred to as being longitudinal.

• Linguists sometimes take an experimental approach to studying children's language development. In an experimental study, linguists use specifically designed tasks to study the development of a particular grammatical structure (e.g., tasks such as judging the truth of pictures, production tasks, imitation tasks; see figures 10.1 and 10.2 on p. 329 for some examples). This type of study is often cross-sectional: that is, children of different ages participate in a single experiment.

**Think ...** Does a naturalistic study have to involve only one child over a long period of time? Some naturalistic studies study several children over a shorter period of time. In what way does this make such studies like experimental studies?

**Now ...** Suppose a researcher collected data from ten different two-year-old children by asking them to name objects presented in a picture. What kind of study is this? What task is the researcher using? Suppose a researcher collects data from three children every two weeks for one year. What kind of study is this? What might be some possible advantages and disadvantages of each study? Think about the time it takes to conduct each study, the children's role in the study, the type of data that is collected, and whether the collected data is representative of children's grammatical knowledge.

# PHONOLOGICAL DEVELOPMENT

Children are born with the ability to perceive the sounds of language, but the ability to produce sounds takes longer.

## Babbling

The onset of babbling at around six months signals the beginning of children's ability to produce sounds. Characteristics of babbling include the following:

⇒ During babbling, children produce repeated CV (consonant vowel) sequences (e.g., [mamama], [dadada], [bababa]).

⇒ Babbled sequences have no meaning attached to them.

⇒ Some sounds (e.g., [p, b, m, t, d, n]) are found in babbling; some sounds are not (e.g., [f, θ, ʃ, r]). See table 10.1 on p. 331 for more examples.

**Think ...** Children exposed to different languages tend to babble using the same sounds. What does this reveal about the relationship between babbling and language development?

## Developmental Order

When children begin to produce sequences with meaning, they acquire the sounds of language gradually. The following tendencies have been observed for the acquisition of consonants.

⇒ **Manner of Articulation.**  Stops are usually the first manner of articulation that children acquire. Liquids are usually the last manner to be acquired.

⇒ **Place of Articulation.**  Children acquire labials first. They then acquire alveolars, velars, and alveopalatals. Interdentals are usually the last place of articulation that children acquire.

⇒ **Word Position.**  Children acquire phonemic contrasts first in word-initial position and later in word-final position.

See table 10.2 on p. 331 for the typical inventory of a two-year-old child. See table 10.3 on p. 332 for the typical inventory of a four-year-old child.

**Try This!** Determine whether each of the following statements regarding the development of sounds is true or false.

1.  [v] is acquired before [d].              TRUE    /    FALSE

2.  [p, b] are acquired before [k, g].       TRUE    /    FALSE

3.  [m] is acquired before [ŋ].              TRUE    /    FALSE

4.  [z] is acquired before [s].              TRUE    /    FALSE

5.  [θ] is acquired before [ʃ].              TRUE    /    FALSE

## CHILDREN'S PHONETIC PROCESSES

While children have fairly regular patterns of pronunciation, their pronunciation is not the same as that of an adult. Differences between child and adult pronunciations are often described using phonetic processes. These are universal in that they are found in children's pronunciations across languages. There are three basic types of processes.

⇒ **Syllable Structure.**  Children may modify the syllable structure found in an adult word. The end result of such modifications is often a CV syllable. Recall from Chapter 8 that this is the unmarked syllable structure.

⇒ **Substitution.**  Children may replace a sound that they have not acquired or find difficult to articulate with one that is easier to articulate.

⇒ **Assimilation.**  Children may change one sound to another so that it is more like a neighbouring sound.

Some specific processes for each type are presented in the following table.

| Type of Process | Process | Definition |
|---|---|---|
| Syllable Structure | Unstressed Syllable Deletion | Children tend to delete syllables that are unstressed and keep those that are stressed. Children are also more likely to delete unstressed syllables before the stressed syllable than after the stressed syllable. See tables 10.4 and 10.5 on p. 333 for some examples. |
| | Consonant Cluster Reduction (CCR) | Children tend to remove one or more members of a complex (branching) onset or coda. See table 10.6 on p. 333 for some examples. |
| | Deletion | Children often delete consonants at the end of a word (which corresponds to the end of a syllable). For example: 'boot' [bu] |
| Substitution | Stopping | Children tend to replace a fricative (or another continuant sound) with the corresponding stop. See table 10.7 on p. 334 for some examples. |
| | Gliding | Children tend to replace liquids with glides. See table 10.7 on p. 334 for some examples. |
| | Fronting | Children tend to replace the more back articulations with front articulations. See table 10.7 on p. 334 for some examples. |
| | Denasalization | Children may replace a nasal stop with its corresponding oral stop. See table 10.7 on p. 334 for some examples. |
| Assimilation | Voicing | Children may voice a voiceless consonant in anticipation of a following vowel (which is also voiced). For example: 'soup' [zup] |
| | Place of Articulation | Children may use the same place of articulation for all the consonants (or vowels) in a word. For example: 'doggy' [gɑgi]. |

**Practice!** Each of the following represents a change from an adult pronunciation to a child's pronunciation. Identify the phonetic process/es that has/have occurred in the child's form. Do this by comparing the child's pronunciation to the adult pronunciation.

1.    show:        adult [ʃow] →          child [sow]

_____

2.    that:        adult [ðæt] →          child [dæt]

_____

3. clean:         adult [klin] →        child [ki]

---

4. duck:          adult [dʌk] →         child [kʌk]

---

5. train:         adult [tren] →        child [wed]

---

6. brush:         adult [brʌʃ] →        child [bʌt]

---

7. ring:          adult [rɪŋ] →         child   [wɪn]

---

8. lamp:          adult [læmp] →        child [jæm]

---

9. delicious:     adult [dəlɪʃəs] →     child [lɪʃəs]

---

## VOCABULARY DEVELOPMENT

Children not only have to learn how to pronounce adult words; they must also learn what words mean.

### Early Vocabulary

Children's vocabularies initially develop quite slowly, but this speeds up rapidly, generally after children acquire fifty or so words. For most children, nouns make up the bulk of their vocabulary, although words from other categories (e.g., verbs, adjectives, social expressions) are also found. See table 10.8 on p. 335 for some examples of common vocabulary items.

### Strategies

Children use three strategies to determine the meanings of nouns.

⇒ **Whole Object Assumption.**  A new word refers to the entire object. For example, when learning the word *cow*, children will assume that this word refers to the entire cow and not just its legs or its tail.

⇒ **Type Assumption.**  A new word refers to a type of object, not a specific object. For example, when learning the word *cow*, children will assume that the word refers not just to a single cow but to other animals sharing the same properties.

⇒ **Basic Level Assumption.**  A new word refers to objects that are alike in some basic way. For example, when learning the word *cow*, children will assume that the word refers only to cows and not to animals in general.

In addition to the above strategies, children also use contextual cues to determine the meanings of new words.

**Errors**

Children make three types of errors when learning the meanings of words.

⇒ **Overextension.**  Children may make the meaning of a word more general. That is, the word includes more members for the child than it does for an adult. For example, children might use the word *juice* to refer to any type of drink. See table 10.9 on p. 338 for some examples of common children's overextensions.

⇒ **Underextension.**  Children may use a word in a more restrictive way than an adult would. For example, children may use the word *kitty* to refer to only the family cat and not to cats in general.

⇒ **Verb Meanings.**  While over- and underextensions describe errors made with nouns, children sometimes also have difficulty determining the meaning of verbs. For example, children sometimes think that *to fill* means *to pour*. This might be because objects are often filled by pouring.

**Think ...** Suppose a child used the word *tunnel* when driving through a tunnel and also when driving under an overpass, and finally, when hiding under a table. What might account for this overextension? Think about the perceptual properties that these instances have in common. Suppose another child used the word *fish* only for goldfish. What might account for this underextension? Think about what might be the prototype or core member of this category.

In addition to nouns and verbs, children also have to acquire adjectives, including those that give information on the dimension of objects. Children acquire these in an orderly fashion: from the more general to the more specific.

$\Rightarrow$ **Any Dimension.** Children first acquire the most general type of adjective: that is, adjectives that can be used to refer to any aspect of size (e.g., *big, small*).

$\Rightarrow$ **Single Dimension.** Children then acquire adjectives that can be used to refer to a single aspect of size (e.g., *tall, short*).

$\Rightarrow$ **Secondary Dimension.** Children then acquire adjectives that can be used to refer to more restricted aspects of size (e.g., *thick, thin*).

See table 10.10 on p. 340 for some more examples of size adjectives and how they can be classified.

**Exercise!** Examine the following vocabulary data from a two-year-old child. Categorize the items into nouns, verbs, adjectives, and social words.

| table | Mommy | cow | yummy | up |
|-------|-------|-----|-------|-----|
| go | coat | allgone | milk | horse |
| piggy | hot | no | dog | boots |
| chicken | juice | jump | Daddy | yucky |
| please | dolly | chair | play | pull |
| banana | sit | hat | bye-bye | kitty |

**Think ...** What type of word is the most common in the above data? Why would children tend to acquire these early? Think about whether these words are concrete or abstract in nature.

**Now ...** Take all of the nouns you found in the data and place them into subcategories (e.g., people, food/drink, animals, clothes, toys, house, etc.). Why would children's early vocabularies contain these types of nouns? Think about the relationship between these objects and what is found in the child's environment.

# MORPHOLOGICAL DEVELOPMENT

Not only do children have to learn the meanings of words, but they also have to learn how to combine morphemes to form words. That is, they have to learn about the internal structure of words.

### Development of Inflectional Affixes

Inflectional affixes are bound morphemes that, in English, provide information on grammatical categories such as number (e.g., singular and plural) and tense (e.g., past).

$\Rightarrow$ **Stages.** Children usually acquire inflectional affixes such as the plural and the past tense in three stages.

1. Children first memorize the inflected form. That is, they are not aware that words such as *hands* or *talked* consist of two morphemes. Since children are simply memorizing words, they will use irregular forms such as *drove*.
2. Children then learn the regular rule and apply it to all words, including words that in the adult language are the exceptions, or irregular forms. *Drove* now becomes *drived*.
3. Finally, children learn the irregular forms. *Drove* once again occurs in children's speech.

⇒ **Overgeneralizations.** The type of error that occurs when children overapply the regular rule, creating words such as *drived,* is called an overgeneralization. It is sometimes also called overregularization, since children are making the language more regular.

**Think ...** Researchers often test the acquisition of inflectional affixes using nonsense words (see figure 10.6 on p. 342). Why would researchers use nonsense words rather than actual words of the language? Think about the developmental stages outlined above.

### Development of Grammatical Morphemes

Inflectional affixes and function words tend to be acquired in a similar order across children. Children usually acquire the *-ing* ending first. They also acquire the plural *-s* before either the possessive *-'s* or the past tense *-ed*. The past tense, in turn, is acquired before the third person singular *-s*. See table 10.12 on p. 343 for the developmental order of seven English grammatical morphemes, and table 10.13 on p. 343 for the frequency of these morphemes in English.

**Think ...** The morpheme *-ing* is typically the first grammatical morpheme that children acquire. Why? Where in a word is it usually found? Is it a syllable? Is it regular or irregular? Does it have any allomorphs? Is its meaning easy to determine? Are there any other *-ing* affixes that have a different function? These are some of the determining factors that have been proposed to account for the order in which children acquire grammatical morphemes.

**Now ...** Ask the same questions for the past tense *-ed*. What is the difference between *-ing* and *-ed*? Can this account for the later acquisition of *-ed* in comparison to *-ing*?

### Development of Word Formation

In addition to acquiring grammatical morphemes, children must also acquire the different processes, such as derivation and compounding, that are used to form words in language.

⇒ **Derivation.** Children typically first acquire the affixes used to form the diminutive (e.g., *-ie*), doer (e.g., *-er*), activity (e.g., *-ing*), and state (e.g., *-ness*). See table 10.14 on p. 344 for some examples.

⇒ **Compounding.** Children acquire the ability to make compounds early. Children's compounds often consist of two nouns. They often make compounds that are not found in adult speech. See table 10.15 on p. 345 for some examples of children's innovative compounds.

**Think ...** Suppose a child used the word *driving wheel* instead of *steering wheel*. Why might a child create such a compound? Is it easier to determine the meaning of the child's compound or the adult compound? Remember that children often create compounds whose meaning is more transparent (at least to them).

**Exercise! Exercise!**   Examine the following data from a three-year-old child and answer the questions that follow.

| Child Sentence | Adult Sentence |
|---|---|
| I going for a walk. | I am going for a walk. |
| Do you like those fishes? | Do you like those fish? |
| The gooses want to play with the fishes. | The geese want to play with the fish. |
| Daddy gave bread to the duckies. | Daddy gave bread to the ducks. |
| Daddy is a good duck-feeder. | Daddy is good at feeding the ducks. |
| I leaving now. | I am leaving now. |

1.  Identify all of the grammatical morphemes from p. 343 of the text in the data.
2.  Which of these grammatical morphemes are missing from the data? Do you think the child has acquired any/all of the missing grammatical morphemes?
3.  Identify any word formation processes being used.
4.  What error does the child make with the plural?
5.  What stage of acquisition with regard to the plural is the child in? What about the past tense? What would you expect to happen next in the acquisition of plural? What about the past tense?

**Reminder!**   Overgeneralizations and overextensions are not the same. An overgeneralization is a morphological error: children use regular endings (e.g., for the plural and the past tense) on irregular words. Overextensions are a semantic error: the meaning of a particular word in children's vocabulary is more general than it would be to an adult.

# SYNTACTIC DEVELOPMENT

In addition to word formation, children learn how to combine words into phrases and phrases into sentences. They must also learn how to form other types of structures such as questions, passives, and relative clauses. Children's acquisition of such structures is gradual, but rapid.

## Stages of Acquisition

Children's ability to combine words into rudimentary sentences proceeds in a very orderly fashion. Three stages can be identified.

⇒ **One-Word Stage.**   In this stage, children's sentences typically consist of a single word called a holophrase. This word expresses the meaning of an entire sentence in adult speech. See table 10.16 on p. 346 for some typical examples of children's holophrases and their meanings. The meanings associated with holophrases are usually identified as semantic relations (e.g., agent of an action, location, etc.).

⇒ **Two-Word Stage.**   In this stage, children's sentences typically consist of two words. See table 10.17 on p. 346 for some typical examples of children's two-word sentences and the semantic relations they express.

⇒ **Telegraphic Stage.**   In this stage, children begin to produce sentences that are longer and more complex. During this stage, children's sentences lack grammatical morphemes such as inflectional affixes and function (non-lexical) words. That is, they consist primarily of content, or lexical, words.

**Exercise!**   Two-year-old Charlie saw his father come in the door and said, "Daddy home." He also watched *Sesame Street* on television and said, "Grover leave," "Ernie funny," and "Tickle Elmo." These utterances are representative of his speech. Answer the following questions regarding Charlie's speech.

1.  What stage of syntactic acquisition is Charlie at?

2.  What is the name of the stage previous to the one Charlie is currently at?

3.  What is the name of the stage after the one Charlie is currently at?

4.  What are the semantic relations evident in Charlie's sentences?

**Remember!**   When children are in the one-word stage, the word they select to express their intended meaning is typically the most informative word in the sentence. So if a child wants to say *I want a cookie,* the child's one-word sentence will probably be *cookie* and not *want*.

### Later Development

Children also acquire the ability to perform syntactic operations that move words and phrases to other positions in the sentence. These operations can be used to create *yes-no* and *wh* questions.

⇒ *Yes-No* **Questions.** This type of question (e.g., *Can we go to the park?*) is formed using Inversion. Being able to apply Inversion requires auxiliary verbs (e.g., *can*).

- Before children acquire auxiliary verbs, they form questions using statements with rising intonation (e.g., *We go park?*).
- After children acquire auxiliary verbs, they are able to move auxiliary verbs to before the subject. However, children may not always move auxiliary verbs when they are first acquired (e.g., *We can go park?*).

⇒ *Wh* **Questions.** This type of question (e.g., *Where are we going?*) is formed using *Wh* Movement and Inversion. Being able to apply *Wh* Movement requires *wh* words.

- Children acquire the *wh* words *what* and *where* first. *Who, how,* and *why* are usually next. *When, which,* and *whose* are generally later acquisitions.
- Children may first use *wh* words outside the sentence (e.g., *Where going? What doing?*). This corresponds to a stage when children have not yet acquired auxiliary verbs.
- Children may initially apply *Wh* Movement without applying Inversion (e.g., *Where we are going?*).

**Try This!**   Examine the following child language data and answer the questions that follow.

> I can't do it.
> Can you feed me?
> What you can feed me?
> I like carrots.
> Baby should eat lunch too.
> Where Baby is?
> I'm eating.
> Can we go now?

Has the child acquired auxiliary verbs? Can the child apply Inversion? Does Inversion happen in both *yes-no* and *wh* questions in the child's speech, or only in *yes-no* questions? You might want to first identify which of the questions are *yes-no* questions and which are *wh* questions. Remember, there are two types of auxiliary verbs: modal and non-modal.

### Sentence Structure Interpretation

Sometimes the meaning of a sentence is related to its syntactic structure. Two such structures are passive sentences and structures with pronominals and reflexives. The relationship between sentence structure and meaning in adult speech for these structures is outlined in Chapter 6.

⇒ **Passives.** Children have a hard time interpreting passive sentences such as *The mouse was chased by the cat.* This is most likely because children expect the first noun phrase in a sentence to be the agent (doer) of the action. In a passive sentence, this is not so: the first noun phrase is the theme (receiver) of the action.

⇒ **Pronominals and Reflexives.** This refers to the distinction, for example, between *me* and *myself,* as in the sentences *You hurt me* and *I hurt myself. Me* is a pronominal, while *myself* is a reflexive. See Chapter 6 for details on the structural difference between these two types of words. As far as language acquisition goes, children make few errors either in understanding or in using these structures.

**Now ...** How would children interpret the sentence *The elephant kisses the lion*? Which noun phrase is doing the action? How would children interpret the sentence *The elephant is kissed by the lion*? Which noun phrase is doing the action? Is this the same as in the first sentence? What strategy is the child using to interpret the sentences?

# FACTORS INFLUENCING ACQUISITION

Some factors that might have an influence on how children acquire language include the following.

⇒ **Adult Speech.** Adults sometimes modify their speech when talking to children. This type of speech is called caregiver speech. See table 10.21 on p. 353 for some features of caregiver speech. While these characteristics may be helpful in acquiring language, they are not necessary to acquire language.

⇒ **Feedback.** Adults also provide feedback to children. Adults may correct children's grammatical errors. They may also repeat the child's utterance, making adjustments to its grammatical structure. But correcting children's grammatical errors has little effect. While adjusting children's utterances may have some effect, the link between these adjustments and language acquisition is still unclear.

⇒ **Cognitive Development.** It does not appear to be the case that the acquisition of language follows from general cognitive development.

⇒ **Inborn Knowledge.** Children may be born with knowledge of the categories, operations, and principles common to all languages (i.e., Universal Grammar). If this is the case, children would only have to learn certain aspects of language (e.g., word order), and they would do this using information available in the input data.

**Think ...** Syntactic development is quite rapid once children are in the telegraphic stage. Children quickly progress from two- and three-word sentences to a variety of morphologically and syntactically complex sentences (see table 10.19 on p. 349 for some examples). Which of the above factors do you think provides the best explanation for the speed of first language acquisition?

Finally, there may be a critical period for language acquisition. This is a period within which children must be exposed to language for normal language development to take place. Individuals not exposed to language during this period typically do not fully acquire grammatical knowledge.

**Think ...** How would having inborn knowledge of language account for such cases?

## REVIEW EXERCISES

1.  Identify the phonetic processes in each of the following child pronunciations.

    a.  sky:       [skaj]   →   [kaj]   _____

    b.  laugh:     [læf]    →   [wæp]   _____

    c.  twig:      [twɪg]   →   [tɪk]   _____

2.  A child looks at the night sky, points to the full moon, and says "ball." This is an example of _____.

3.  A child looks at a picture of a goat in a book and hears the word *goat*. The child assumes that the word *goat* means an animal. Which meaning-acquisition strategy is the child using? _____.

4.  Give the order in which children acquire the following morphemes: the/a, past tense *-ed*, *-ing*, plural *-s*, and possessive *-'s*. _____
    _____

5.  What are the three stages of syntactic acquisition? What are the characteristics of children's typical sentences in each stage?

**STAGE**                              **CHARACTERISTICS**

_____          _____

                                        _____

_____          _____

                                        _____

_____          _____

                                        _____

---

**REVIEW! REVIEW!**   Make sure you know ...

–   the difference between naturalistic and experimental studies
–   what babbling is
–   how to identify children's phonetic processes
–   the strategies children use to acquire meaning
–   the different types of meaning errors children make
–   what overgeneralizations are
–   the determining factors affecting the acquisition of grammatical morphemes
–   how children acquire derivation and compounding
–   the different stages of syntactic acquisition
–   how children acquire Inversion and *wh* questions
–   the different factors that may influence language acquisition

# QUESTIONS?  PROBLEMS?  DIFFICULTIES?

_____

_____

_____

_____

_____

_____

_____

_____

_____

_____

# CHAPTER 11.
# SECOND LANGUAGE ACQUISITION

The field of second language acquisition examines how people acquire a language other than their first language. Important topics and concepts found in this chapter include the following:

1. Communicative competence
2. Interlanguage
3. Role of the first and second language
4. Second language phonology
5. Second language syntax
6. Second language morphology
7. Factors influencing second language acquisition
8. The second language classroom
9. Bilingual education

## COMMUNICATIVE COMPETENCE

Communicative competence refers to the linguistic and social rules that a speaker needs in order to successfully communicate in a particular language. Many different aspects together make up communicative competence. Four of these components are outlined below.

⇒ **Grammatical competence.** This refers to knowledge of phonetics, phonology, morphology, syntax, and semantics. A second language (L2) learner needs to acquire these core components of a grammar.

⇒ **Textual competence.** This refers to knowledge of how to put sentences together to form a larger text. An L2 learner needs to be able to organize and link sentences together to form a cohesive whole.

⇒ **Sociolinguistic competence.** This refers to knowledge of how to produce and comprehend different social dialects. A social dialect is a variety of language that is appropriate to a particular context (e.g., formal or informal situations). L2 learners need to be able to use language in a way that is appropriate to a particular social situation.

⇒ **Illocutionary competence.** This refers to knowledge of a speaker's intent in producing a sentence. An L2 learner needs to be able to comprehend a speaker's intent and to produce sentences that convey a particular intent in a particular social situation.

See figure 11.2 on p. 366 for how these different types of competency are part of a larger model of communicative competence.

**Remember!** Models of communicative competence are important in studying second language acquisition. They allow for the following:

- the measuring of second language knowledge and ability
- the construction of second language proficiency tests
- the design of balanced second language classrooms

## Try This!

1. An L2 learner of English may say, "I went to the store. I bought some apples. They tasted great. I will go back to the store. I will buy some more." Such sentences indicate that the learner has not yet acquired what type of competence?

2. Suppose someone said: "It would be amazing if you could get him to work for you." If an L2 learner only interpreted this statement as positive, what type of competence has the learner not yet fully acquired?

# INTERLANGUAGE

Communicative competence is the final state (i.e., the ultimate goal) when acquiring a second language. The initial state is the first language: adults acquiring a second language have already acquired their first, or native, language. Interlanguage (IL) refers to the intermediate state between the first (L1) and second language (L2).

Here are some important things to keep in mind about interlanguages.

⇒ **Systematic.** A learner's IL is a mental system of rules and representations: a grammar. The IL grammar will contain features from both the learner's first and second languages.

- Learners will often transfer properties of their first language into their IL grammars. See tables 11.1 and 11.2 on p. 364 for some examples of phonological transfer. See table 11.4 on p. 366 for some examples of lexical, morphological, and syntactic transfer.

- Learners will also use features of their L2 in their IL grammars. See table 11.3 on p. 365 of the text for an example that contains features of both the learner's L1 and L2.

⇒ **Dynamic**. The IL grammar changes as the learner's knowledge of the second language changes.

⇒ **Fossilization.** When a learner's IL grammar stops changing, it is said to have fossilized.

**Think ...** If fossilization happens before the learner has fully acquired all the properties of the L2, the IL grammar will still contain properties of the L1. Will the L2 learner always sound like a native speaker of the L1?

**Practice!**   Learners often transfer aspects of their L1 knowledge to their IL grammars. The use of learners' L1 knowledge in their L2 output can cause errors (sometimes called transfer errors). Each of the following sentences contains this type of error. For each sentence, state which aspect of the learner's L1 grammar is responsible for the error.

1.  I bought some fruits at the store.
2.  I told a funny yoke.
3.  What do you think what George eats?
4.  You need to transport those plants.
5.  What he is trying to say?

---

### REMINDER! REMINDER!

While many errors that L2 learners make are the result of the influence of their first language on their interlanguage, L2 learners make more errors with a particular grammatical structure at some times than at others. This type of variation is often called a performance error. When learners are focused on the form of a particular structure, they make fewer errors than when there are extra processing demands on the learner, such as trying to carry on a conversation in a noisy room.

---

## SECOND LANGUAGE PHONOLOGY

The study of second language phonology examines both the acquisition of phonological properties and the role of markedness in explaining the acquisition process for different learners.

### Acquisition of Phonology

⇒ **Segments.**  Individual languages only use a subset of all possible speech sounds found in the world's languages. Languages will therefore vary in the sounds that they contain. This means that L2 learners will most likely have to learn to produce and perceive some new sounds.

⇒ **Features.**  Sometimes the acquisition of a sound in the L2 that is not in the L1 requires that the learner acquire a particular feature. Features are individual phonetic properties such as voice or continuancy. Sounds are a collection of these features. Since inventories of sounds can differ across languages, so can features. This means that L2 learners may have to learn new features in order to produce and perceive sounds not in their L1. Studies have shown that L2 learners can do this.

⇒ **Syllables.**  Syllable structure can vary across languages. Some languages allow complex onsets and codas (e.g., English), while others do not (e.g., Arabic, Chinese). Languages may also have restrictions on which segments can go into onsets and codas (e.g., Japanese only allows nasal codas). L2 learners will most likely have to learn a new set of restrictions on syllable structure.

⇒ **Stress.** How stress is assigned also differs across languages. For some languages, stress is predictable (always on a particular syllable), while for other languages, it must be learned on a word-by-word basis. L2 learners will probably have to learn a stress pattern that is different from that of their L1.

**Think ...** What kinds of transfer errors might L2 learners make? Think about differences in sounds, syllable structure, and stress between an L1 and an L2. What strategies might L2 learners use when attempting to pronounce words whose phonology is different from their L1? What results if the L2 learners' interlanguage grammars fossilize before the L2 learner fully acquires the phonology of the L1?

### Role of Markedness

Some sounds of language may be harder for the L2 learner to acquire than others. Markedness has been used to explain this difference. Sounds that are more marked are more complex and less common in language than are those that are less marked (see Chapter 8).

There are two different hypotheses regarding the role of markedness in L2 learning.

⇒ **Markedness Differential Hypothesis.** This hypothesis is based on differences in the markedness of a particular property in the L1 and L2. The hypothesis makes two predictions:

- Learners will find it more difficult to learn a property that is more marked in their L2 than is the corresponding property in their L1.
- Learners will find it easier to learn a property that is less marked in their L2 than what is found in their L1.

⇒ **Similarity Differential Hypothesis.** This hypothesis is also based on differences between the L1 and L2, and makes the following prediction:

- Learners will learn a property in their L2 that is unlike what is found in their L1 faster than they will learn a property that is similar to what is found in their L1.

**Think ...** Why would an L2 learner first acquire properties that are different from the L1? Why would they not first acquire properties that are similar?

## Exercise! Exercise!

1.  Long and short vowels are contrastive (i.e., they make a meaning difference) in German, but not in English, which has only contrastive short vowels. Would it be harder for a German speaker to acquire English short vowels, or would it be harder for an English speaker to acquire German long vowels? Think about which is more marked, contrastive long or contrastive short vowels. Remember that languages do not have contrastive long vowels unless they also have contrastive short vowels.

2. Suppose an L2 learner's L1 contains the fricatives / s / and / f /, while the L2 contains, in addition to these sounds, the fricatives / θ / and / x /. Which will the L2 learner learn first, / θ / or / x /? Justify your answer.

3. Consider the difference in how Cantonese and Mandarin speakers would pronounce the following English words.

| English Word | Cantonese Speaker | Mandarin Speaker |
|---|---|---|
| desk | [dɛs] | [dɛs.kə] |
| test | [tɛs] | [tɛs.tə] |
| friend | [frɛn] | [frɛn.də] |
| five | [faj] | [faj.və] |
| league | [li] | [li.gə] |

   a. What strategy is the Cantonese speaker using to pronounce the English words?
   b. What strategy is the Mandarin speaker using to pronounce the English words?
   c. How do these different strategies affect the English word? Think about the syllable structure that results.

4. Suppose a learner's L1 contains the velar sounds / k / and / x /, while the learner's L2 contains, in addition to these sounds, the velar sounds / g / and / ɣ /. Will the learner find it easy to acquire / g / or / ɣ / in the L2? Why? Justify your answer. Think about the markedness relationship between stops and fricatives.

5. In Hungarian, stress is always on the first syllable. Which of the following words would a Hungarian L2 learner of English have difficulty pronouncing like a native English speaker?

| | | | |
|---|---|---|---|
| scorned | macaroni | informative | genius |
| dictate | duplicate | explode | discover |

## SECOND LANGUAGE SYNTAX

Languages differ in the types of syntactic structure they allow. The study of second language syntax examines how learners acquire different syntactic structures and the role of markedness in explaining how they do this. Two examples are outlined below.

### Acquisition of Syntax

⇒ **Null subjects.** Some languages (e.g., French and English) require all sentences to have an overt subject. For example, in English, *He ran home* is grammatical but *(He) ran home*, with an implied subject, is not. Other languages (e.g., Spanish and Italian) allow sentences without a subject, so the Spanish equivalents of both *He ran home* and *(He) ran home* are grammatical. English speakers acquiring Spanish would have to learn that sentences can have an implied subject, while Spanish speakers learning English would have to learn that this is not permissible.

⇒ **Verb Raising.** Verb Raising refers to taking a verb from within the verb phrase and moving, or raising, it to I (see Chapter 5). Languages (e.g., English and French) differ in whether or not verbs can move: English does not allow main verbs to move past adverbs: *He usually runs home* is grammatical in English, but *\*He runs usually home* is not. English speakers learning French would have to learn that structures such as *He runs usually home* are grammatical, while French speakers learning English would have to learn the reverse!

**Role of Markedness**

Markedness can be used to explain learners' difficulty or ease in acquiring L2 syntactic structures. One example of how markedness can do this is the Subset Principle. There are three important aspects to this principle.

⇒ **The subset relationship.** Some grammars are in a subset-superset relationship to each other. Languages in subset A allow fewer grammatical structures (along a particular dimension) than do languages in superset B.

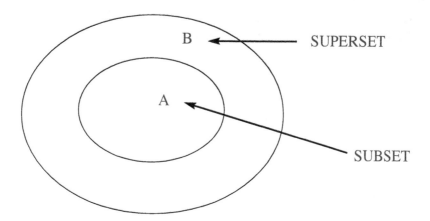

⇒ **The role of evidence.** Learners need evidence to decide whether a language allows or does not allow a particular structure. There are two types of evidence.

  • Positive evidence refers to observations that indicate which structures are possible in a language. For example, hearing sentences with subjects is positive evidence that sentences can have a subject. Positive evidence is usually readily available in the input data.

  • Negative evidence refers to observations that indicate which structures are missing or are not possible in a language. For example, being told that a particular structure is not grammatical in the language constitutes direct negative evidence. Negative evidence can also be indirect: inferring that a particular structure is not possible because no one ever says it.

⇒ **The acquisition task**. Learners whose L1 is the subset language must acquire the superset language. Learners whose L1 is the superset language must acquire the subset language as their L2.

- Moving from the subset (A) to the superset (B) requires positive evidence.
- Moving from the superset (B) to the subset (A) requires negative evidence.

Learners generally find it easier to move from the subset to the superset, since this can be done using positive evidence. See pp. 376 to 378 for an example of how the Subset Principle can be used to explain the acquisition of null subjects by L2 learners of Spanish and Italian, and the acquisition of overt subjects by L2 learners of English and French (whose L1 is Spanish or Italian).

**Try This!**   French and English differ in adverb placement. French allows structures such as *The man is drinking slowly his coffee,* while English does not.

1. Which is the superset language? Which is the subset language?
2. Which learner would require positive evidence? Which would require negative evidence? What might be some examples of the negative evidence that the learner might need.
3. What kinds of errors would you expect a French speaker learning English to make?

## SECOND LANGUAGE MORPHOLOGY

The type and number of grammatical morphemes found in languages can vary. The study of second language morphology examines how learners acquire such differences, along with explanations of how learners do this.

### Acquisition of Morphology

⇒ **Morpheme order.** Adults acquiring English as a second language acquire grammatical morphemes (e.g., *-ing*, plural *-s*, possessive *-'s*, third person singular *-s*, past tense *-ed, the/a,* auxiliary *be*) in a different order than do children acquiring English as a first language. See table 11.7 on p. 378 for the L1 order, and table 11.8 on p. 379 for the L2 order.

### Role of Complexity

For children, factors such as frequency, word position, syllabicity, number of allomorphs, and so on help to determine the order in which grammatical morphemes are acquired.

For adults, differences in complexity may determine acquisition order. Three levels of complexity can be identified.

⇒ The presence of a morpheme is determined by the word itself (least complex).
⇒ The presence of a morpheme is determined by a phrase (more complex).
⇒ The presence of a morpheme is determined by a sentence (most complex).

See figure 11.8 on p. 380 for how the structure of these three levels increases in complexity. Adults usually acquire the least complex structure first.

**Think ...** What level of complexity can explain the occurrence of the past tense *-ed* ending in English? Is this word, phrase, or sentence complexity? Why? Can this type of complexity explain the later occurrence of this ending?

### Morphology and Syntax

One common error that L2 learners make involves omitting inflectional endings such as the past tense *-ed* or the plural *-s*. Two hypotheses attempt to explain this error.

⇒ **The Impaired Representation Hypothesis.** This hypothesis argues that learners lack or have an impaired representation of a particular structure.

⇒ **The Missing Surface Inflection Hypothesis.** This hypothesis argues that learners have the correct representation but have difficulty mapping inflection onto their structures.

Since morphology and syntax are closely related, both of these hypotheses provide possible explanations. This is because the presence of morphological phenomena such as inflection is often dependent on the syntactic structure.

**Think ...** When L2 learners acquire English morphemes, they often make errors such as using *taked* instead of *took* or *haves* instead of *has*. Are these errors similar to the errors children make when acquiring English? If so, could you classify this type of error as a transfer error? Why or why not? If not, how could you classify this type of error?

## FACTORS AFFECTING SECOND LANGUAGE ACQUISITION

There is a great deal of variation in the grammars of second language learners as well as in their overall success in acquiring a second language. Age and individual differences are two factors that may help in accounting for this variation.

⇒ **Age.** Studies have shown that adults can acquire native-like or near native-like syntactic and phonological competence. There is no known biological reason to prevent them from doing so. However, adults may use different learning mechanisms (e.g., general problem-solving skills) than do children (e.g., inborn knowledge).

⇒ **Individual differences.** Differences in the characteristics of learners may have more of a role in explaining differences in success than age. Individuals may vary in their affective and their cognitive characteristics.

- Affective factors include motivation to learn the L2. Learners who want to learn the L2 for a specific goal or reason are instrumentally motivated, while learners who want to learn the L2 to learn more about a culture are integratively motivated. Studies have shown that degree of motivation is more important to success in the L2 than is the type of motivation.

- **Cognitive factors.** L2 learners may be field independent or field dependent. Field-independent learners are more focused on the specific, while field-dependent learners are more focused on the general.

**Think ...** What is the difference between affective and cognitive factors in second language acquisition? Which are more likely to focus on the accuracy of grammatical structures, field-independent or field-dependent learners? Which type of learner is more likely to focus on fluency? Does the successful L2 learner need both accuracy and fluency?

Cognitive factors also include learning and communication strategies. Learning strategies are strategies used to fill gaps in L2 knowledge, while communication strategies are strategies used to keep communication going despite gaps in L2 knowledge. Think of an example of each type of strategy. What is the difference between learning and communication strategies and being either field independent or field dependent?

**Now ...** Think about the relationship between age and phonological acquisition. While L2 learners can achieve native-like pronunciation, this is not the norm. What is the relationship between age and the ability to achieve this? Think about the critical period for acquiring language.

## THE SECOND LANGUAGE CLASSROOM

Adults often acquire a second language in a classroom setting. Three important characteristics of the second language classroom are discussed below.

⇒ **Modified input.** Foreigner talk refers to adjustments native speakers make when talking to second language learners. Teacher talk, a subset of foreigner talk, takes place in the classroom. The goal of teacher talk is to provide comprehensible input to the L2 learner. This is crucial so that students know what is being talked about.

⇒ **Modified interaction.** L2 teachers may use comprehension checks, prompts, and expansions to encourage or help students use the L2. L2 teachers may also use recasts: they may reformulate a learner's incorrect utterance so that it is correct.

⇒ **Focus on form.** Instruction in the L2 typically includes not only instruction on the form of the L2, but also correction of L2 learners' inaccuracies when using the L2.

**Think ...** Why are recasts more useful to more proficient L2 learners than less proficient learners? Why do less proficient learners benefit more from correction than from recasts? Why does correction of the use of lexical items have a greater effect on an L2 learner's IL grammar than the correction of grammatical structures?

## Try This!

1. Give two reasons why the classroom is a good environment in which to learn a second language.
2. Describe what teacher talk involves and why it may not be matched to some L2 learners' language proficiency.
3. Explain three strategies that teachers use to help foster interaction in a second language classroom.
4. Describe three issues that researchers need to think about when considering how a focus on form affects the learning process.

## BILINGUAL EDUCATION

Bilingualism is the study of how children simultaneously acquire two languages. The goal of bilingual education is to produce bilingual children. There are two types of bilingual education.

⇒ **Minority language maintenance programs.** In these programs, children who speak a minority language (e.g., Mandarin) are placed in a classroom setting where they initially receive all of their education in the minority language. Gradually instruction in the majority language (e.g., English) is introduced and increased. Students become bilingual, performing equally well in both the minority and majority languages.

These types of programs are also called Heritage Language Programs or L1 Maintenance Programs.

⇒ **French immersion programs.** These programs involve immersing a student who speaks the majority language (e.g., English) in a program where all instruction is given in a minority language (e.g., French). Children become bilingual, learning both English and French.

French immersion programs are not submersion programs in that an English-speaking student is not placed in a class with native speakers of French. Rather, all students in a French immersion program are native English speakers.

**Think ...** What is a dual-language program? How are these language programs the same or different from minority language maintenance programs? What is an advantage of each type of program?

**REVIEW! REVIEW!**  Make sure you understand the terms and concepts listed below.

- accuracy, fluency
- bilingualism
- communication strategies
- communicative competence
- field independent, field dependent
- impaired representation hypothesis
- immersion programs
- instrumental and integrative motivation
- interlanguage
- learning strategies

- markedness differential hypothesis
- minority language maintenance
- missing surface inflection hypothesis
- negative evidence
- positive evidence
- similarity differential hypothesis
- subset principle
- transfer

## QUESTIONS?  PROBLEMS?  DIFFICULTIES?

_____

_____

_____

_____

_____

_____

_____

_____

_____

_____

# CHAPTER 12.
# PSYCHOLINGUISTICS: THE STUDY OF LANGUAGE PROCESSING

Psycholinguistics is the study of the mechanisms that underlie language processing. Psycholinguists use various techniques to understand how language happens: that is, how the mind breaks down what it reads or hears, and what processes are behind how it puts language together for production. Psycholinguists use various techniques to investigate these mechanisms. Insights provided by psycholinguistic research have confirmed aspects of the structure of language (phonology, morphology, syntax, and semantics) as understood by linguists. Important topics and concepts found in this chapter include the following:

1. Priming
2. Lexical decision task
3. Frequency effect
4. Priming effect
5. Event-related potentials
6. Slips of the tongue
7. Bottom-up processing
8. Top-down processing
9. Psycholinguistic modelling

## METHODS OF PSYCHOLINGUISTIC RESEARCH

Psycholinguists dedicate a lot of time to devising appropriate methods for investigating language processing. Remember that ...

⇒ Language processing is subconscious – we are not aware of the mental activities that make language comprehension and production possible. You do not know how your mind is able to understand the sentence you are reading, how it interprets the characters on a page, or how it interprets sound vibrations as meaningful messages.

⇒ Slips of the tongue (sometimes called spoonerisms) are naturally occurring speech errors. We can gain insight into language production by analyzing speech errors such as slips of the tongue; for example, they tell us that an utterance has to be planned out before it is spoken. The study of phenomena such as slips of the tongue is known as a *field technique*, since the examples can only be observed as speakers naturally produce them (we cannot control their occurrence by experimental methods).

⇒ Because language processing cannot be observed directly, the investigation of language processing is challenging for researchers. Psycholinguists design experiments that enable them to control as much as possible the conditions under which language processing happens. In this way, they can indirectly gain an understanding of the cognitive operations that underpin language processing.

## EXPERIMENTAL METHODS

Various experimental paradigms are discussed in Chapter 12. Some methods are more suitable for investigations into particular aspects of language processing. You should be familiar with the following concepts and terms:

| TERM | DEFINITION |
|---|---|
| lexical decision task | An experimental paradigm in which a participant indicates whether or not a word on a computer screen (the stimulus) is a real word in his/her language by pressing a button. |
| response latency | One of the two items typically measured (dependent variables) in a lexical decision task. Response latency refers to the time (in milliseconds) that it takes for the participant to respond to the stimulus. |
| response accuracy | One of the two items typically measured (dependent variables) in a lexical decision task. Response accuracy measures the correctness of a participant's responses to stimuli. |
| frequency effect | The experimental finding (in a lexical decision task) that participants respond more quickly to more frequently occurring words than to less common words. We understand from this that we process frequent words more quickly (have easier access to them). |
| priming effect | The experimental finding that participants respond more quickly to a word (target) if they have first been exposed to a semantically related word (prime). The word *student* is said to prime the word *teacher*. |
| spreading activation | The process related to the priming effect. When a participant is exposed to a prime, the prime 'activates' not only that word, but other words associated with it (the activation 'spreads' to related lexical items). The activation of the prime *student* results in the activation of the target *teacher*. |
| ERP | Event-related potential (ERP) experiments measure changes in the electrical activity in the brain. The electrical activity is monitored by electrodes placed on the scalp. Changes in the electrical activity, in response to a specific auditory or written stimulus, are recorded and calculated. The electrical potentials related to the stimulus (event) are separated from 'background noise' and presented as wave forms that display negative and positive voltage, and the intervening time (in milliseconds) between the stimulus and the effect. |
| N400 | The N400 refers to a negative (voltage) peak at 400 milliseconds. The N400 ERP peak has been very well studied: a negative peak is observed at 400 milliseconds after the presentation of a semantically anomalous stimulus. The more semantically anomalous the stimulus, the greater the (voltage) effect as measured by the N400 peak. |

**Exercise!**  See how many details about experimental methods in psycholinguistics you can recall. Complete the following statements, based on the discussion on pp. 399 to 407.

1. Native speakers take less than a third of second to recognize a _____.
2. Experimental findings and tip-of-the-tongue phenomena suggest that the _____ must be flexible.
3. The average adult reads at a rate of _____ words per minute.
4. Two common methods for exploring how words are organized and accessed are the lexical decision task and _____.
5. The response time for more frequently used words is _____ milliseconds.
6. Psycholinguists have found that participants take more time to reject _____ non-words.
7. _____ have been found not only for words that are associated semantically, but for morphologically and phonologically related words.
8. The type of automatic computation that is thought to be at the core of sentence processing is called _____.
9. Sentence-processing experiments show that participants have longer bar-pressing times when processing _____ and _____.
10. Eye-tracking experiments have shown that difficult sentences result in participants having longer fixation times and significantly more _____ .

**Now ...**  Imagine that you are preparing a priming experiment in which you would like to investigate if the responses of non-native speakers of English are similar to those of native speakers. In order to explore the effects of a semantically related word, you will also need to compare response latency and response accuracy when you give a semantically unrelated word. Below are the target words for your experiment. Provide an example of a semantically related prime and an unrelated prime. Compare your answers to those of your classmates. How similar are your responses?

| Target | Semantically related prime | Unrelated prime |
|---|---|---|
| paper | | |
| nurse | | |
| floor | | |
| train | | |
| pear | | |
| leaf | | |
| foot | | |
| photo | | |

**Try This!**  Consider the following examples, many of which are semantically anomalous. Imagine that you are preparing an ERP experiment. Indicate which sentences you would expect to provoke a **positive ERP** response (because they do not contain a semantic anomaly); which would produce a **moderate N400** response (they are semantically anomalous and not what we would anticipate); and which would produce a **large N400** response (they are semantically highly anomalous and very much unanticipated). Place a P (positive), M (moderate), or L (large) next to each sentence.

1. Would you like some freshly squeezed coffee?
2. The book is on the large desk.
3. The juice is in the oven.
4. It was too late to call.
5. He was asked a question by a fish.
6. I spoke to her jar.
7. The poodle didn't finish the wine.
8. I study linguistics and fruit.

**Think ...** It is mentioned in Chapter 12 that some studies have shown that syntactic anomaly results in the P600 wave (a positive peak at 600 milliseconds after a syntactically anomalous stimulus). We would expect that a sentence that is both syntactically and semantically anomalous would provoke both the P600 and N400 ERP signature waves. If this were the case, what would this tell us about semantic and syntactic processing?

## LANGUAGE PROCESSING AND LINGUISTICS

Experimental findings in psycholinguistics support many of the concepts and units that linguists use to describe phonology, morphology, syntax, and semantics, such as features, phonemes, syllables, roots, affixes, verb phrases, noun phrases, and structural ambiguity. Make sure that you are familiar with any new terminology presented in this section, including the following terms:

| parsing | Parsing is the automatic process that segments sentences presented in linear strings and arranges them into hierarchically organized structures. |
|---|---|
| bottom-up processing | In bottom-up processing, a listener or reader builds up larger units incrementally through the analysis of the smaller units (e.g., phonemes) as they unfold. This is sometimes referred to as *lower-level processing*. Bottom-up processing interacts with top-down processing. |
| top-down processing | In top-down processing, a listener or reader uses their expectations (based on conceptual and/or contextual knowledge) to interpret what is being said or read as it unfolds. This is sometimes called *higher-level processing*. Top-down processing interacts with bottom-up processing. |
| cohort model | According to the cohort model, listeners retrieve from the mental lexicon all the words (a cohort) that correspond to the sequence of sounds unfolding in the speech signal. This process takes place until a uniqueness point in the word is reached: that is, until there are no further matches in the mental lexicon. |

**Exercise!**   How many details about language processing and linguistics can you recall? Indicate whether the following statements, based on the discussion on pp. 407 to 416, are true or false.

1.  According to the post-lexical decomposition view, whole-word access occurs after the activation of constituent morphemes (morphological parsing).
2.  The cohort model suggests that the phoneme is a fundamental unit of word recognition.
3.  Phonological features are at the core of top-down processing.
4.  Lexical decision experiments have shown that in the case of words that have more than one meaning, priming effects are present even for the meaning(s) not favoured by the context.
5.  In fact, experiments have shown that the priming effects discussed in the previous question (the activation of all meanings of a word) last for a significant period of time.
6.  Experimental findings suggest that processing times for morphologically permissible (legal) and morphologically impermissible nonsense words are the same.
7.  Garden path effects are said to result in part from the principle of minimal attachment: Assume (or build) a simple syntactic structure if possible.
8.  There is a direct correlation between syntactic complexity and processing (parsing) difficulty.

**Try This!**   Many slips of the tongue tell us something about how we assemble the parts of an utterance. The assemblage errors provide clues to how language is organized. The following slips of the tongue provide evidence for the existence of particular linguistic units (e.g., morphemes, phonological features). Identify the linguistic units.

1.  animals and teddy bears → anibals and teddy mears
2.  spoon feeding → foon speeding
3.  bake the cookies → cake the bookies
4.  I spoke to Sam and Bill. → I spoke to Zam and Pill.
5.  The charges were filed. → The files were charged.
6.  reading list → leading rist
7.  It's been done quickly enough. → It's been done quick enoughly.
8.  cognitive modeling → cognitive moleding

**Now ...**   According to the cohort model, we reduce the number of words in a cohort until we find a uniqueness or recognition point: that is, until all 'competitors' are eliminated, and only one match remains (the target word). For each of the following lexical items, indicate what occurs according to the cohort model, as shown in the first example.

| Target | Possible cohort after first two phonemes | Uniqueness/recognition point |
|---|---|---|
| victimize | video, victor, vigor, villa, vinegar, vim | victim**i**ze (*no more competitors after phoneme* /aj/) |
| sheep | | |
| medication | | |
| badminton | | |
| kneecap | | |

**Think ...** You are preparing the stimuli for an experiment whose aim is to compare your participants' responses to nonsense words to responses discussed in psycholinguistic studies. In this experiment, you are interested in selectional restrictions and the role they play in the processing of new, morphologically complex words. Below, you will find four new nonsense roots (two nouns and two verbs), followed by several examples containing derivational affixes that have been attached to those roots. Write GD (greater difficulty) next to the words you anticipate will present greater processing difficulty for your participants. If you need to review English derivational affixes, see Chapter 4. After completing the table, answer the questions that follow.

**new nouns:** *mern, jat*
**new verbs:** *flum, strod*

| New form | GD? | New form | GD? |
|---|---|---|---|
| strodable | | unmern | |
| flumly | | flumer | |
| mernful | | deflum | |
| jatish | | merner | |
| jatless | | reflum | |
| jatness | | strodful | |
| ex-mern | | reflumness | |
| reflumable | | mis-strod | |

1. Explain why you anticipate that the words you've labeled GD would present greater processing difficulty.
2. Identify a phonological factor that may affect participants' responses.
3. Name an additional morphological factor that may affect participants' responses.

**Exercise!** Read the following garden path sentences. For each example, indicate where the misanalysis occurs, as shown in the example. Then rewrite the sentence so that it would be easier to process.

Example: He confessed his crimes harmed many people.
**Reason for misanalysis**: The reader interprets *his crimes* as the complement (direct object) of the verb *confessed* rather than the subject NP of the VP *harmed*.
**Rewritten form**: He confessed that his crimes (had) harmed many people.

1.  The student forgot the answers were in the back of the book.

    **Reason for misanalysis**: _____

    _____

    **Rewritten form**: _____

2.  The defendant questioned swore he was innocent.

    **Reason for misanalysis**: _____

    _____

    **Rewritten form**: _____

3.  After Pat ate the chicken turned out to be bad.

    **Reason for misanalysis**: _____

    _____

    **Rewritten form**: _____

4.  Without her donations failed to appear.

    **Reason for misanalysis**: _____

    _____

    **Rewritten form**: _____

5.  While Anna dressed the baby splashed in the bathtub.

    **Reason for misanalysis**: _____

    _____

    **Rewritten form**: _____

**Think ...** Two principles of parsing are put forward in the chapter to explain the difficulty we have with garden path sentences: late closure and minimal attachment. Here are the sentences from the previous exercise. Explain what *principally* motivates the garden path effects in each case: late closure, minimal attachment, or both.

1. The student forgot the answers were in the back of the book. _____
2. The defendant questioned swore he was innocent. _____
3. After Pat ate the chicken turned out to be bad. _____
4. Without her donations failed to appear. _____
5. While Anna dressed the baby splashed in the bathtub. _____

**Now ...** For each of the following sentences, draw tree diagrams that show (a) the garden path effects and (b) the correct interpretation.

1. The defendant questioned swore he was innocent.
2. The student forgot the answers were in the back of the book.

## PSYCHOLINGUISTIC MODELLING

Psycholinguistic models are diagrammatic representations of what is believed to occur during language processing. Diagrammatic representations are meant to simplify and summarize many findings and to generate hypotheses about language processing.

**Exercise!** Test your knowledge about psycholinguistic modelling by answering the following questions.

1. What model of language production and perception hypothesizes that different levels of processing – phonological, syntactic, and semantic – operate simultaneously?
2. What model of language processing hypothesizes that comprehension operates in stages: that is, that smaller units, such as phonological features, are progressively transformed into larger units (words and syntactic structures)?
3. Which type of processing model better handles bottom-up processing?
4. What do we call any processing model that hypothesizes that at least two competing mechanisms are operational in any processing task?
5. What competing mechanisms are understood to underpin the processing of multimorphemic words?
6. What do we call models of language processing that depend on abstract structural concepts such as features, phonemes, phonological rules, and syntactic categories?
7. What is the term for models of language processing that consist of multiple associations that link simple processing units (based on a representation of the transmission of information via neural networks in the brain)?
8. Draw your own parallel processing model.
9. Draw your own serial processing model.
10. Draw symbolic and connectionist representations for the words *love* and *live*.

# CHAPTER 13.
# BRAIN AND LANGUAGE

Neurolinguistics is a subfield of linguistics that studies the relationship between the brain and language. Important terms and concepts in this chapter include the following:

1. The cerebral cortex
2. The cerebral hemispheres
3. The lobes of the cerebral hemispheres
4. Autopsy studies
5. Studies of the living brain
6. Dichotic listening tasks
7. Split brain studies
8. Fluent and non-fluent aphasia

## BRAIN STRUCTURES AND ORGANIZATION

The brain consists of lower and higher structures. Lower brain structures are common to almost all animals and control functions essential to survival (e.g., respiration). The lower brain structures comprise the brain stem and the cerebellum. The cerebral cortex constitutes the higher brain structure, and it is this structure that is responsible for language processing and so much more!

⇒ **Cerebral cortex.** The cerebral cortex is a wrinkled grey mass that sits on top of the lower brain structures. It gets its wrinkled appearance from being folded in upon itself many, many times.

- Sulci (singular: sulcus): Areas where the cerebral cortex is folded in – the hidden areas
- Gyri (singular: gyrus): Areas where the cerebral cortex is folded out toward the surface – the visible folds
- Fissures: Very deep sulci

⇒ **Cerebral hemispheres.** The cerebral cortex is divided into two hemispheres, the left and the right. See figure 13.1 on p. 426 for an illustration of how the longitudinal fissure separates the cerebral cortex into the left and right brains.

- Lateralization refers to the fact that each hemisphere is associated with distinct cognitive functions. The left brain tends to be more involved in analytical tasks, while the right brain tends to be more involved in tasks that require more holistic processing.

- Contralateralization refers to the fact that each hemisphere is responsible for movement and sensation on the opposite side of the body. That is, the left hemisphere controls the right side of the body, while the right hemisphere controls the left side of the body.

The corpus callosum joins the two hemispheres together, allowing them to communicate with each other. See figure 13.2 on p. 427 for an illustration of the lower and higher brain structures as well as the corpus callosum.

⇒ **Lobes of the cerebral hemispheres.** Each hemisphere is divided into four lobes: frontal, temporal, parietal, and occipital. Each hemispheric lobe is associated with its own specialized function. See figure 13.3 on p. 428 for the location of the four hemispheric lobes and the functions associated with each.

**Reminder!** While a specific function might be lateralized within a particular hemisphere, we actually use both hemispheres for most things we do. For example, for most right-handed individuals, language is lateralized in the left hemisphere. However, the right hemisphere is also used in everyday language processing. We need the right brain so that we can correctly interpret prosodic cues such as loudness and intonation, which tell us whether someone is angry or not.

**Colour Your Brain!** Using different colours, shade in the four lobes found in each cerebral hemisphere. Label each lobe. Label the folds of the brain that separate the different lobes: the lateral fissure, the central sulcus, and the angular gyrus.

# EVIDENCE FOR BRAIN ORGANIZATION

There are at least three different techniques for investigating how the brain represents, organizes, and processes language.

⇒ **Autopsy studies.** This is the oldest, and until recently, the only way to investigate brain organization. This technique involves observing individuals with a brain injury, recording their deficits, and upon death, examining their brains to determine which areas were damaged. Researchers then make correlations between the deficit and the damaged area of the brain.

⇒ **Studies of the living brain.** This technique investigates the living brain. Examples of this type of study include the following:

- computerized axial tomography (CT scanning)
- positron emission tomography (PET scan)
- functional magnetic resonance imaging (fMRI)
- magnetoencephalography (MEG)

These techniques typically require specialized and expensive equipment.

⇒ **Hemispheric connections.** This technique also investigates the living brain, but does so by examining the type of behaviour that can be associated with a particular hemisphere.

- In a dichotic listening task, subjects are presented with different stimuli to both ears at the same time and must report which they hear first. Typically, the right ear shows an advantage for words, while the left ear shows an advantage for the perception of melodies and other sounds.

- Split brain studies examine the cognitive functions of individuals who have had their corpus callosum surgically cut. When the corpus callosum is cut, the two hemispheres of the brain can no longer communicate with each other. This means that information from the left side of the body goes to the right hemisphere and stays there. Similarly, information from the right side of the body goes to the left hemisphere and stays there.

Both dichotic listening tasks and split brain studies are based on contralateralization: the control of each hemisphere of the brain by the opposite side of the body.

**Think ...** Investigations of the brain have revealed a great deal about how the brain represents and organizes language. For example, autopsy studies have revealed that the frontal lobe is involved in speech production. PET scans have also revealed that blood flows to this area during speech. See figure 13.5 on p. 431 for an illustration of the differences in blood flow when hearing words, seeing words, speaking words, and generating words. Does this mean that all language is processed in the same area of the brain, or are different areas of the brain involved in different language tasks?

## Try This!

1. The sound of a cat meowing is presented to the right ear of a subject, while the sound of a car engine is presented to the left ear. Assume that the subject is a normal, healthy right-handed individual. Which sound will the subject report hearing first? Explain why in terms of brain structure and organization. What about when the sounds are reversed (i.e., the cat meowing in the left ear and the car engine in the right ear)?

2. The sound of the word *lamp* is presented to the right ear of a subject, while the sound of the word *frog* is presented to the left ear. Assume that the subject is a normal, healthy right-handed individual. Which word will the subject report hearing first? Explain why in terms of brain structure and organization.

3. Assume that the subject undergoing the test in (1) and (2) is a split brain patient. The subject will no longer be able to process both sounds. Which sound in (1) will the subject no longer be able to process and interpret? What about in (2)? For both instances, explain why in terms of brain structure and organization.

## LANGUAGE PROCESSING

The different techniques for studying the brain, whether living or not, all reveal that the left hemisphere is generally responsible for language and that within the left hemisphere, there are a number of specific areas dedicated to language representation and processing. The major areas of the brain involved in language representation and processing include the following:

⇒ **Broca's area.** This area is located in the frontal lobe of the left hemisphere (for most individuals) and is primarily responsible for speech production.

⇒ **Wernicke's area.** This area is located in the temporal lobe of the left hemisphere (for most individuals) and is primarily responsible for comprehension.

⇒ **Angular gyrus.** This is a visible fold of the cerebral cortex in the parietal lobe and is involved in reading.

See figure 13.4 on p. 429 for the approximate location of each of these language areas. Both Broca's area and Wernicke's area were discovered through autopsy studies.

In addition to these dedicated language areas, three cortical areas of the brain are also involved in processing language.

⇒ **Auditory cortex.** This is located in the temporal lobe of each hemisphere and is responsible for processing auditory input.

⇒ **Visual cortex.** This is located in the occipital lobe of each hemisphere and is responsible for processing visual input.

⇒ **Motor cortex.** This is located in the frontal lobe of each hemisphere and is responsible for movement.

**Colour Your Brain!** Using different colours, shade in the approximate locations of Broca's area, Wernicke's area, the angular gyrus, the primary visual cortex, the primary auditory cortex, and the primary motor cortex. Label each of these areas.

**Think ...** Is brain organization random? The motor cortex, responsible for movement, is located in the frontal lobe, as is Broca's area, which is responsible for speech production. The visual cortex, in the occipital lobe, is located near the angular gyrus, which is used in reading. The auditory cortex, in the temporal lobe, is located near Wernicke's area, which is responsible for comprehension, both oral and written. Brain organization is not random!

## BRAIN SCENARIOS

Since the motor cortex, auditory cortex, and visual cortex are also involved in processing language, a person could, in theory, experience language difficulties without actually damaging the main language areas.

Consider each of the following scenarios. Assume that the individual named in each is an otherwise normal right-handed person. For each scenario, answer the question in terms of the structures and properties of the brain.

1. Hilda has had a stroke during the night that destroyed her right visual cortex as well as her corpus callosum. Will she be able to read in the morning?
2. Ronald was in an accident that destroyed only his left auditory cortex. Can he still hear and understand language?
3. Hillary received a blow to the head that destroyed her left visual cortex as well as her corpus callosum. Will she still be able to read?
4. Thomas is a split brain patient. If he holds a spoon in his left hand without having seen it, will he be able to name it? Will he be able to draw it? If so, with which hand(s)?

# APHASIA

Aphasia refers to the loss of language ability due to damage to the brain. Stroke, head injuries, infections, brain tumours, and brain hemorrhage are some of the causes of aphasia. Patients with aphasia typically all experience some difficulty in speaking, listening, writing, and reading. The amount of difficulty depends on where the damage is and the extent of the damage.

Some types of aphasia involve more specific language loss such that some skills are lost and others remain intact. These incidences are of interest to neurolinguists, as they can tell us much about how the brain represents and processes language.

⇒ **Non-fluent aphasia.** This type of aphasia results from damage to parts of the brain in front of the central sulcus. This area of the brain contains Broca's area, which is responsible for speech production. Damage can result in Broca's aphasia, which has the following characteristics:

- slow, halting speech
- lack of normal sentence intonation (dysprosody)
- speech errors, such as the simplification of consonant clusters (phonemic paraphasia)
- the omission of functional words and inflectional affixes
- difficulty determining the grammaticality of sentences
- difficulty comprehending certain types of syntactic structures, such as passives

The word *agrammatism* is often used to refer to the omission of function words and inflectional affixes, combined with difficulty in comprehension related to syntactic structure. This term simply means that the patient has lost grammatical ability.

**Now ...** An active sentence and its passive counterpart are paraphrases of each other in that they have the same meaning. Cross out the words and endings that a Broca's aphasic would have difficulty processing in the following active sentence and passive sentence.

The flies bothered the boy.
The boy was bothered by the flies.

Do the sentences have the same meaning for someone suffering from Broca's aphasia? Why would a Broca's aphasic still be able to identify the correct meaning of the passive (second) sentence? Why would a Broca's aphasic be unsure of the meaning if the sentence was *The boy was bothered by the girl*?

⇒ **Fluent aphasia.** This type of aphasia results from damage to the left cortex of the brain behind the central sulcus. This area of the brain contains Wernicke's area, which is responsible for language comprehension. Damage can result in Wernicke's aphasia. A Wernicke's aphasic will have no difficulty in producing speech or in using intonation, and will not omit function words and inflectional affixes.

Instead, Wernicke's aphasics will have trouble putting together sentences that make sense and understanding the speech directed at them. This means that they probably will not be able to respond appropriately to questions and that their sentences will be unrelated to each other (and to sentences of other speakers) in a conversation.

⇒ **Relationship to linguistic theory.**  Aphasia provides theoretical linguists with an opportunity to test theories about the structure of language. This type of research has provided evidence for phonological structures such as features, rules, and processes, along with the morphological distinction between inflection and derivation. It also raises questions about the nature of function words and syntactic theory, indicating that more research into these areas is necessary.

**Reminder!**   Broca's and Wernicke's aphasia are not the only types of non-fluent and fluent aphasia. Both are less severe types of aphasia. More severe types of non-fluent and fluent aphasia include global aphasia and jargon aphasia, respectively.

## Exercise!

1.  Circle the word that a Broca's aphasic will have more trouble producing. Justify your choice.

    tallest (as in *Jeff is the tallest man in his family.*)
    beautiful (as in *Gloria is very beautiful.*)

2.  Each of the sentences below is passive. For each, give the meaning that a Broca's aphasic would assign to the sentence or specify that a Broca's aphasic would be unable to assign a meaning.

    a.  The dog was broken by the window.
    b.  The leopard was eaten by the tiger.
    c.  The bear was chased by the man.

3.  Suppose you asked a Wernicke's aphasic, "What time is it?" How might he or she respond to this question?

## ACQUIRED DYSLEXIA AND DYSGRAPHIA

Brain trauma can also cause impairments in reading (acquired dyslexia) and writing (acquired dysgraphia). These impairments can occur in conjunction with Broca's and Wernicke's aphasia. Acquired dyslexia can also occur as the only language deficit.

⇒ **In conjunction with aphasia.**  People with either Broca's or Wernicke's aphasia exhibit the same difficulties with reading and writing as they do with spoken language.

• Broca's aphasics will not be able to spell all words correctly. They will also omit function words and inflectional affixes in their writing. Broca's aphasics will not have trouble reading silently but will have difficulties reading aloud.

- Wernicke's aphasics will not have any difficulty spelling, but what they write will not make much sense. They will also have difficulty in comprehending written language.

⇒ **As the only language deficit.**   This occurs when the angular gyrus is damaged. There are two types of acquired dyslexia: phonological dyslexia and surface dyslexia.

- Patients with phonological dyslexia can only read words they have seen before. This is because they have lost the ability to use spelling-to-sound rules, which we use to read new words aloud.

- In contrast, patients with surface dyslexia must use spelling-to-sound rules for all words. They have lost the ability to recognize words as whole units. They will also have difficulty in understanding irregularly spelled words.

**Think ...** In words such as *through* and *light*, the 'gh' is silent. What about in the word *ghost?* What difficulties might this cause for someone with surface dyslexia? Think of examples where the same letter or combination of letters corresponds to different sounds. What difficulties would this cause for someone with surface dyslexia?

---

## WHAT ABOUT WORDS?

All types of aphasia typically include difficulties in finding words. So where are words located in the brain? Different kinds of words (e.g., nouns and verbs) might actually be represented in different parts of the brain! Words may also be represented as a network of linguistic and non-linguistic associations. See figure 13.6 on p. 442 for an example of a difference in the representation of action-related and vision-related words.

---

## Exercises! Exercises!

1. For each area of the brain listed below, identify its location in the brain and state its role in language processing.

| AREA OF THE BRAIN | LOCATION IN THE BRAIN | ROLE IN LANGUAGE PROCESSING |
|---|---|---|
| Broca's area | | |
| Wernicke's area | | |
| angular gyrus | | |
| auditory cortex | | |
| visual cortex | | |
| motor cortex | | |

2.  What is the difference between fluent and non-fluent aphasia?

3.  Name one general characteristic of each of the following types of aphasia.

Broca's aphasia

Wernicke's aphasia

acquired dyslexia

4.  What is the difference between phonological and surface dyslexia?

---

**REVIEW! REVIEW!** Make sure you understand the terms and concepts listed below.

- acquired dyslexia/dysgraphia
- agrammatism
- angular gyrus
- autopsy and living brain studies
- Broca's aphasia
- cerebral cortex
- corpus callosum
- dichotic listening tasks
- dysprosody
- fluent (sensory) aphasia

- hemispheric lobes (four)
- left and right cerebral hemispheres
- non-fluent (motor) aphasia
- phonemic paraphasia
- phonological dyslexia
- split brain studies
- sulci, gyri, and fissures
- surface dyslexia
- Wernicke's aphasia

# QUESTIONS? PROBLEMS? DIFFICULTIES?

_____

_____

_____

_____

_____

_____

_____

_____

_____

_____

# CHAPTER 14.
# LANGUAGE IN SOCIAL CONTEXTS

Sociolinguistics is the systematic study of the relationship between language and society. Sociolinguists explore the many ways in which languages display variation and what motivates the variation. Important topics and concepts found in this chapter include the following:

1. Speech variety
2. Dialectology and dialect geography
3. The sociolinguistic variable
4. Variable rules or constraints
5. Apparent-time versus real-time methods
6. Code switching
7. Borrowing
8. Language contact
9. Pidgins and creoles
10. Overt and covert prestige
11. Discourse analysis
12. Ethnography of communication
13. Linguistic accommodation
14. Diglossia
15. Language planning

## SPEECH VARIETY

Sociolinguists study speech communities and speech varieties. People may have strong opinions and attitudes toward certain speakers and speech varieties, attitudes that are based not on linguistic criteria but rather on political, cultural, historical, socioeconomic, or other non-linguistic factors. To avoid the value judgments often associated with the terms *dialect* and *language*, sociolinguists use the neutral term *speech variety*.

⇒ Mutual intelligibility is sometimes used as a criterion to identify speech varieties as dialects of the same language, but this criterion is not a straightforward one. Political, cultural, and historical factors have been known to play a significant role in shaping speakers' perceptions of what is a dialect and what is a language, and whether another speech variety is understandable to them. Speakers can treat mutually intelligible varieties as different languages (Swedish and Norwegian) or mutually unintelligible varieties as dialects of one language (varieties spoken in China).

⇒ The term *slang* refers only to particular words or phrases typically used by younger members of the speech community. Most slang is short-lived, but some terms can be popular for several decades (e.g., *cool*).

⇒ The term *accent* refers only to those features of pronunciation that enable us to identify a speaker as belonging to a different (regional or social) speech community. From a linguistic perspective, all speakers have an accent.

## LANGUAGE VARIATION AND SOCIAL DISTINCTIONS

Variationist sociolinguistics examines and attempts to explain the linguistic and social factors that motivate language variation and to make sense of the patterns behind language variation. Make sure that you are familiar with new concepts and terms, including the following:

| TERM | DEFINITION |
|------|------------|
| sociolinguistic variable | A sociolinguistic variable is any linguistic unit that displays variation and that can be subjected to a systematic analysis based on linguistic and social factors. The linguistic unit that displays variation is the variable; the possible ways the unit can be realized are the variants. |
| variable rules or constraints | A variable rule or constraint specifies the conditions under which a particular variant appears. Variable constraints are typically probabilistic, since a linguistic variable can be realized in a number of ways. Variable rules capture what is more likely to happen given a particular condition or environment rather than what necessarily happens. |
| real time versus apparent time | Both real-time and apparent-time methods enable us to study language change. In real-time studies, groups of speakers are interviewed at various points as they age (for example, at age twenty, at forty, and at sixty) to track how they use a particular feature. Apparent-time studies offer a shortcut to the real-time method: the speech of speakers from different age groups is compared at the same time. The hypothesis behind this method is that a change in progress can be captured by comparing the speech of younger speakers to that of older speakers at the same point in time. |

## LANGUAGE VARIATION AND PLACE, TIME, AND ISOLATION

Sociolinguists are also interested in regional variation, the study of linguistic differences based on geographical location (place), and in what synchronic variation can tell us about language change (what happens to language over time). The linguistic characteristics of some speech communities are sometimes the result of isolation. In Canada, we have speech varieties that are the result of physical, linguistic, and social isolation: Newfoundland English, Quebec French, and African Nova Scotia English, respectively. Make sure that you are familiar with any new terminology introduced in these sections, including the following terms:

| TERM | DEFINITION |
|------|------------|
| dialect geography | Dialect geography and dialectology refer to the systematic study of dialects, particularly regional dialects, in order to identify dialect areas. The results of this work are often presented in the form of a series of maps that illustrate the features or forms that predominate in particular areas. |
| dialect levelling | Dialect levelling refers to a process whereby one realization for a linguistic unit 'wins out' over competitors (other options) available in the speech community, leading to less variation for that particular unit. Typically, the most frequent variant is the one selected. |
| isogloss | An isogloss is a line on a map that marks the boundary of an area in which a particular linguistic feature (phonetic, morphological, lexical, etc.) is used. Isogloss bundles—several isoglosses in the same place—are used to indicate the boundary between different dialect areas. |
| linguistic isolate | In sociolinguistics, the term *linguistic isolate* is used to refer to a language that is physically isolated from its source. An example of this is found in the Dominican Republic. The descendants of African Americans in the Samaná Peninsula of the Dominican Republic continue to speak a variety of English even though Spanish is the majority language. In historical linguistics, the term *linguistic isolate* is used to refer to a language that appears to have no known relatives. For example, Basque is an isolate because it cannot be shown that Basque shares a common ancestor with any other language or languages that linguists have studied. |

**Exercise!** See how many details about regional variation, language change, and language isolation you can recall. Complete the following statements, based on the discussion on pp. 450 to 459.

1. Research in the area of dialect geography has historically focused on the speech of _____ on the assumption that these speakers preserve older speech features.

2. American English, particularly the _____ dialect, provided a lot of the linguistic input to Canadian English.

3. Newfoundland was settled early, predominantly by speakers from two regions: _____ and _____.

4. The phonological feature that distinguishes Canadian English from many varieties of American English is _____.

5. Would *fear* and *fire* be homophones in Newfoundland English? _____

6.   Provide the first, second, and third person forms for the verb *like* in Newfoundland English.
     _____

7.   What does *I'm after telling him to do it* (Newfoundland English) mean? _____

8.   This approach can capture language change. It has been used to illustrate how speakers of Canadian English have increasingly merged the phonemes /ʍ/ and /w/ such that the youngest speakers use almost exclusively /w/. The method or approach is called _____.

9.   Which of the following feature(s) is/are typical of Quebec French?

     a.  the diphthongization of many nasal vowels

     b.  the extensive use of formal *vous*

     c.  the use of [va] for several persons of the verb *go*

10.  Show two phonological differences between Par  isian French (PF) and Quebec French (QF) by providing the phonetic transcription for both varieties of the feminine form of the adjective *petite*: _____ (PF) and _____ (QF).

11.  The speech of descendants of African Americans living near _____ preserves features of earlier stages of African American English.

12.  Sociolinguists have found that the language of communities with _____ social networks is more resistant to change.

**Now...** The textbook mentions several lexical items typical of Canadian English, such as *tuque*, *running shoes*, and *double-double*. How aware are you of terms used in other varieties of English? How many of the following do you know? What does one say for ...

   1.  *running shoes* in South African English?               _____

   2.  *cooler* in New Zealand English?                        _____

   3.  *single parent* in New Zealand English?                 _____

   4.  *cantaloupe* in Australian and New Zealand English?      _____

   5.  *pick-up truck* in South African English?               _____

   6.  *sweater* in Australian English?                        _____

   7.  *sidewalk* in Australian English?                       _____

   8.  *stoplight/traffic light* in South African English?     _____

   9.  *candy* in Australian and New Zealand English?          _____

  10.  *speed bump* in New Zealand English?                    _____

**Try This!** The Northern Cities Vowel Shift, discussed on p. 455, refers to a series of vowel changes (shifts) that have taken place or are taking place in the speech of those from Buffalo, Cleveland, Detroit, Chicago, and other northern US cities. As a result, 'shifted' and 'unshifted' varieties of North American English can sound strikingly different from one another. Here are some of the vowel changes that are part of the Northern Cities Shift:

⇒ The low back vowel [ɑ] is fronted, so that it comes very close to sounding like [æ].

⇒ The front vowel [æ] is fronted and raised, so that it approximates [ɛ], [eə], or [iə].

⇒ The vowel [ɛ] is pronounced further back and lower, almost as [ʌ].

⇒ The vowel [ʌ] is pronounced so that it approximates [ɔ].

Use the following table to compare your pronunciation of the words in the first column to that of a speaker involved in the Northern Cities Shift, as demonstrated for *bat*. Do you think some of the differences could result in miscommunication?

| Example | Phonetic transcription of my pronunciation | Possible transcription for speaker involved in Northern Cities Shift |
|---------|---------|---------|
| bat | [bæt] | [bɛt]/[beət]/[biət] |
| father | | |
| stuck | | |
| bet | | |
| stack | | |
| cot | | |
| bus | | |
| block | | |

# LANGUAGE CONTACT

Language contact – when two or more languages are used within a speech community – can result in a variety of phenomena. Mixed languages, pidgins, and creoles have emerged from language contact situations. Make sure that you are familiar with any new terminology introduced in this section of the chapter, including the following terms:

| TERM | DEFINITION |
|------|-----------|
| code switching | A speaker who uses more than one language or variety within a conversation is said to be code switching. |
| matrix language | The matrix language is the dominant language in a code-switched utterance. |
| borrowing | A borrowing is a word that is adopted and adapted from another language. Borrowed words are adapted to the borrowing linguistic system in terms of phonology, morphology, and so on. In language contact situations, speakers of one language will often borrow words from another language; the borrowers are rarely aware that the word is from another language. |
| lingua franca | A lingua franca is a language adopted as a means of communication among speakers of different languages. Typically, the lingua franca is the second (or third) language of the speakers who use it. Today, English is the international lingua franca of technology, science, and business. |
| mixed language | A language with features from two distinct sources. Mixed languages are believed to be rare. An often-cited example is Michif, the mixed language of the Métis, in which the nominal morphology is based on Métis French and the verbal morphology of Cree. |
| pidgin | Pidgin languages emerge when there is a need for speakers of different languages to communicate (for trade purposes, for example). In comparison to non-pidgins, they are generally characterized as having a limited vocabulary and a reduced grammar. A pidgin is usually not the native language of the speakers who use it. |
| creole | A creole is generally defined as a pidgin that has become the first language of a speech community. In order to become the first language of the community (and to fulfill all communicative functions), pidgins undergo creolization: grammatical, lexical, and stylistic expansion. |
| lexifier language | A lexifier language is the language that provides the majority of the vocabulary to a creole (or a pidgin). The lexifier language for Haitian Creole is French; the lexifier language for Jamaican Creole is English. |

**Exercise!**   How well do you know the language contact section of Chapter 14? Indicate whether the following statements are true or false.

1. All contact situations lead to the formation of pidgins.

2. Some linguists attribute the similarities across creoles to the language bioprogram: the innate biological capacity to acquire language.

3. Some linguists believe that all creoles emerged from a single ancestral language, a proto-pidgin.

4. The most commonly borrowed lexical items are nouns and verbs.

5. Generally, function words are not borrowed.

6. In situations where a creole continuum exists, the variety that is closest to the creole is called the acrolect.

7. Intermediate varieties within a creole continuum are mesolects.

8. All pidgins necessarily become creoles.

9. Creoles are mixed languages.

10. Code switching occurs because speakers cannot think of words and phrases in one of the languages—they have lexical gaps.

**Try This!** Make sure that you are familiar with the creole features discussed in Chapter 14. Now consider the following examples from an English-lexifier creole (Jamaican Creole) and pidgin (Nigerian Pidgin English): the first five examples are from Jamaican Creole; the last three examples are from Nigerian Pidgin English. Comment on the examples, particularly on the underlined forms. The examples are not given in phonetic transcription but are intended to be representative of how they are pronounced.

1. <u>Mi</u> neve(r) <u>tell</u> im. 'I didn't tell him.'
2. Tell <u>we</u> di trut. 'Tell us the truth.'
3. <u>Dem</u> no so bad. 'They are not so bad.'
4. A di <u>bway</u> boat. 'It's the boy's boat.'
5. <u>Im say</u> di <u>boat no good</u>. 'He said the boat is no good.'
6. He <u>tok</u> tru. 'He speaks the truth.'
7. Your money <u>don kom</u>. 'You've hit the jackpot!'
8. He <u>don go</u>. 'He went.'

## DISTINCTIONS WITHIN A COMMUNITY

There can be a lot of variation within a speech community based on factors such as socioeconomic class, ethnicity, and gender. It is important to remember that social factors do not contribute in isolation to language use. For example, gender and ethnicity, or class and gender, can together contribute to language variation in complex ways.

**Exercise!** Familiarize yourself with any new terms and concepts that are introduced in this part of the chapter. Then complete the following statements using the words and phrases suggested below.

| careful style | insecurity |
|---|---|
| change from above | overt |
| community of practice | prestige |
| covert | rapport |
| hypercorrection | report |

1.  Sociolinguistic studies have shown that there is a strong correlation between _____ and prestige variants, regardless of socioeconomic class.

2.  Upper-class speakers often use _____ norms taken from outside the speech community. For example, Americans and Canadians may adopt features of British speech.

3.  Labov's New York City studies showed that speakers in the second-highest socioeconomic class dramatically increased their use of prestige variants when paying close attention to speech. This type of overcompensation, attributed to linguistic _____, is called _____.

4.  Many studies have shown that women use more variants associated with _____ prestige, whereas men use more non-standard forms.

5.  An interesting finding is that, generally, men not only use more non-standard variants than women, but believe that they use non-standard variants even more than they do in reality. The term _____ prestige has been suggested for the positive value that men attach to non-standard forms.

6.  _____ is the term used for language change that spreads from the upper classes to the lower classes. Sociolinguistic research has shown that women tend to be leaders in this type of change: women use more new forms than men.

7.  Researchers have called the discourse style of women a _____ style: in general, women's conversational goals appear to include collaboration and building relationships.

8.  The conversational style of men has been called a _____ style, since it suggests a tendency to use language more for the purpose of conveying factual information.

9.  The term _____ is used to refer to speakers who share speech practices because they participate in a common activity.

## DISTINCTIONS WITHIN A COMMUNITY: ETHNICITY

The discussion in section 14.6.2 makes reference to the fact that non-standard varieties can encode subtle distinctions that cannot be expressed in the same way in the standard counterpart. Two features of African American English (AAE) stand out for the distinctions they make possible: zero copula and habitual *be*.

⇒ *Zero copula* (or *copula deletion*) refers to the deletion of the linking verb (usually the verb *to be*) in certain contexts. In AAE, copula deletion can *only* occur where Standard English (SE) permits contracted forms:

| | |
|---|---|
| Example: | She is going to school. |
| SE: | She's going to school. |
| AAE: | She going to school. |

⇒ If the verb *to be* cannot undergo contraction in Standard English, then copula deletion does not take place in African American English. Neither the SE nor the AAE example is acceptable:

| | |
|---|---|
| Example: | They know how great she is. |
| SE: | *They know how great she's. |
| AAE: | *They know how great she. |

⇒ *Habitual be* enables speakers of AAE to make an aspectual distinction through verb forms alone that speakers of standard varieties of English cannot make without using adverbs or adverbial expressions. When *habitual be* is used, it indicates that the action usually (habitually) or often occurs. AAE *She <u>be</u> on time* would be *She is usually on time* in SE.

⇒ Note how *copula deletion* and *habitual be* together enable speakers of AAE to concisely and precisely distinguish punctual versus habitual action.

| | | |
|---|---|---|
| *punctual* | They busy. | 'They are busy (right now).' |
| *habitual* | They be busy. | 'They are usually busy.' |

**Now ...** Use your knowledge of African American English to interpret and judge the acceptability of the following sentences. Place an asterisk before any sentence that you deem unacceptable in AAE (use the left column). Use the column on the right either to explain why you think a particular example is ungrammatical in AAE or to rewrite the AAE sentence according to SE norms.

| | Example | Explanation of ungrammaticality or SE version |
|---|---|---|
| | 1. She be telling lies. | |
| | 2. I have to good. | |
| | 3. He be going today. | |
| | 4. We waiting for you. | |
| | 5. Some of them nice. | |
| | 6. They be home by five. | |
| | 7. That's where he. | |
| | 8. They be eating right now. | |

# DISTINCTIONS WITHIN A COMMUNITY: AGE AND GENDER

**Try This!** People often have negative attitudes toward aspects of the language of younger speakers. For example, according to a BBC report, actor Emma Thompson has complained about the sloppy use of language among teenagers, such as their use of *like*.[1] A non-linguist might perceive younger speakers' use of *like* in discourse as arbitrary and meaningless (when *like* is used differently from the accepted usage, as in *He looks like his brother,* in which *like* expresses similarity). Sociolinguists studying *like* in the conversations of younger speakers have identified special discourse uses of *like*. The following exercises provide examples of these uses. Examine sentences 1 to 15; then answer the questions below.

1.  We can do *like* all kinds of things.
2.  And do they take *like* debit?
3.  Let's do that *like* as soon as possible.
4.  You can *like* try yoga.
5.  They *like* paid for the whole thing.
6.  That's *like* so unfair.
7.  I need *like* a good friend.
8.  They asked me *like* how I did it.
9.  Can you *like* give me ten examples using 'like'?
10. *Like* what did he say?
11. Could I *like* come by around four?
12. It's not *like* great, but it's okay.
13. He's *like* cool, but a bit strange.
14. And *like* they talked all night.
15. I'm hoping to get into *like* speech path.

1.  Although the use of *like* in these examples may appear arbitrary to non-linguists, there are constraints governing where it can appear. Identify the syntactic positions in which *like* can occur.
2.  What is the purpose of *like* in these examples?
3.  Do you use *like* in this way? Can you provide three examples of your own for this usage of *like*?

**Now ...** Look at the following conversational excerpt, which contains three examples of *like*. Compare the use of *like* in these examples to its use in the examples above. Discuss the properties and function of *like* in these examples. Can you provide additional examples?

| Speaker A: | Are you okay? |
|---|---|
| Speaker B: | I can't believe my sister. She said, "What's wrong?" And I'm *like*, "I should've passed the midterm. I studied a lot." And she's *like*, "Yeah, right – you never study." And I'm *like*, "No, really, I studied a lot ..." |

**Think ...** Imagine that you have conducted a research project in which your goal was to examine the distributional patterns of the two discourse uses of *like* illustrated above. You collected two hundred speech samples containing the two types of *like* and organized them according to age and gender. You have tabulated your results and plotted them on graphs. Figure 1 shows the distribution by age and gender of *focuser like* (as in the example *You can like try yoga*), which we have labelled *usage 1*. Figure 2 shows the distribution by age and gender of *quotative like* (as in the example *And I'm like, "I should've passed the midterm"*), which we have labelled *usage 2*.

Examine the following graphs; then answer the questions below.

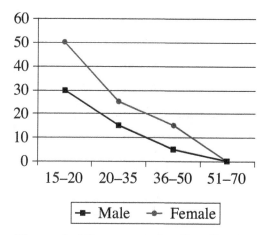

**Figure 1.** *Like: usage 1* – **distribution by age and gender**

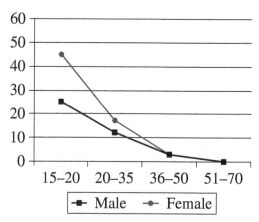

**Figure 2.** *Like: usage 2* – **distribution by age and gender**

1.  What method of sociolinguistic analysis is represented in these distributions?

2.  What conclusions about language change and language use among male and female speakers could you tentatively draw based on these results?

3.   Use the following table to plan a follow-up study so that you can confirm your hypotheses.

| type of study |
| --- |
| speech community: details |
| data collection methods |
| data analysis |

4.   What type of study would you propose to gauge attitudes toward these uses of *like*?[2]

## SOCIAL INTERACTION AND LANGUAGE

Discourse analysis is the study of how language works beyond individual sentences. For example, we can analyze the language of a conversation by attempting to answer certain questions. Who speaks and when? How are conversations organized? How do the participants speak: in other words, what linguistic – phonological, syntactic, lexical – choices do participants make, and why? What do the linguistic choices tell us about the relationship between speakers? What do the linguistic choices reveal about the status of the participants?

**Exercise!** Familiarize yourself with any new terms and concepts introduced in this part of the chapter by completing the following statements with the words and phrases suggested on the next page.

| accommodation | key |
| communicative competence | register |
| diglossia | speech events |
| genre | style |
| jargon | turn-taking cues |

1. Ethnography of communication analysis is a methodological tool that enables linguists to study the norms and conventions that govern _____.

2. The ability to use language in accordance with the norms governing what is socially appropriate is known as _____.

3. The adjustment of one's language so that it is more like that of someone we are speaking with is called linguistic _____.

4. The mood or emotional tone of a speech event is known as the _____.

5. The term for the type or category of a speech event is _____.

6. A speaker with communicative competence is able to control his or her speech in terms of _____: that is, the speaker knows when it is appropriate for speech to be more formal or informal, and whether it should be careful or casual.

7. When one makes linguistic choices – phonological, syntactic, and lexical – based on their suitability for a particular speech situation (e.g., particular stylistic and linguistic choices are associated with marriage ceremonies), this is called using the appropriate _____.

8. Research in conversational analysis has shown that _____ are culture specific rather than universal.

9. _____ refers to a situation in which different varieties of the same language, or different languages, are used for very different purposes or domains within the same speech community. One variety is used in more formal settings (government, education), while the other is reserved for informal or casual situations (among friends and family).

10. Vocabulary that is occupation specific or activity specific is called _____.

**Now ...** For the next few days, conduct some conversational analyses of your own. Observe closely both conversations in which you are a participant and those in which you are not. Try to observe what happens in as many different speech situations as possible: a student and professor talking before or after class, a client and a clerk in a bank, a customer service representative and a customer, patients and medical staff in a doctor's office or hospital, two colleagues talking about work, interviews on the news. As you observe different conversations, try to keep the following questions in mind.

1. What style and register are the participants using?

2. If you are able to observe a conversation in its entirety, what openings and closings are used?

3. Are you able to identify some turn-taking cues? Are the exchanges equal in terms of duration? Does one speaker dominate the conversation?

4. Do the speakers seem to have the same status, or is it clear that there is a power imbalance?

5. What forms of address are used? Are participants using reciprocal or non-reciprocal naming?

6. Can you identify other ways (besides naming practices) in which language is used either to demonstrate solidarity (shared status) or to maintain distance between speakers?

7. If it is clear that one of the participants is a non-native speaker of English or speaks a different variety of English (other than what is dominant in the speech community), what strategies are being used to show solidarity or maintain distance?

8. Is there evidence of linguistic accommodation? Who is doing the accommodating?

9. How do you use language to show distance between you and another speaker?

10. How do you use language to express closeness or solidarity?

## HOW SOCIETIES DEAL WITH LANGUAGE

Sociolinguistics also examines what societies do with languages. What are the attitudes toward the varieties available in the broader speech community? How is a particular variety selected and promoted within the society? What are the consequences for the other varieties when this happens?

⇒ A standard language is best defined from a social perspective: it is the prestige variety spoken by the educated, the upper socioeconomic classes, and the media. It is the language selected to serve official purposes: for example, it is the language of government and education.

⇒ How a language comes to be the standard has nothing to do with its inherent linguistic properties: languages do *not* become standards because they are objectively superior to other varieties. The standard develops as the prestige variety as a result of sociopolitical and socioeconomic factors. Sometimes this happens 'naturally': that is, the language of the powerful or dominant group becomes the prestige variety over time. In some cases, the selection of a standard is the result of a deliberate process (language planning).

⇒ Language planning involves the systematic regulation of the use of different languages in a society. It involves the creation of legislation (language policy) that controls which variety (or varieties) will serve official purposes. This can involve the establishment of norms for the official variety (standardization). When a language is deemed 'official', its use increases; as a result, the use of varieties not selected for official status decreases or is limited.

⇒ The establishment of a standard in a society leads to the marginalization of other varieties. Since non-standard varieties do not have the support of the powerful and their domain of use is limited, they can be the object of negative attitudes and ridicule. In many circumstances, the marginalized varieties lose progressively more speakers over time, potentially leading to language death.

⇒ The asymmetrical power relationship between standard and non-standard languages leads to the view that the standard is more 'grammatically correct'. Prescriptive grammars are written to reinforce the perceived correctness of certain ways of speaking. Some speakers fear that the 'real language' is in a state of decay.

**Exercise!**  Do you know which languages have official or national status in the following countries or territories? Sometimes a language has de facto official status or national status: there is no policy mandating its acceptance and use, but in practice it is widely accepted and used. Use the *Ethnologue: Languages of the World* website[3] to find out if you are not sure.

Afghanistan: _____

Bolivia: _____

Botswana: _____

Democratic Republic of Congo: _____

Djibouti: _____

Fiji: _____

Finland: _____

Irish Republic: _____

Mozambique: _____

New Zealand: _____

Paraguay: _____

South Africa: _____

**Now ...**  Imagine that you come across an Internet forum dedicated to 'proper English usage'. Someone has just posted the following commentary.

When I think of what is happening to English today, I want to cry. Everyone makes careless errors when speaking. Do people not realize that one is supposed to say 'everyone forgot <u>his</u> manners,' not 'everyone forgot <u>their</u> manners,' because <u>everyone</u> is grammatically singular? One also routinely hears sentences such as 'I don't know what he's talking <u>about</u>.' When did we forget that it is a serious violation to strand a preposition? When I ask for someone over the phone, I never hear the correct response 'It is <u>I</u>'; I only hear the vulgar sounding 'It's <u>me</u>.' And does no one remember the English subjunctive? I only hear 'I wish I <u>was</u> ...,' although I am sure everyone was taught that this structure requires the subjunctive: 'I wish I <u>were</u> ...' I fear that the failure to use English properly will affect other areas of life. It's just the beginning!

Carelessness in language will lead to carelessness in other areas of life, such as government, education, business and health care. I fear for the younger generations. I hope it's not too late to change what's happening.

What would you post in response? Write your own commentary using your knowledge of sociolinguistics in general (regional and social variation, language change) and what you know about standard languages and prescriptivism in particular.

---

[1] Reported in *BBC News Magazine*, 28 September 2010. http://www.bbc.co.uk/news/magazine-11426737.

[2] If you're interested in exploring this topic further, please see the following studies: Robert Underhill, "*Like* is, Like, Focus," *American Speech* 63, 3 (1988): 234-46; Suzanne Romaine and Deborah Lange, "The Use of *like* as a Marker of Reported Speech and Thought: A Case of Grammaticalization in Progress," *American Speech* 66, 3 (1991): 227-79; Kathleen Ferrara and Barbara Bell, "Sociolinguistic Variation and Discourse Function of Constructed Dialogue Introducers: The Case of *be + like*," *American Speech* 70, 3 (1995): 265-89; Jennifer Dailey-O'Cain, "The Sociolinguistic Distribution of and Attitudes toward Focuser *like* and Quotative *like*," *Journal of Sociolinguistics* 4, 1 (2000): 60-80; and Sali Tagliamonte and Alex D'Arcy, "*He's Like, She's Like*: The Quotative System in Canadian Youth," *Journal of Sociolinguistics* 8, 4 (2004): 493-514.

[3] M. Paul Lewis (ed.), *Ethnologue: Languages of the World*, 16th ed. (Dallas, TX: SIL International, 2009). Online version: http://www.ethnologue.com/.

## QUESTIONS? PROBLEMS? DIFFICULTIES?

_____

_____

_____

_____

_____

_____

_____

_____

_____

_____

_____

# CHAPTER 15.
# WRITING AND LANGUAGE

Writing is the graphic or visual representation of speech. Although spoken language is acquired without explicit teaching, writing systems do require formal instruction. The development of writing is a relatively recent human development. In fact, many languages around the world do not have a writing system, and illiteracy exists in societies with well-established writing systems.

Important terms and concepts found in this chapter include the following:

1. Logographic versus phonographic writing
2. Syllabic writing and syllabaries
3. Alphabetic writing
4. Abjads and abugidas
5. Pictography
6. The rebus principle
7. Cuneiform writing
8. Hieroglyphs
9. The acrophonic principle
10. English orthography

## TYPES OF WRITING

In the writing systems that have developed, we identify two basic types: logographic and phonographic systems.

⇒ In logographic writing, the oldest type of writing, the symbols used represent entire words or morphemes (for this reason, logographic writing is sometimes called word writing). All writing systems have logographic elements: contemporary English makes use of many logograms, including &, #, $, £, and the symbols for the Arabic numerals 1, 2, 3, and so on. Since these symbols stand for concepts and do not have a particular phonetic value, many other languages also make use of them.

⇒ In phonographic writing, symbols represent sounds. If the symbols represent speech segments, the phonographic system is an alphabetic system; if they represent syllables, the system is syllabic.

⇒ In alphabetic writing, each symbol generally corresponds to a particular consonant or vowel segment. The symbols of an alphabetic system are called *graphemes*. Alphabetic systems are not meant to capture sub-phonemic (or allophonic) details; rather, each grapheme ideally corresponds to a consonant or vowel phoneme. In practice, alphabetic systems rarely display a one-to-one mapping of graphemes to phonemes. In English, the grapheme *c* can represent the phonemes / k / or / s /, as in *cat* and *city*; *s* can represent several sounds, including / s /, / z /, and / ʃ / as in *soup, leaves,* and *sugar*; the phoneme / f / can be represented by *f, gh,* or *ph: fish, cough, philosophy.*

⇒ In syllabic writing, each symbol represents a syllable. The group of symbols that make up the syllabic inventory of a language is called a *syllabary.* Syllabic writing is most suitable for languages that have limited syllable types (CV or CVC). Languages that use syllabic writing include Cherokee, Cree, and Japanese.

**Exercise!** See how many details about types of writing you can recall. Complete the following statements, based on the discussion on pp. 479 to 481.

1. A segmental writing system that gives as much importance to the representation of vowels as it does to consonants is a(n) _____ system.
2. A segmental writing system that is based on consonants, with vowels obligatorily represented with diacritics, is called _____.
3. A segmental writing system that is based entirely on consonants, with vowels optionally represented with diacritics, is called _____.
4. In Indic languages that use Devanagari script, all vowels must be represented except the default vowel, which is typically _____.
5. The symbols % and € in English are examples of _____ writing.
6. The use of *CU* for 'see you' is an example of the integration of _____ writing into English, which otherwise has a(n) _____ writing system.
7. Arabic and Hebrew employ a(n) _____ writing system.

## THE EARLY HISTORY OF WRITING

We know that early writing developed out of picture writing, or pictograms. Important links have been made between record keeping and the emergence of writing.

⇒ The earliest stage we can identify in the evolution of writing is a system for representing objects.

⇒ Petroglyphs, scenes depicted on stones, may represent a pre-literate stage in the evolution of writing.

⇒ An important stage in pre-writing is the use of clay tokens for the purpose of record keeping.

⇒ All writing has ultimately developed out of picture writing, or pictograms. Pictograms are still in use today.

**Exercise!** The following pictograms are commonly used in airports around the world. Can you identify the message in each case?

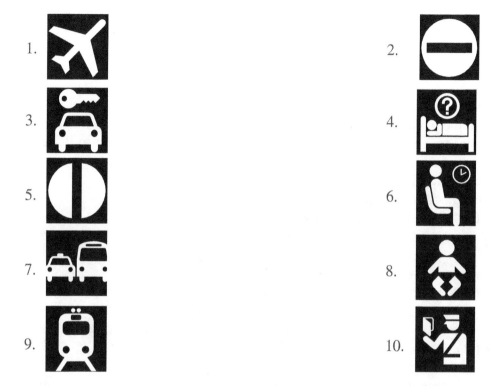

1. [image]  2. [image]
3. [image]  4. [image]
5. [image]  6. [image]
7. [image]  8. [image]
9. [image]  10. [image]

**Think ...** Think of messages in everyday life that are expressed through pictograms. Consider road signs, emoticons, and institutional signage. Why do you think we continue to use so many pictograms in the modern world, even in highly literate societies?

## THE EVOLUTION OF WRITING

This section of the chapter provides an overview of the development of writing, from Sumerian pictographic writing, to cuneiform writing, to the development of syllabic and alphabet writing. Make sure that you are familiar with the following terms:

| TERM | DEFINITION |
|------|-----------|
| rebus principle | The rebus principle is the process by which a symbol comes to be associated with a sound or syllable in a particular word; the symbol is then used to represent other words having that sound/syllable. A good example in English is use of the logographic symbol 2 for all instances of the syllable / tu /: *nd2cu* ('need to see you'). |
| cuneiform writing | Cuneiform is an ancient writing system in which symbols were created by pressing a wedge-shaped stylus into soft clay. Cuneiform symbols consist of short strokes. |
| hieroglyphs | The pictographic system that emerged in Egypt was based on symbols called *hieroglyphs*. Egyptian hieroglyphs developed into both logographic and phonographic writing. |

**Exercise!** How familiar are you with some facts concerning the emergence of writing? Indicate whether the following statements are true or false.

1. The earliest known pictographic writing comes from Ethiopia.
2. The earliest known pictographic writing is from approximately five thousand years ago.
3. Sumerian is believed to have been logographic from a fairly early stage because it seems to have been written in a linear order representing the order of words in speech.
4. The modern use of smilies in netspeak is an example of the rebus principle.
5. Rebuses are the precursor to syllabic writing.
6. Cuneiform writing always maintained its pictographic nature.
7. Egyptian hieroglyphs developed into a mixed system of word writing and phonographic writing.
8. Cuneiform writing was a precursor to Egyptian hieroglyphs.
9. Hieroglyphic symbols were eventually used to represent particular consonant phonemes.
10. According to the acrophonic principle, the letter *b* in English could be called *bear*.
11. The Etruscans developed the first full alphabet based on the Phoenician writing system.
12. It is believed that the Romans acquired their alphabet through the Etruscans.

**Try This!** Identify the meaning expressed by the following rebuses. Assume that the hand symbol stands for the English sound sequence [fɔr].

1.

2.

3.

4.

5.

**Now ...** Invent five rebuses of your own. Can your classmates interpret them? Consider using the following symbols (but add others of your own).

| | |
|---|---|
| 1. | |
| 2. | |
| 3. | |
| 4. | |
| 5. | |

## SOME NON-EUROPEAN WRITING SYSTEMS

To this point, we have focused on the origins of European writing systems. Not all writing systems originated in the Middle East. This section of the chapter discusses the writing systems that emerged in China, Japan, and Korea, as well as a script developed for Cree.

**Exercise!** Familiarize yourself with the facts surrounding non-European writing systems. Complete the following statements using the words and phrases suggested below. (Note: One of the suggested words or phrases will not be required.)

| | |
|---|---|
| coda consonants | literary script |
| direction | logographic |
| hanja | oracle texts |
| hangul | phonetic determinatives |
| hiragana | pictograms |
| kanji | romaji |
| katakana | vowel length |

1. The modern Chinese writing system developed from _____.
2. The oldest Chinese inscriptions, known as the _____, are from approximately 1200 BC.
3. Since many monosyllabic words are represented by a single symbol in Chinese writing, we can call the system a truly _____ system.
4. The modern Chinese writing system requires the use of _____ in combination with semantic radicals to identify the morphemes that they represent.
5. Despite some inherent complexities, the same _____ can be understood by speakers of different Chinese languages.
6. The Japanese writing system incorporates three distinct scripts: two syllabaries and a set of Chinese characters called _____.
7. The Roman alphabet, called _____ in Japanese, is becoming quite prevalent in modern advertisements in Japan.
8. In Japanese, onomatopoeic words and words borrowed from other languages are written in the _____ syllabary.
9. The standard Korean alphabetic script (originally commissioned by King Sejong in the fifteenth century) is called _____.
10. Korean also makes use of Chinese characters, called _____.
11. The Cree syllabary can be called partially alphabetic, since _____ can have their own symbols.
12. In the Cree writing system, vowel differences are indicated by changing the _____ of the syllabic symbol.
13. In Cree writing, a superposed dot indicates _____.

**Try This!** As you have learned, hangul is the alphabet of the Korean language. Each hangul symbol represents a phoneme in the sound system of Korean. The phoneme-based symbols are combined in syllabic blocks according to the syllable patterns of Korean phonology. Hangul consists of twenty-four characters (or letters) in all, called *jamo*: fourteen consonant symbols and ten vowel symbols. This exercise introduces you to many of the characters of hangul.

The rules for creating syllabic blocks reflect the following principles:

⇒ Each syllable has three positions: initial, medial, and final.

⇒ Initial position (the syllable onset) is reserved for any consonant.

⇒ Medial position (the syllable nucleus) is occupied by a vowel (or diphthong).

⇒ Final position (the syllable coda) can either be filled by a consonant or be left empty (it is also possible to have codas of two consonants).

⇒ Vowel symbols that are 'vertical' are placed to the right of the initial consonant.

⇒ Vowel symbols that are 'horizontal' are placed under the initial consonant.

Here are some examples:

The sounds [k], [i], and [o] are represented respectively by the symbols ㄱ, ㅣ, and ㅗ. Note that the symbol for [i] is vertical, but the symbol for [o] is horizontal. The following examples of the syllables [ki] and [ko] illustrate how syllable building or stacking works (the boxes and arrows are intended to help you visualize the building process):

 [ki]

[ko]

Consider the following Korean examples, which are given in both hangul and phonetic transcription, and then answer the questions that follow.

1. 나무      [namu]      'tree'
2. 삼         [sam]        'three'
3. 사무      [samu]       'office work'
4. 속         [sok]         'inside'
5. 구         [ku]          'nine'
6. 국         [kuk]         'soup'

   a. What is the hangul symbol that represents the sound [a]?
   b. What is the hangul symbol that represents the sound [m]?
   c. What is the hangul symbol that represents [u]?
   d. What is the hangul symbol that represents [s]?
   e. What is the hangul symbol that represents [n]?

Now consider the following additional examples:

7. 아무      [amu]        'any'
8. 우리      [uri]         'we'
9. 아니      [ani]         'no'
10. 일상     [ilsaŋ]       'daily'

   f. What is the hangul symbol that represents [r]?
   g. What is the hangul symbol that represents [l]?
   h. Comment on the answers you've provided regarding the symbols for [l] and [r].
   i. What have you observed about the hangul symbol ㅇ?

So far, ten hangul symbols have been introduced, representing seven consonants and four vowels. Use the following table to organize what you have learned so far.

| Hangul symbol | Phonetic value | Hangul symbol | Phonetic value |
|---|---|---|---|
|  |  |  |  |
|  |  |  |  |
|  |  |  |  |
|  |  |  |  |
|  |  |  |  |

Write the following words in hangul:

| | | |
|---|---|---|
| j. | [son] | 'hand' |
| k. | [kon.lan] | 'trouble' |
| l. | [ki.rin] | 'giraffe' |
| m. | [al] | 'egg' |

Consider these additional Korean examples in hangul.

| | | | |
|---|---|---|---|
| 11. | 간 | [kan] | 'liver' |
| 12. | 뱀 | [pɛm] | 'snake' |
| 13. | 누구 | [nugu] | 'who' |
| 14. | 새 | [sɛ] | 'bird' |
| 15. | 바다 | [pada] | 'sea' |
| 16. | 달 | [tal] | 'moon' |
| 17. | 소금 | [sogɨm] | 'salt' |
| 18. | 소고기 | [sogogi] | 'beef' |
| 19. | 기름 | [kirɨm] | 'oil' |

n. What new symbols are introduced in examples 11 to 19?

o. What sounds do these symbols represent?

p. What can you conclude regarding the status of voicing in Korean stops?

q. Given what you have observed for other stops, what would you expect the symbol for the sound [b] to be?

Write the following words in hangul.

| | | |
|---|---|---|
| r. | [kɨrigo] | 'and' |
| s. | [nɛmsɛ] | 'smell' |
| t. | [masida] | 'to drink' |
| u. | [irɨm] | 'name' |
| v. | [alda] | 'to know' |

# ENGLISH ORTHOGRAPHY

This section of the chapter presents some of the factors that have shaped the development of the English orthographic system. Challenges to reforming the system are also considered, as are reasons why the English orthographic system makes sense from a morphological perspective.

## Why is English spelling so irregular?

There used to be a closer connection between sounds (phonemes) and alphabetic symbols in English. Several internal factors (i.e., stemming from within the language system) and external factors (i.e., coming from outside the language system) contributed to creating the irregularities we observe in English orthography today. These reasons help explain why English orthography does not represent the one phoneme-one symbol principle to the extent that it used to.

External factors that led to the weakening of the one phoneme-one symbol nature of English orthography include the following:

⇒ Many French words were introduced following the Norman invasion. Along with French vocabulary, spelling changes modelled on how French words were written were also introduced.

⇒ Etymological spelling altered the written form of many English words. This type of spelling reflects the remote origin of the word, even if it does not at all coincide with how the word was ever pronounced. In the history of English, etymological spelling can be seen in the words *debt* and *island*, among others. The *b* in *debt* was introduced to acknowledge that the word ultimately came from Latin *debitum*, even though English speakers have never had a [b] in the pronunciation of the word. The word *island* is historically an Anglo-Saxon word (it used to be written *yland*) and has never had [s] in its pronunciation; it has a different history from *isle*, which the English borrowed from the French and which is ultimately derived from Latin *insula*. Etymological spelling, on the wrong assumption that *island* and *isle* are historically related, is responsible for introducing the *s* in *island*.

⇒ Various spelling rules were introduced by different prominent individuals, particularly in the late 1500s and early 1600s. For example, in 1582, Richard Mulcaster proposed the use of a silent final *e* to indicate that the preceding vowel was long (tense), as in the word *name*. Learners of English will be familiar with this orthographic principle: *mat* has a short vowel sound, but *mate* has a long vowel sound, as indicated by the final *e*. Of course, this is not as straightforward as it appears: *give* is not pronounced [ gajv ].

Some internal factors led to the weakening of the one phoneme-one symbol nature of English orthography. In other words, the spelling system used to capture relatively faithfully the spoken language, but the spoken language changed and the orthography did not. Here are two significant speech system changes that are not reflected in English orthography.

⇒ One of the most striking changes in the history of English is the Great Vowel Shift. This term covers a series of changes in the vowel system of English that occurred over approximately two hundred years, roughly the fifteenth century to the seventeenth century. During this time, all the long vowels of English (at the time, vowel length was phonemic in English) systematically changed: low and mid long vowels raised, and the highest long vowels diphthongized (see Chapter 7 for more details). The spelling system of modern English does not reflect the 'shifted' pronunciation.

⇒ English speakers stopped producing some sounds in certain contexts, but the corresponding written symbols for such sounds were not removed. For example, speakers long ago stopped pronouncing [k] in words such as *knee* and *knight*, yet such words continue to be written with 'silent *k*'. Word-medial *gh* typically represented a palatal or velar fricative, sounds that are no longer part of the phonological inventory of English: the *gh* in words such as *light, right,* and *thought* used to correspond to [ç] or [x]. In these examples, too, English orthography continues to convey a former sound, now 'silent'.

**Exercise!** Look up the long vowel changes involved in the Great Vowel Shift (see Chapter 7 for details). Complete the following table, which captures the principal Great Vowel Shift changes. In the table, from top to bottom, the front long vowels (from low to high) appear first, followed by all the back vowels (from mid to high). For some changes, you do not need to identify an intermediate phoneme since there was only one major change overall (these are marked '—' in the table).

| Middle English vowel phoneme (pre-GVS) | Intermediate phoneme | Final phoneme |
|---|---|---|
| | /æː/ | /eː/ |
| /æː/ | | /iː/ |
| /ɛː/ | | /iː/ |
| /eː/ | — | |
| | — | /aj/ |
| /ɔː/ | — | |
| /oː/ | — | |
| | — | /aw/ |

**Now ...** Using your knowledge of the Great Vowel Shift and your insights regarding the English orthographic system (it does not reflect the 'shifted' pronunciation), provide the Middle English and Modern English vowel phonemes for the following words, as is done in the first two examples. This exercise will help you to make sense of some of the symbols for vowels in the English writing system. Remember that vowel length is not phonemic in English today: the length distinction of older English gave way to a tense-lax distinction. Therefore, Modern English reflexes of older long vowels are tense vowels.

| Example | Pre-GVS vowel phoneme | Modern English phoneme |
|---------|----------------------|------------------------|
| bite | /iː / | /aj/ |
| boat | /ɔː/ | /o/ = [ow] |
| boot |  |  |
| mate |  |  |
| time |  |  |
| see |  |  |
| out |  |  |
| sea |  |  |
| house |  |  |
| goat |  |  |
| tooth |  |  |
| fame |  |  |

**Try This!** Now that you are familiar with the relationship between certain orthographic symbols and some pre-GVS phonemes, consider the following words: *break*, *great*, *good*, *book*, and *police*. According to the GVS, *break* and *great* should be pronounced /brik/ and /grit/, *good* and *book* should be pronounced /gud/ and /buk/, and *police* should have the diphthong /aj/, as does *polite*. Why do you think these do not contain the 'shifted' phonemes?

**Exercise!**   In many cases English has a one-to-several mapping of phonemes to alphabetic symbols. For example, the /u/ phoneme of English can be represented orthographically in at least eight ways: *sp**oo**n*, *s**ou**p*, *wh**o**, n**ew***, *sh**oe**, tr**ue**, r**u**le, s**ui**t*. Think of at least six ways in which the following vowel and consonant phonemes of English can be represented orthographically.

/aj/ _____     _____     _____

_____     _____     _____

/ʃ/ _____     _____     _____

_____     _____     _____

**Now ...** Propose reforms to the English writing system that would eliminate the numerous cases of one-to-several mappings of phonemes to symbols. Start by suggesting a single written symbol for the phonemes from the previous exercise. What problems do you encounter?

**Think ...** In the previous exercise you were asked to propose orthographic reforms. Chapter 15 mentions existing obstacles to reforming the English writing system. What are these obstacles? Can you think of others?

**Morphology and Orthography:** Chapter 15 outlines some morphologically motivated advantages of the English writing system.

⇒ The English writing system captures the derivational relationship between words. Spelling helps us to see that *sign* is related to *signature*, and that *musician* is derived from *music*. In other words, the orthography represents root morphemes consistently, even though the same root can have different pronunciations.

⇒ The English writing system tends not to permit a word-final single *s* unless it represents an inflectional morpheme (e.g., the plural morpheme or the third person singular morpheme). If the written final *s* does not represent an inflectional morpheme, then either it is doubled (*kiss*) or it is followed by an *e* (*mouse*).

⇒ The English writing system does not allow word-final double *ll* in polysyllabic words except in certain morphologically motivated cases: compounding (*landfill*) and derivation (*resell*).

⇒ The orthographic change of a final *y* to *i* occurs before affixes, as in the examples *carried* and *beautiful*.

**Now ...**   Conduct a survey on attitudes toward English orthography. Ask the same questions both to classmates and friends who have learned English as a first language and to those who have learned English as a second language. Review the morphological aspects of English orthography with each person, and then ask the following questions:

1. Were you aware of these aspects of English orthography?
2. Do you find the morphological aspects of English orthography helpful?
3. Do you think the English writing system should be reformed? Why or why not?

Compare the responses. Are there differences based on whether speakers are first or second language learners of English? What are your own views on English orthography?

## WRITING AND READING

This section of the chapter considers logographic, syllabic, and alphabetic writing systems from the perspective of reading and learnability. Remember that each writing system captures a different type of linguistic unit.

⇒ The symbols in logographic systems correspond to morphemes or words.

⇒ The symbols in syllabaries represent the syllabic units of a language.

⇒ The symbols in alphabets correspond, to a greater or lesser extent, to consonant and vowel phonemes.

**Exercise!** Familiarize yourself with the discussion on reading and writing on pp. 500 to 502, and then complete the statements below.

1.  People who suffer brain injuries that result in phonological deficits do not lose the ability to write and read _____ symbols.
2.  The major advantage of a _____ writing system over a _____ writing system is that all of the symbols can be mastered in a relatively short period of time and quickly used to produce and understand many new words.
3.  It seems that children can recognize _____ more easily than they can identify _____. As a result, _____ are generally easier to master for children.
4.  Educated people typically know _____ Chinese characters, but knowledge of _____ Chinese characters is required even to read a newspaper.
5.  _____ is a disability of neurological origin that affects the processing of written symbols and the relationship between those symbols and sounds and words.
6.  A language with numerous complex syllable types is least suitable for a _____.

**Think ...** As mentioned at the beginning of the chapter, written communication is a relatively recent phenomenon and is quite different from oral communication. Having examined writing from different perspectives, describe in your own words the differences between oral and written communication.

## QUESTIONS? PROBLEMS? DIFFICULTIES?

_____

_____

_____

_____

_____

_____

_____